AF506284

Engineering
Artificial Intelligence
Software

Engineering
Artificial Intelligence
Software

Derek Partridge
Department of Computer Science
University of Exeter

intellect
Oxford, England

First published in Great Britain in 1992 by
Intellect Books
Suite 2, 108/110 London Road, Oxford OX3 9AW

First published in the US in 1992 by
Ablex Publishing Corporation
355 Chestnut Street
Norwood, New Jersey 07648

Copyright © 1992 Intellect Ltd.

All rights reserved. No part of this publication may be reproduced,
stored in a retrieval system, or transmitted, in any form or by any
means, electronic, mechanical, photocopying, recording, or otherwise,
without written permission.

Consulting editor: Masoud Yazdani
Copy editor: Pamela Clements
Cover design: Mark Lewis

British Library Cataloguing in Publication

Partridge, D. (Derek) 1945-
    Engineering Artificial Intelligence Software
    1. Computer systems. Software. Design. Applications of
    artificial intelligence
    I. Title
    005.12

ISBN 1-871516-06-4

Library of Congress Cataloging-in-Publication Data

Partridge, Derek. 1945-
  Engineering Artificial Intelligence Software / by Derek Partridge.
    p. cm.
  Includes bibliographical references and index.
  ISBN 0-89391-778-8
  1. Artificial Intelligence--Software. I. Title.
0336.P37
006.3'0285'5--cc20   90-26630
                                CIP

Printed and bound in Great Britain by Billing & Sons Ltd, Worcester

Contents

List of figures

Preface

This book is aimed at the computer-literate person who wishes to find out about the reality of exploiting the promise of artificial intelligence in practical, maintainable software systems. It cuts through the hype, so commonly associated with discussions of artificial intelligence, and presents the realities, both the promise and the problems, the current state of the art, and future directions.

It is not another expert systems book. Expert systems are viewed as just one manifestation of AI in practical software; the issues raised in this book are much broader. Expert systems are discussed, but as a source of lessons about the dangers as well as the beneficial possibilities for adding AI to practical software systems.

In the opening three chapters, we take a long hard look at the conventional wisdom concerning software engineering - what the goals are, the rationale behind them, and the realities of the situation. This is done in part because efforts to engineer AI-software appear to undermine the accepted foundations of conventional software engineering so we need to determine how solid the foundations really are; it is also done because in attempting to engineer AI-software we subject the standard procedures of software design and development to close scrutiny - our attempts to build robust and reliable AI-software provides a magnifying glass on the conventional procedures.

Chapter 4 elaborates on the prototyping schemes described in Chapter 3 and uses this well-accepted methodological strategy to take us on into the more contentious domain of evolutionary and exploratory software design and development. This move places us squarely within the general paradigm (i.e. incremental system development) from whence an effective model for engineering AI software will emerge. This chapter concludes with a presentation of the conventional paradigms for software development which sets the scene for the 'new paradigms' which constitute the next chapter.

Chapters 1 to 4 are somewhat polemical in nature, unashamedly so. Is this appropriate in a text book? Clearly, I believe that it can be, and it is in this case. As attractive as it might be to provide an unbiased presentation of how to build AI software, it is just not possible. How best to build AI software, and even whether it is a reasonable endeavour to embark on in the first place, are controversial topics. I have attempted to present the major competing alternatives whenever possible, and I haven't tried too hard to hide my personal preferences. I don't think that this style of writing is necessarily out of place in a text book. In fact, I think that it is sorely needed in this particular subject area. The prevalence of uncritical texts is largely responsible for the current state of passive acceptance of what should really be hotly debated issues, e.g. that software construction should mirror conventional engineering practice, or that the single key component is an abstract specification which can be complete.

I clearly don't have an exclusive insight into the problems that permeate the software world; many before me have seriously questioned elements of the conventional wisdom and offered a possible remedy. In Chapter 5 I present just a few of the new paradigms that have been proposed in recent years. This serves to open up the problem, to emphasize the particularly problematic elements, and to reassure you that there is no quick fix that I have overlooked.

In Chapter 6 I refocus the narrative and examine specific components of an effective incremental software design and development paradigm - a discipline of exploratory programming. None of these component features appear to be readily available, and some seem to offer little hope of availability, ready or otherwise. One of the intentions of this chapter is to show that despite the actual difficulty of realizing these essential component features, the appearance of impossibility is only an unfortunate illusion.

The next two chapters present two, very different, sources of reason for guarded optimism for the engineering of AI software. Chapter 7, on Machine Learning, reviews several facets of this complex AI subfield that have had an impact on practical software development. Chapter 8 comprises the main concession to expert systems' technology. As I said at the very beginning, this is not an expert systems book, but this new technology cannot be ignored in a book that deals with the design and development of AI software. However, we do not retell the famous exploits of the star performers in this field, nor do we examine particular mechanisms used to achieve expert-level performances. What we do is to look at how, in general terms, these celebrated AI-software systems were developed, and equally important why so many of them have failed to surmount the prototype stage. The lessons are both positive and negative, and it may be the negative ones that are the most instructive.

The penultimate chapter attempts to draw together many of the lines of reasoning developed earlier. It attempts to organize these threads of argument into a more coherent whole - the umbrella of software support environments. To conclude this chapter two other seemingly desirable styles of approach to the problems of engineering AI software are examined.

In the final chapter, Chapter 10, we bring in the `societal' aspects of the general problem. It is people that build software systems (and that may be **the** problem, the advocate of automatic programming might be tempted to interject), and for any significant system it is definitely people rather than a single person. Just as software systems are not built in a personless vacuum, they are seldom used in one either. It is all too easy for the `technician' to focus exclusively on the technical problems and forget that many people are in fact bound up with the problem, and in many different ways. So this last chapter, in addition to providing a summation of all that has gone before, briefly reviews these `societal' problems of software development. For they cannot be temporarily shelved to be tackled after the technical ones have been solved: they are part and parcel of the technical problems of engineering AI software - indeed, of engineering all large-scale software. And to neglect the people aspect may leave us attempting to solve fictitious, purely technical problems.

Finally, the embryonic state of the art in the engineering of AI-software (despite what you might hear to the contrary) means that this is not, and cannot at the present time be, a `manual' to guide the interested reader through a detailed procedure for constructing robust and reliable AI-software products. Although I do present and discuss specific systems (even a few commercially available systems) whenever possible, the book is by no means saturated with expositions of the shells, tools or environments that you can just go out and buy in order to get on with engineering some AI-software. What you will find (I hope) is a comprehensive and coherent examination of the many problems that engineering AI-software involves, as well as a consideration of the alternative routes to solution of these problems. This book is certainly not the last word on this important subject, but it may be a good start.

Acknowledgements

As with all substantial pieces of work the author cannot take 100 per cent of the credit, only of the blame. I would like to thank several anonymous reviewers who helped curb my excesses and Sue Charles who drew most of the figures.

Derek Partridge

1
Introduction to Computer Software

1.1   Computers and software systems

Software systems are programs, usually large ones, running on a computer. Despite several decades of concerted effort, the design, implementation, and maintenance of such systems is more of an art than a science. That is to say, the development and maintenance of such systems are processes dominated by loose guidelines, heuristic principles and inspirational guesswork, rather than formally defined principles and well-defined techniques.

The advent of electronic digital computers and the subsequent, almost miraculous, advances in electronic circuitry technology have provided mankind with an amazing tool. It has taken humanity into a new age. Electronic computers have opened up possibilities that were hardly dreamed of just a few decades ago. We have rockets that can be accurately guided to the outermost planets and can then take pictures to send back to us. We have a banking system, involving plastic cards and remote automatic tellers, that provides us with astounding financial flexibility, and so on.

In sum, computers have moved us into domains of unbelievable complexity, and enable us to manage them fairly successfully - most of the time. In fact computers don't just enable us to deal with situations of far greater complexity than we could possibly manage without them, they positively lure us into these domains of excessive complexity. The modern computer is an exceedingly seductive device: it tempts us with the promise of its great power, but it also entices the unwary to overstep the bounds of manageable complexity.

Computer systems designers are well aware of this danger, and that small specialist sector of society whose role is to construct software systems has laboured to produce a framework from which reliable, robust, and maintainable, in a phrase, practically useful software systems are likely to be forthcoming. This framework is the central feature of the discipline of **software engineering**. Observance of the strictures of software engineering *can* lead to the production of high-quality software systems, but there are no guarantees. Software system design and construction is thus a skilled art (i.e. a blend of artistic flair and technical skill), but then so is much of science in all domains, despite the widespread, naive views to the contrary. So what exactly is software engineering?

1.2   An introduction to software engineering

What is software engineering? Well according to one source:

> Software engineering is the introduction of formal engineering principles to the creation and production of software. A scientific or logical approach replaces the perhaps more traditional unstructured (or artistic) methods.
>
> DTI, *Software Engineering Newsletter*, Issue No. 7, 1988

This definition is on the right track, but is perhaps more a definition of some future desired situation than the current reality. And clearly I have some reservations about the 'scientific' aspirations explicitly mentioned in the definition. I don't really know what this word means, but I suspect that it is being (mis)used as a synonym for 'logical'. A further point of contention that will emerge later when we come to a consideration of the promise and problems of artificial intelligence (AI) in practical software systems is that the desire for 'a scientific or logical approach' may be born of a fundamental misconception, and one that AI illuminates.

Ince (1989) presents an altogether less slick but far more realistic characterization of the essence of software engineering.

> Software engineering is no different from conventional engineering disciplines: a software product has to meet cost constraints; the software engineer relies on results from computer science to carry out system development; a software system has to carry out certain functions, for example in a plant monitoring system those of communicating pressure and temperature readings to plant operators;   and a software developer has to work under sets of constraints such as budget, project duration, system response time and program size.
>
> Ince (1989) p. 4

This definition (or description) again tries to account for the 'engineering' part of the label, but it avoids the mythological associations of the term instead of stressing them as in the previous definition. Engineering is not an exact science; it is not a discipline characterized by formal techniques; the 'logical approach' (under any formal interpretation of 'logical') has no major role in most types of engineering. In fact, much engineering is saturated with rule-of-thumb procedures which experience has shown will mostly work, i.e. it is just like much of the practice of software system building. Precise calculation and use of formal notations certainly have a role in engineering (as Parnas, 1989, for example stresses) and they also have a role in software engineering. The unanswered questions are: do they have central roles and do they have similar roles within these two disciplines?

Yet, it is undeniable that software systems crash with amazing regularity whereas bridges and buildings very seldom fail to perform adequately over long periods of time. This is the crucial difference between these two disciplines that leads us to think that software builders have useful lessons to learn from bridge builders, i.e. real engineers. But coining the name 'software engineering' and yet setting a course for the realms of the logicist does not seem to be a rational way to capitalize on the success of real engineers.

Can we reasonably expect to be able to exploit engineering know-how? Are software systems like bridges, or buildings, or complex machinery? Or is the depth of similarity merely wafer thin? These are difficult questions and, moreover, ones that will intrude on our deliberations quite starkly when we bring AI into the picture. So, before launching into an investigation of software life cycles, I'll indulge in a minor diversion which will be seen to pay off later on in this text.

1.3 Bridges and buildings versus software systems

Let me tabulate a few differences and similarities between these two sorts of artefacts. First some similarities:

1. they are both artefacts, i.e. man-made objects;
2. they are both complex objects, i.e. have many interrelated components;
3. they are both pragmatic objects, i.e. are destined for actual use in the real world - contrast works of art;

but there are, of course, some significant differences.

bridges and buildings	software systems
concrete objects objects	formal-abstraction-based
non-linguistic objects	linguistic objects
non-malleable objects	malleable objects
simple or relatively unconstrained functionality	precise, complex functionality

Some explanation of this tabulation is required, I suspect. There are clearly important differences between an elaborate pile of reinforced concrete and steel (say, a bridge or building) and a computer program (i.e. a software system). The former is a solid physical object which is typically difficult and expensive to change. If, for example, you're curious about the ramifications of two span-supports rather than three, or about the implications of doubling the thickness of a steel girder, the chances of being able to satisfy your curiosity on the engineered product are very slim. The engineer must resort to modelling (i.e. constructing small-scale models, rather than mathematical models - although this is done as well) to answer these sorts of questions, or verify predictions of this nature, as they so often do. Notice that such modelling is an alternative to formal analysis, and not the preferred alternative - it's more expensive, slower, and less accurate. At least, it would have all of these less desirable characteristics *if formal analysis were possible*, but it usually isn't except in terms of gross approximations (the mathematical models) that need to be supported by empirical evidence such as model building can provide.

So, because of the fact that engineering is not a formal science, the notion of modelling, of building prototypes, is heavily exploited. Take note of the fact that typically the model (or prototype) and the final engineered product are totally different objects, and they have to be because the impetus for this type of modelling is to be found in the nature of the non-malleability of the engineered final product.

Software-engineered products (i.e. programs) are quite different with respect to malleability. Programs are very easily alterable. Tentative changes typically cost very little in time, money, or effort. In fact, programs are much too easily alterable; in my terminology, they are highly malleable objects. Thus it would seem that the need to build models in order to explore conjectures, or verify deductions, is absent. Yet modelling, in the sense of building prototypes, is common practice in software engineering. "Have the software engineers misunderstood the nature of their task?" we ask ourselves. I'm very tempted to answer "yes" to this question, but not with respect to the need for prototype model building. Why is this?

First, notice that a model of a software system *is itself* a software system. This fundamental difference between engineering and software engineering leads to the conclusion that seemingly similar processes (i.e. prototype model building) may serve rather different purposes within these two classes of engineering. At the very least, it should serve as a warning against over-eagerness in equating the activities of real engineers and software engineers, even when they seem to be doing quite similar things.

An important difference between the products of engineering and of software engineering stems from the precise nature of the abstract medium used to build programs - it is a linguistic medium. A software system is a statement in a language. It is not a statement in a natural language, and it may appear quite alien to the average linguistically competent, but computationally illiterate, observer. Nevertheless, a software system is a linguistic statement, and although natural languages and formal languages have much less in common than their names would suggest (formal languages: another readily misinterpretable label), there are some significant similarities. One consequence of this feature of software engineered products is that we may be tempted to entertain the view that programs might also be theories - we don't typically spare much thought for the suggestion that bridges might be theories (in structural mechanics?) or even that they might contain their designs (the blueprints are in there somewhere!). Similarly, software engineers are typically not tempted too much to view their artefacts as theories, but, when we later let AI intrude into these deliberations, we'll see that this odd notion gathers considerable support in some quarters.

A most important consequence of the fact that programs are composed of formal linguistic structures - i.e. programs are formal statements- is that they therefore invite being mauled with mechanisms that can boast the unassailable attribute of mathematical rigour. In particular, they are constantly subjected to logical massage, of one sort or another - especially the sorts that hold a promise 'proof of correctness.'

The last-listed point of difference concerns the functionality of acceptable objects - i.e. how they behave in the world. You might be tempted to observe that many engineered objects don't behave, they just are. The function of a bridge is purely passive: it doesn't act *on* the world, it just sits there and allows things to run over it. So it does have this passive functionality (which is a point of difference with software systems), but more importantly the functionality is relatively simple - crudely put, its function is to sit there without breaking or cracking and let things run over it (not much of an existence I admit, but that's about the extent of it if you're a bridge).

"Ah, but certain engineered objects, such as steam engines, do have a complex, active functionality just like software systems." you might respond. "Yes and no," I would reply. They do have complex, active functionality, but it's very different from the functionality of software systems in several crucial respects. It's less tightly constrained and it's much more modular - i.e. engineered products have relatively broad ranges of acceptable functionality, and the overall functionality can be decomposed into relatively independent components. Thus, a building must exhibit complex functionality, both active and passive, but to a good first approximation the adequacy of the doors, doorways, corridors and stairs in supporting movement throughout the structure is independent of the adequacy of the central heating system, and of the performance of the toilets, and of the performance of the roof, etc. The undoubted complex functionality can be broken down, *to a reasonable approximation*, into relatively independent functional components - this results in a reduction in effective complexity. And, although the doors, doorways, etc. must conform to building codes, almost any reasonably large hole in the wall will operate adequately as a door: something pretty drastic has to happen before it will fail to support the necessary function of providing access from one space to another. Software systems are rather different. We strive for modular functionality and achieve it to varying degrees dependent upon the nature of the problem as well as the skill of the software engineer. But the medium of programming lends itself to a hidden and subtle interaction between components that is not possible (and therefore not a problem) when building with nuts, bolts, concrete, steel, plastic, etc. There is also a positive inducement to employ functional cross-links: they can buy software power cheaply in terms of program size and running time (the important issue of software power is considered fully later).

Finally, there are usually tight constraints on what functionality is acceptable: software systems typically operate under precisely defined functional constraints, if the actual functionality strays from the tight demands of the system specification then it is likely to be inadequate, incorrect, even useless in its designated role. Notice that not all (or even most) of these constraints are explicitly stated; many tight functional requirements become necessary in order to realize the specified requirements given the particular implementation strategy selected. They just emerge as the software engineer strives to develop a correct computational procedure within the web of constraints on the task. These are the implicit functional constraints on the particular software system; they have to be actively searched out and checked for accuracy.

In his polemic on what should be taught in computer science, Dijkstra makes the preliminary point that modern computer technology introduces two "radical novelties". The particularly relevant one here "is that the automatic computer is our first large-scale digital device" and consequently "it has, unavoidably, the uncomfortable property that the smallest possible perturbations - i.e. changes of a single bit - can have the most drastic consequences." Whereas most engineered artefacts "are viewed as analogue devices whose behaviour is, over a large range, a continuous function of all parameters involved" (Dijkstra, 1989, p. 1400).

In sum, there are a few similarities between bridges and software systems, but there are many salient differences. So why this general exhortation to try to build and design programs in the mould successfully used for bridges? Is it a misguided campaign fuelled by little more than desperation? What the software people really hope to import into their discipline is product reliability. But are bridges, buildings, and steam engines reliable because the technology is well understood, in the sense of well defined, or because the artefacts are produced as a result of rigid adherence to a complete and precise specification of desired behaviour? The answer is not clearly 'Yes'. And yet we find many advocates of "formal methods" in the world of software design and development who appear to subscribe to something like this view. The term "formal methods", when used in the software world, focuses attention on the notions of abstract formalized specifications for software, and provable correctness of a program with respect to such a specification. Gibbins (1990) discusses the question "What are formal methods?" and quotes with approval from an Alvey Software Engineering Strategy Document:

> "A formal method is a set of rigorous engineering practices which are generally based on formal systems and which are applied to the development of engineering products such as software or hardware". (p. 278)

Here we see again an attempt to roll formal techniques and engineering practices and products all into one ball, as if it's indisputable that they meld together well. One question we really ought to ask ourselves is, 'do they?' Is the use of formal techniques the key to engineering reliability? Or could it be that well-engineered products are reliable because of a long tradition that has allowed the heuristics to be refined? More importantly, are they reliable because their relative functional simplicity permits the incorporation of redundancy in a similarly simple way? If you want to be sure that the bridge will function adequately, then, when you've finished the crude calculations, you double the size of the spanning girders, pour more concrete into the supporting pillars, etc. What you don't do is set about trying to prove that your calculations will guarantee adequate functioning. The functional complexity of software systems seems to make them unamenable to a similar coarse-grained style of adding redundancy to safeguard performance requirements - i.e. you can't just double the number of statements in a program, or beef up the supporting procedures by adding more of the same statements. So, while the engineering paradigm in general (i.e. formal approximation bolstered by added redundancy and a wealth of experience) may be appropriate, it can be misguided to look too closely and uncritically at the details of engineering practice, and even worse to aspire to a fiction of supposed formal practice.

The main point to take from this introductory discussion is that the very basics of the field of software engineering are by no means settled. There is no clear agreement as to what it is exactly that the software engineers ought to be importing from conventional engineering practice, nor how it is best applied for the effective generation of robust and reliable software products. There is general agreement that use of "rigorous engineering principles" and "engineering judgement" are good things, but beneath this most general level of agreement consensus is much harder to find.

Enough 'setting the scene', it is time to quickly review the orthodox view of the framework for software engineering.

In the UK, a substantial report from a joint working party of The British Computer Society and The Institution of Electrical Engineers on undergraduate curricula for software engineering gives us the following answer to the question: what is software engineering?

> Software engineering requires understanding and application of engineering principles, design skills, good management practice, computer science and mathematical formalism. It is the task of software engineering to draw together these separate areas of expertise and bring them to bear upon the requirements elicitation, specification, design, verification, implementation, testing, documentation and maintenance of complex and large-scale software systems. The software engineer thus fulfils the role of architect of a complex system, taking account of user requirements and needs, feasibility, cost, quality, reliability, safety and time constraints. The necessity to balance the relative importance of these factors according to the nature of the system and the application gives a strong ethical dimension to the task of the software engineer, on whom the safety or well-being of others may depend, and for whom, as in medicine or in law, a sense of professional morality is a requirement of the job. Sound engineering judgement is required.
>
> BCS and IEE report on Undergraduate Curricula for Software Engineering, June 1989, London, p. 13.

Now, this is something more like an attempt to capture the nature of software engineering concisely, if not exactly in a nutshell. This characterization makes it clear that the topic is a diverse one, and that the relationship of this discipline to engineering may not be fundamental (just one of many peripheral concerns that impinge on the task of software development). A similar observation can be made about "the logical approach" which is covered, presumably, by "mathematical formalism" in the above. So "engineering principles" and mathematics have a part to play, but neither have been given the lead role, although I'm surprised by the prominence given to "engineering judgement" (whatever that might be) in the last sentence.

In addition, what this description of software engineering brings out is the sequence of component activities that are generally agreed to constitute the practice of software engineering: requirements elicitation, specification, design, verification, implementation, testing, documentation and maintenance. This sequence actually mirrors quite closely the general sequence of activities known as the **software life cycle**. The minor exceptions concern verification and documentation. To some, verification suggests the largely academic, toy-program exercise of formally verifying that an algorithm is correct (with respect to the specification) in some absolute sense; it might then be considered inappropriate (or, at least, premature) to include it in a characterization of practical, large-scale software engineering. Validation, with its connotation of checking but without the implication of formal establishment of truth in an absolute sense, is sometimes the preferred term, and each stage of the software development process is validated not just the algorithm that is the final outcome of the design process. The process of documentation is similarly (or certainly should be) a more dispersed one than the simple sequence given above would suggest. The major documentation effort is probably made after the system has been tested and before it has to be maintained, but documentation details should be generated at every stage of software development. After successful testing, it should be mostly a matter of organizing and polishing the documentation for the users of the product.

So, software engineering can be characterized by the following sequence of processes with the proviso that validation and documentation run throughout the whole sequence.

Requirements elicitation, analysis or even **engineering** is the first stage after the decision to construct a software system for some application. Apart from the software people, it primarily involves the future users of the proposed software system. After all, it is for the user that the system is being constructed - isn't it? In any long, drawn-out, complex task, such as software design and construction, mistakes are sure to be made. Extensive studies have made it very clear that the further along you are in the process of completing the task when an error becomes apparent, the more costly it is to correct it. Hence, much emphasis and attention is lavished (or should be) on the requirements phase - it's the cheapest place to find and fix the errors.

But what errors could you have here? You've not produced any code and no design either (certainly not a detailed design), so how could you have made a mistake? What you get from the requirements stage is the details of what the user does and doesn't want in the desired software system. Therefore, as long as you check the final requirements document with the user: "These are the features you want, right? And these are things you definitely don't want, right?", and the user nods and signs on the dotted line - how could you have made a mistake?

Well the requirements document will be a complex object, and it is easy, for example, to include in your list of desirable features two that are incompatible, or even inconsistent. You might want to concede this, but maintain that the user signed off on these requirements so it's the user's problem and not yours. But such a hard-nosed view is not really acceptable when you are the systems expert not the user. You are being paid to develop the software system and so you shoulder the major responsibility for the correctness of the requirements as well as all subsequent stages in the process. Both parties have to agree 'in good faith' to work together. It is not helpful to view these early stages as geared towards the production of a formal contract whose precise wording can be subsequently exploited by either party (we shall see the poverty of this approach when we look more closely at specifications in Chapter 3). And, of course, in a complex document there are many hidden problems. For example, it may be that the consequences (either logical or just practical ones) of the requirements conflict. It is true that such a conflict of consequences should be predictable from the document, and in principle I guess the logical ones are, and the practical ones as well, to some reasonable degree. But when dealing with objects of high complexity what may be possible in principle is likely to be impossible in practice.

So there certainly is room for mistakes in the requirements phase, and there's a high probability that whatever cross-checking and analysis of the requirements you perform, some mistakes will elude you and make their unwelcome presence known at some later (and more costly) stage. Nevertheless, the software engineer can (and should) work to minimize the errors in the system requirements document.

What happens to the requirements document? It becomes the basis for the system specification. A **specification** is a statement of what the eventual software system is supposed to do. In an effort to obtain a precise and unambiguous specification, formal or semi-formal notations are typically used for the system specification.

This is easily illustrated for problems that are simple and well-defined functions like sorting. The user might conceive of the problem as:

> I want a computer program to maintain the stock inventory as a list of items ordered in terms of their part numbers.

That's a specification of a problem, but not a formal one, and one, moreover, that despite its apparent triviality could well repay the software engineer the cost of a little requirements analysis. Why does the user think that this system will be useful? Is an ordered list really the structure that will best serve the user's needs? And should it really be ordered according to part number? Taking another tack: how big a list are we contemplating? How changeable is it? In what ways does it change? For example, does it grow only from the bottom - i.e. by the addition of new items with new part numbers that are greater than any already on the list? Are the part numbers objects that have an obvious ordering - e.g. simple integers that can be ordered numerically?

These are the sorts of information that a process of requirements elicitation should uncover. There is general information about whether what the user conceives of as the desired system will really solve the actual problem. And there is more specific information about the special nature of the problem in the user's environment. But let us assume that the simple problem specification survives the requirements analysis intact. The task is then to transform it into a formal specification of **WHAT** the desired system will do. This is often viewed as a **rigorous functional specification (RFS)**, where the "functional" attribute refers to the fact that the essence of the problem is a functional (i.e. input-output or I-O) relationship. The user knows what information will be input and what the desired system should output. It is the difficult and demanding task of the software engineer to determine **HOW** to realize the specified function within the multitude of surrounding constraints.

So what is the RFS for this particular problem? Essentially this is a sorting problem. What the user wants is an implementation of **SORT(x)** which gives **y**, where

the list **y** is a *permutation* of the list **x**
and the list **y** is *ordered*

and this is an RFS provided that the terms *permutation* and *ordered* are formally defined (which can easily be done - I will not bore you with the details, just take it on trust).

Now we know exactly what the programming task is: it's to design a correct implementation of the **SORT** function within the constraints of the particular context of the user's problem - e.g. there will be efficiency considerations of both time and space. But these constraints are typically considered to be secondary to the task of designing a correct implementation of the function. After all, if it's not correct, then what good is the fact that it runs fast and takes up little space in the computer memory? So, the focus on program (or algorithm) correctness seems eminently sensible. We can summarize this view as follows:

> **Conventional software-system design** (i.e. conventional programming in looser parlance) is the process of devising correct implementations of well-specified problems.

This takes as on to the **design** stage - the process of designing an algorithm to implement the specified function. The emphasis switches from **WHAT** is to be implemented (captured in the specification) to **HOW** it is to be implemented, the computational process to be executed by a computer in order to realize the function. Stated in terms of **WHAT** and **HOW**:

> **Conventional software-system development** is the process of designing a correct HOW for a well-defined WHAT.

There are many ways to realize any given function, good ones and bad ones. It is the software engineer's task to design one of the good ones, where 'good' is an ill-defined notion but characterized by the set of constraints for the task, constraints such as efficiency and maintainability of the final system. This is where the art of software engineering begins to intrude on the task. It is true that there are formal techniques for developing an algorithm from a specification that minimize the necessity for creativity and, more importantly, guarantee that the resultant algorithm is a correct procedure for computing the specification. But these techniques, like so many of their formal brethren, don't (yet?) scale-up to the point where they are usable for the design of practical software systems.

This leaves the software engineer with the task of designing a computational procedure on the basis of loose guidelines and some firm principles which collectively often go under the name of **structured programming** or **structured design**. Apart from principles of modularity, and stepwise decomposition the software engineer typically has an elaborate framework such as SSADM (Structured Systems Analysis and

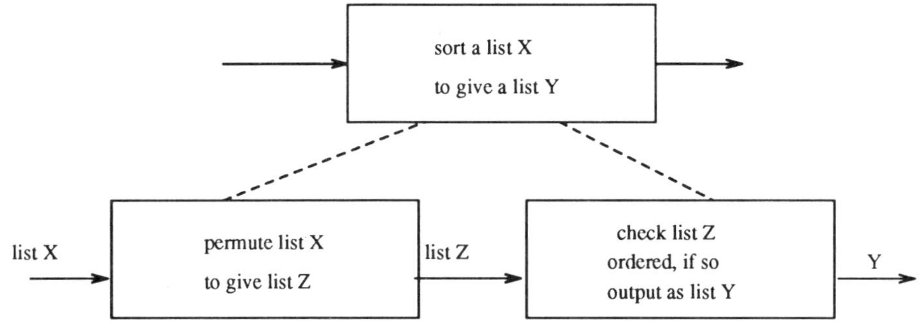

Fig 1.1 A specification and a first attempt at a general design

Design Method, see Ashworth and Goodland, 1990) that encompasses general principles as well as formal notations and includes a two-dimensional graphical notation (such as data flow diagrams - see later) for diagramming the designs developed.

The design of a large software system is usually broken down into a number of design steps. At the very least there will be a general system design (a general decomposition of the total system into major functional subsystems) and then a detailed design (in which each of the functional subsystems is decomposed into primitive computational components that will realize the desired subfunction).

Thus, to continue with our trivial example, the general design might be to decompose the problem into two subsystems: one to compute permutations of lists, and the other to check ordering in lists. The detailed design can then focus on these two subfunctions quite independently (once the necessary interface has been specified - in this case the permutation subfunction must generate a list and the order-checker module must accept that list as input). We might diagram the general design as in Figure 1.1.

Now that's the beginnings of a design for an algorithm to realize the **SORT**   function. (As a matter of fact it's a bad beginning, but we'll get to that later.) We have two subsystems: one that does permutations and one that checks for ordering, and the interface between them is a list structure. So we are free to work on designing the details of each of these modules quite independently provided that we adhere to the interface constraint: the permutation module must output a list and the ordering-checker must accept this list as input.

But, as the reader who's paying attention will have noted, this design has some problems. If the list z just happens to be ordered then everything works fine, but if not, the computation is left dangling - i.e. it is not clear what will happen when the ordering check on list z comes out negative. So we must take care of this eventuality; this has been done in Figure 1.2.

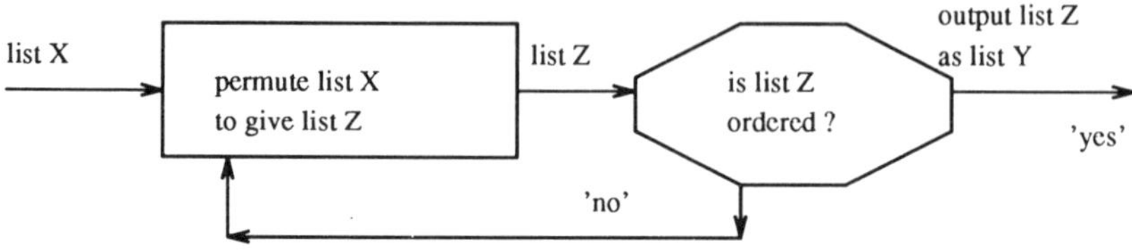

Fig 1.2 A better design for the **SORT** algorithm

Now, Figure 1.2 is a definite improvement over Figure 1.1 (provided that we take note of the newly emerged implicit constraint on the permutation process - i.e. it must generate a *new* permutation of list **x** every time it is re-entered). I have used a structured form of English and a flow-chart-type layout to represent my design, and this works quite well for simple examples but more sophisticated notational schemes seem to be required for large-scale designs. Simple flow-charting can support perspicuous representation of designs that are not too complex (which is perhaps the way all designs should be, but many are not and perhaps some never can be). But as designs become more complex, simple flow-charting can all too easily give rise to conceptually opaque representations - the powerful image here is of a bowl of spaghetti when faced with a superabundance of arrows criss-crossing each other both up and down the flow-chart.

Such a situation may be indicative of two things: firstly, a bad design, in which case the designer needs to think again, and secondly, the inadequacy of flow-charts as a representation medium for the problem at hand. The prevalence of bad designs is a continuing problem throughout the engineering world. Good design is hard to define, hard to teach, and hard to do. In the world of software design there has been much concerted effort directed towards the problem of software design. Many design strategies now exist and are composed of principles and guidelines which if applied with care (and flair) should channel software designs into the 'good' rather than the 'bad' category. A further crucial component of most design schemes is a representation structure, a design language, a means of representing with maximum clarity the designs developed (and this feature addresses the second problem mentioned at the head of this paragraph). A good design representation language, sometimes called a program-design language (PDL), can itself do much to keep the software designer on the path towards a good design. A PDL can do this by, for example, making bad design features awkward or impossible to represent.

PDLs begun to emerge at the very birth of the term software engineering, i.e. in the late 60s. The HIPO chart (Hierarchy plus Input-Process-Output) was one popular early PDL. SADT (Software Analysis and Design Techniques) from SoftTech Inc. is a graphical scheme, based on hierarchically structured sets of diagrams, for systems analysis and

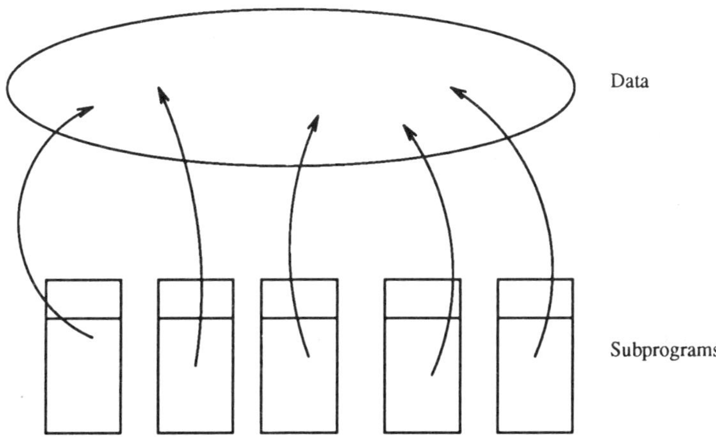

Fig 1.3 Program design of the early 60s

design. Another example is Jackson Design Methodology, developed by Michael Jackson, which assumes that system structure design should reflect the data structures to be used. Finally, I can refer you forward to Chapter 5 where data flow diagrams are used to represent a specific design.

There is now considerable support for the view that much of the foregoing (on design strategy and representations) is not only old technology but fast becoming obsolete (or at least severely limited in scope of applicability). As Yourdon (1990, p. 257) puts it: "Structured techniques, for example, were hailed by some as the productivity solution of the 1970s and 1980s. Computer-aided software engineering (CASE) was promoted in the same way during the second half of the 1980s. Now, some people are suggesting that object orientation is the salvation of the 1990s." And he seems to be one of these people, for he concludes his article on **object-oriented analysis** (OOA) and **object-oriented design** (OOD) with: "Object orientation is the future, and the future is here and now" (p. 264).

So what is this OOA and OOD which has sprung from OOP, **object-oriented programming**, which first saw light in the form of the language Smalltalk? The first question is: what is an object in the current context?

An **object** is a module that encapsulates both function and data.

That's not much of a definition, but it does capture a particularly salient feature of the object-oriented paradigm: OOP brings together and accords roughly equal status to both the procedural and the data structure aspects of computational problem-solving. The precursor paradigms tended to focus on function and give data a secondary status. Objects unify the ideas of algorithmic and data abstraction. They own the data which they

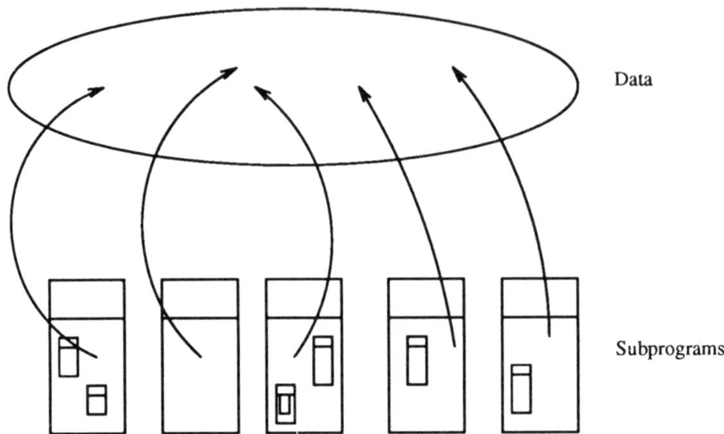

Fig 1.4 Program design of the late 60s

encapsulate and it is only indirectly visible external to the object. Finally, objects typically exist in the well-defined context of other, more general objects, and from which they can inherit certain properties. This inheritance feature has particular significance for us in the context of software reuse, and thus we shall look at it more closely when come to consider questions of software reuse later in this book (Chapter 6).

Booch (1991) in his book on OOD presents an illuminating sequence of figures that neatly depicts the history of change in program-design schemes (although he presents them in terms of programming language development which is, of course, closely correlated with design considerations).

In Figure 1.3 we see a program as a collection of code modules that reference one common pool of global data.

In Figure 1.4 we see further sophistication of the basic idea of code-data separation. In this scheme we see nested subprograms and notions of the scope and visibility of program elements.

In Figure 1.5 we see the problems of programming-in-the-large being explicitly addressed. Large programs are developed by teams and thus there was a need to enable different parts of the program to be developed independently. This need was met by what Booch calls "modules", and he carves up the program into modules, as illustrated in Figure 1.5.

Despite the increasing sophistication of techniques for dealing with the code, data was still given nothing like the same amount of consideration. This was the point where object-oriented ideas began to emerge and to reach their first culmination in the Smalltalk languages - Smalltalk 80 being the best known. Figure 1.6 illustrates early program design based on OOP.

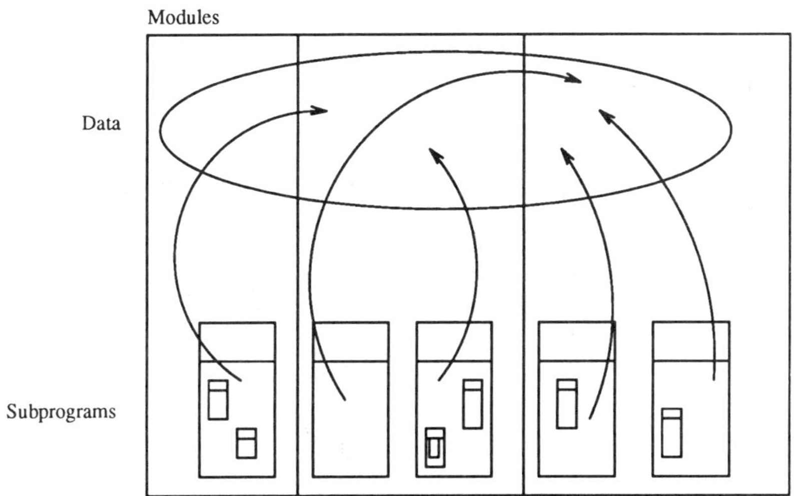

Fig 1.5 Program design of the 70s

Here we see that there is little or no global data. In this scheme, function and data are united such that the building blocks are no longer primarily subprograms, blocks of code, but integrated code-data elements, i.e. objects. Notice also that the underlying program structure is no longer a tree-structured hierarchy but a network.

Finally, programming-in-the-large has grown to become programming-in-the-colossal (as Booch nicely puts it) and the object-oriented model scales up to give programs composed of clusters of abstractions built in layers on top of one another (see Figure 1.7).

In order to conclude this brief review of software design methodology let me give you Booch's definitions of OOA and OOD.

Object-oriented analysis is a method of analysis that examines requirements from the perspective of the classes and objects found in the vocabulary of the problem domain.

Object-oriented design is a method of design encompassing the process of object-oriented decomposition and a notation for depicting both logical and physical as well as static and dynamic models of the system under design.

Booch (1991) p. 37

Returning to our own (relatively trivial) design problem: having completed the general design, the detailed design would amount to realizing each of these two modules in some formal or semi-formal language which is composed of 'computational primitives'. This means that the elements of the detailed design are structures that each have a relatively straightforward representation within typical programming languages - e.g. assignment statements and IF-THEN-ELSE statements.

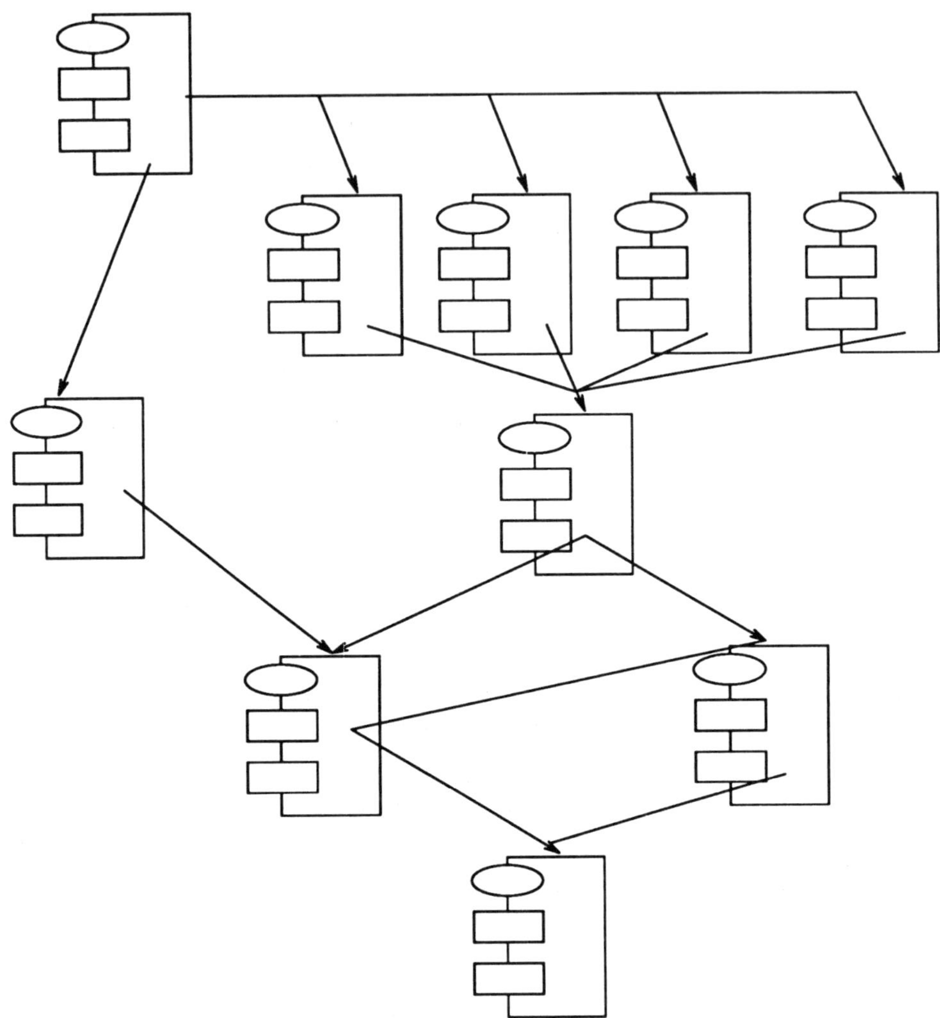

Fig 1.6 Early program design based on OOP

The detailed design is an algorithm, and, as you will have gathered from the rather woolly explanation in the preceding paragraph, this important term is not easy to define. An **algorithm** is a well-specified computational procedure which is independent of any particular computational device. That is to say, it defines the **HOW** of a specification without the inevitable clutter of a real, executable program - e.g. no declaration statements. Its value and importance lies in the attempt to capture the essence of the computational process in a crisp and clean

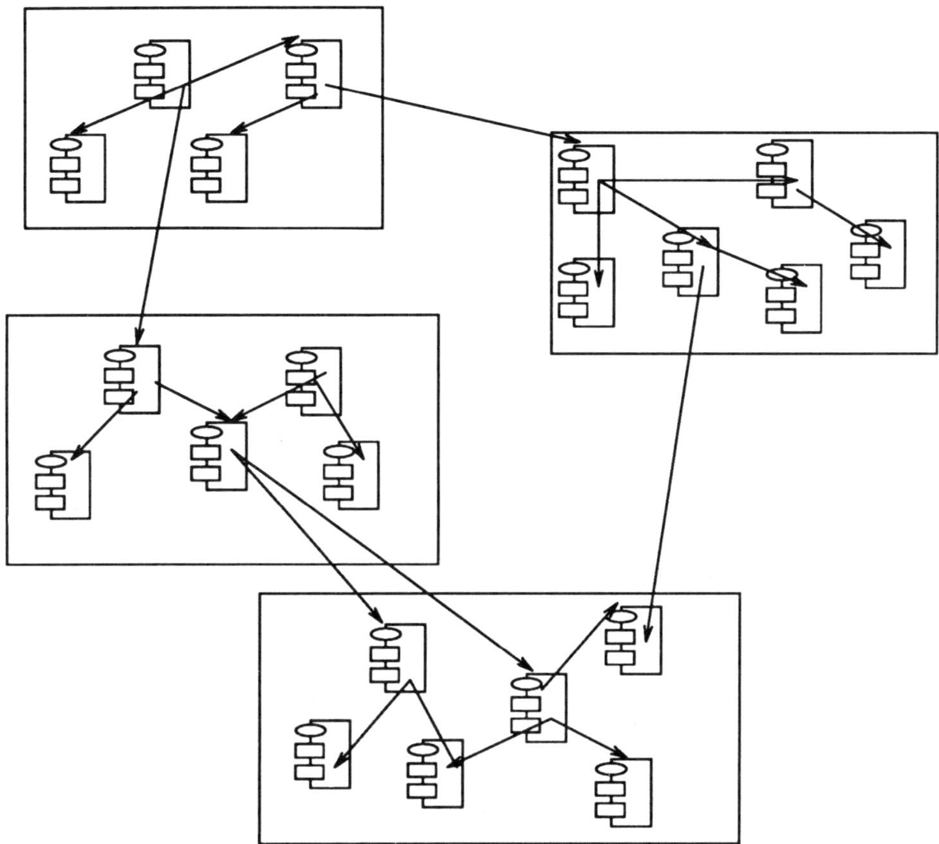

Fig 1.7 The OOP approach to programming-in-the-colossal

way. Its fuzziness comes from the fact that what is a computational primitive depends upon what style of computation (e.g. declarative versus procedural) is being contemplated. In more general terms: as soon as we concretize an algorithm, i.e. display it in terms of some representation scheme (usually a formally defined language), we cannot avoid using the particular representational structures that the chosen scheme offers us, and we are barred from using any construct that is not in the representation-language chosen. Hence non-essential (with respect to the original problem) information must become manifest in the chosen representation of the algorithm.

For purely historical reasons the generally expected (and accepted) language for expressing algorithms is derived from the programming language ALGOL - it is an implementation independent ALGOL. Hence the facetious (but telling) definition:

An **algorithm** is a program written in pidgin ALGOL.

As an illustration, the detailed design of (i.e. an algorithm to realize) the order-checking module of our sorting system might be:

input list **z**;
assume list is ordered;
for each element in the list,
except the last
   begin
            if current element > next element
                  then signal list not ordered
   end;
report list **z** ordered, or list not ordered

For those readers who use procedural languages like Pascal, FORTRAN, COBOL, this representation is close to an executable program. But if you're contemplating a final implementation in, say, LISP or Prolog, then this algorithm will need major remodelling before it is useful. In fact, if a Prolog program is the ultimate goal, then the original specification was virtually an executable program; it was certainly an algorithm. Just add some syntactic sugar:

sort(X,Y):- permute(X,Y), ordered(Y).

and four clauses to define **permute** and **ordered** and we have an executable PROLOG program.

So, a specification can be an algorithm, a specification can even be an implementation. This observation lies behind much of the current interest in **logic programming**. Problems can be formally specified in logic, and Prolog is close to a computational notation for logic.

From the design stage then we obtain an algorithm - a statement of **HOW** to compute the desired function. This is the critical point to verify that the algorithm is indeed correct, although many would maintain that really the design and algorithm development process should be composed of correctness-preserving transformations thereby automatically providing the guarantee that we now seek. Gries (1981, p. 299) gives a brief history of programming methodology in which he maintains that "When the theory [of proof of program correctness] was first presented, it seemed terribly difficult to prove an existing program correct, and it was soon admitted that the only way to prove a program correct was to develop the proof and program hand-in-hand - with the former leading the way." But although he subscribes to the proof-before-program view, he admits that "one *should* develop a proof and program hand-in-hand, but the proof should be a mixture of formality and common sense" p. 300. Dijkstra is a major force in the proof-before-program movement, and he promoted it with his notion "weakest preconditions" as a basis for a "calculus for the derivation of programs" (Dijkstra, 1976).

So, the **verification** stage is one of proving that the algorithm is a correct procedure for computing the function specified originally. There are many ways to go about this verification, from developing the proof hand-in-hand with the algorithm to application of the proof rules associated with each algorithmic primitive and thus demonstrating that the necessary input is always transformed into the desired output. One thing that is common to all such verification and proof techniques is that they are not yet usable on typical software systems. A variety of reasons are offered to explain this state of affairs. Some maintain that the proofs promise to be more complicated than the programs, and so mechanical proof checking (which is a distant possibility, at best) is essential. Others (such as Dijkstra, 1989, p. 1414) counter this with the assertion that "the presumed dogma that calculational proofs are an order of magnitude too long to be practical has not been confirmed by my experience. On the contrary, well-chosen formalisms provide a shorthand with which no verbal rendering can compete." A more sweeping line of attack challenges the foundations of the verificationists' programme: it claims that "The differences between a program and a proof are so many and so profound ... that it is hard to think of any relevant respect in which they are alike" (Halpern,1990, p. 47, who does detail a wealth of the claimed differences). Let me list a few of the claimed differences:

proofs	**programs**
objective (the theorem) stated formally known unambiguously	objective not often at all (outside model CS problems)
objective stated in terms of proof calculus	objective not stated in programming terms but in terms external to the program
fit into the fabric of mathematics - they tend to be interrelated	do not form one continuous fabric - each is relatively unique
often has value in its own right - establishment of a theorem may be quite secondary	very rarely has any value in itself merely a means to an end, if a better program appears former is discarded without a pang
subsequent new proofs of a theorem can be significant for a variety of reasons - e.g., more elegant, or innovative approach	new programs duplicating function of an available one seldom add much to the discipline, only worth is likely to be in efficiency gain

So "Why," we have to ask (as Halpern does), " do so many people think that proofs and programs are in an important sense similar?" The answer seems to rest on the observation that both proofs and programs appear to be formal syntactic entities. But we should be careful that such appearances are not misleading or just superficial - Halpern argues for both of these qualities in this alleged similarity. Halpern, who argues at length and with great skill, also provides full references back into the literature that comprises this debate. Suffice it to say that what formal verification may deliver for practical software systems, and even how exactly it may make the delivery, are hotly debated issues about which informed opinion can be found at both extremes.

So, for whatever reason, the software engineer must currently forego the certainties that verification techniques aspire to deliver one day. That is not to say that formal verification techniques have no place in practical software engineering today: right now, well-defined components of the system maybe verifiable and verification-based design schemes can provide a useful framework for design even if the verifications themselves have to be a mixture of "formality and common sense", as Gries admits.

On the other hand, even this middle-of-the-road standpoint might well be unacceptable to those who hold that verification is a misconceived notion because it applies only to static abstractions, and software systems are seldom static and are never abstractions - they are objects in the real world and as such can never be subject to 100 per cent guarantees (e.g. certainly Halpern, 1990, and De Millo, Lipton and Perlis, 1979, and to a lesser extent, Fetzer, 1988). And this observation brings us to the real world and the next stage of the software engineering process, implementation. **Implementation** is the transformation of a design into a machine-executable notation - i.e. transformation into a program.

The program is a real-world object and thus it can't be verified, but it can be tested. **Testing** is the process of running the program with a specific set of input data and seeing if it gives the correct answer for that particular input.

There are several points to note about the testing stage: first, the very fact that a software system can be tested relies on the assumption that its behaviour can (in principle, and usually in practice as well) be evaluated as correct or incorrect. At first sight, the necessary existence of such a property of a proposed software system would seem to be no real obstacle at all - but, once again, wait for AI to show its hand for then we shall see that correctness of specific program behaviour can easily become a non-resolvable issue.

Second, there is the much-quoted disparaging remark of Dijkstra's that "testing only shows the presence of errors, not their absence". Testing is thus seen as a weak stop gap, the best that we can do for the moment. The best that can be said of a tested piece of software is that it is free from known error. And in order to make this a strong statement software engineers have developed elaborate testing schemes. There are guidelines about what data values to test (e.g. the barely legal and the barely illegal); there are principles concerning the control structure within the software (e.g. all alternative control paths must be exercised); and there are more global principles about separating the system designers and the testers (e.g. the test data should be constructed by someone who was not involved in the system design and only has the specification to rely on - this sort of strategy tends to eliminate the propagation of implicit, but incorrect assumptions, from specification, through design and implementation, into the finished product). Other testing strategies include such bizarre activities as actively bugging (i.e. purposely introducing errors) software to assess the quality of the tests by the number of these introduced errors the testing strategy actually uncovers.

When the software has survived the testing phase, it is nearly a product ready for sale on the open market. But what first needs to be done is to generate and organize all the supplementary information that must go with the actual program code. This is information to enable the users (probably not computer experts themselves) to use the system effectively; it may also be detailed technical information to support the subsequent maintenance of this software system over time by, presumably, persons who are computer experts. The generation and organization of all the necessary information is the **documentation** stage of software engineering. A lot of it may be done by technical writers, rather than the software engineers, but the system designers and implementors should clearly have a significant input into the documents generated.

Finally, when the tested and documented product has been sold, or delivered if built especially for a particular user, we enter the maintenance stage. Software **maintenance** is the process of keeping the system going and serving a useful purpose for as long as necessary, or possible, whichever is shorter. In involves two major subprocesses: tracking down and removing (or at least disabling) the errors that show up during day-to-day usage of the software, and changing the software to meet changing user needs.

That (fairly) quick tour of software engineering will serve as a grounding in the nature of the task. We can now build on it, extend it, augment it, change it, question it, and even contradict it.

As mentioned much earlier, the great quest - the driving force behind the push to imbue software practice with engineering principles and judgement - is for reliability of software systems. The lack of such reliability was recognized in the late 60s and the resultant state of affairs was known as the software crisis.

1.4   The software crisis

So now we have sketched out the general framework within which software engineering operates, and we've also briefly examined the notion of introducing "engineering principles" to reinforce the technology. Why is there this drive to beef up the practice of software engineering? Why is it that, everywhere we look in the software world from academics, for whom computation is an abstract notion way above the trivializing clutter of actual computers, to hard-core systems designers and programmers, people actually working at the code face (as it were), we encounter this urge to apologize for the current techniques and to seek improvement? We all know that striving for improvement is an edifying occupation, always to be encouraged, but the ubiquity of this phenomenon does not account for the passion and commitment found among software people. Fundamentally, this common yearning for better methods of software production springs from the recognition that the technology is in a state of crisis - in a phrase, the software crisis.

What is this software crisis, this driving force that impels both academia and industry alike to seek constantly to improve their tools and working methods? The **software crisis** is the name given to the state of the software industry to emphasize the fact that most practical software systems contain errors and are inherently unreliable, and yet many crucial functions within our society rely on the accuracy of such systems.

The name was coined and accepted as an accurate reflection of the current state of affairs in the late 60s. In the past twenty years much concentrated effort, resulting in more disciplined programming languages, principles and guidelines for good system design, sophisticated support software, improved design-and-development languages, and advances in formal techniques, has taken a good deal of the edge off the original crisis. But, working in precisely the opposite direction, the moves to more ambitious software projects (such as real-time and safety-critical applications as well as simply larger and more complex systems) has undermined, perhaps negated, the impact of the general improvements. So despite enormous advances within both the science and the technology of software design, it is not clear that the nature of the crisis has changed much, or lessened in severity.

If there were, say, a similar long-term crisis in regular engineering then we would think twice before driving over a new bridge, resist the impulse to slam doors in buildings, and generally proceed with caution in order that these edifices and erections should not crack, split, break off at the edges, or even collapse into a more stable state of lower potential energy. Software products are typically not treated with a great deal of circumspection, but then neither do they seem to kill many people or cause the collapse of significant sectors of society. Why is this? Perhaps there isn't really a software crisis after all? Or perhaps the significance of software systems within society is overrated, as such things often are by the people who are responsible for them?

I think that neither of these proffered answers is correct, but that they both have a significant element of truth in them. For the software purist, the technology is in crisis. We can't prove that our software systems do what they're supposed to do, and we can guarantee that they contain errors which may, or may not, be obvious when they occur. Added to the difficulty of findings errors, which we know must be there, we can't guarantee to correct them either, certainly not without introducing other errors that offer no more promise of being findable or fixable than the original ones. This sort of description does begin to sketch out a state of affairs that may merit the label "crisis".

On the other hand, the competent software practitioner can challenge the "crisis" descriptor. If software is constructed in accordance with a stringent development methodology, validated at every step, thoroughly tested before use, and used wisely then we can guarantee software reliability - at least, to the same degree that we can guarantee any complex artefacts in the real world. From this viewpoint, the only reason for "crisis" in the industry is sheer professional incompetence somewhere along the line. This is not to say that there are not a lot of very bad software systems around. It is just to say that the existence of bad products is due to the prevalence of professional incompetence rather than flaws in the basic methodology.

Our practitioner might continue with something like: software systems are objects in the real world, they are not mathematical abstractions.Thus it is foolish to expect proofs of correctness, and hence guaranteed correctness in some absolute sense. So if you want to call this state of affairs one of "crisis", then there will always be a software crisis. The more rational view is to work towards a technology that will maximize confidence in the products but always bear in mind, with respect to application area and usage, that the software is not guaranteed in some absolute sense.

And formalism does, of course, have an important part to play in the development of a software technology that regularly delivers robust, reliable and maintainable products. We have every reason to expect valuable contributions from formal semantic definitions of the various languages used (from requirements and specification languages through to implementation languages), from formal analytical techniques for increasing our understanding of these complex objects (i.e. large programs), and from formal proof techniques (for clearly some system components can be based on proven abstractions).

In sum, the problems that constitute the software crisis have by no means all been solved, but the worst effects of the crisis can be avoided by a combination of a professional approach to system development, and sensible application and use of the systems so constructed. In addition, further progress will undoubtedly be made in the development of tools and techniques both formal and purely methodological. But the point that we have to bear in mind is: what does AI do to this situation? And we shall get to this issue later in this book.

1.5   A demand for more software power

One of the contributing forces to the continued impact of the software crisis is, as mentioned above, the desire for more ambitious software systems - we can view this as a demand for more software power. So what is the nature of this desired increase in software power? It takes a number of forms. Let me list them and then consider each one in turn.

1. Responsiveness to human users

2. Software systems in new types of domains

3. Responsiveness to a dynamic usage environment

4. Software systems with self-maintenance capabilities

Before attempting to explain this list, I should make it clear that this is very much a wish list for what will be achievable at some future date in terms of increasing software power; it is not a statement of current possibilities. But what we do currently see is various attempts in the software world to move in the direction of one or more of these types of increases in software power.

1.6   Responsiveness to human users

Software that is responsive to its users should be self-explanatory. But there is broad range of degrees of responsiveness in various dimensions. It might be said that user-responsive software has been with us for years. The bank's computer system, for example, treats its customers as individuals: it recognizes them (by means of a plastic card and a code number); it accesses their personal account; and deals with it in the manner that they request. It is thus responsive to each customer as an individual, but not in the same way as a human cashier is. There is a qualitative difference in user responsiveness between the computer system and the human. The human approach (in its better manifestations) typifies the level of user responsiveness to individuals that we should work towards. And when we have made some significant progress down this particular road we shall similarly have increased the power of software systems.Currently they are limited to treating everyone as much the same (some sort of average human being); when, in the future, they can recognize and respond subtly to some of our many individual differences, we shall have entered a new age of software systems.

What advances would such a move necessitate? Basically, the computer system would have to be capable of building and maintaining an up-to-date model of each individual user, and then the more familiar a person was to the system, the more individual treatment he or she could expect. But currently we have little idea of what the basic information that characterizes an individual is (let alone how to represent it within the computer system). In addition, we have similarly sparse knowledge of what sorts of perception and automatic modification mechanisms would be necessary to keep the user models up to date.

1.7   Software systems in new types of domains

This aspect of increased software power is based on the observation that if the range of applicability of a technology is increased then the power of that technology can be said to have increased. The construction of robust and reliable software systems in domains which were previously beyond the state of the art implies that more powerful software systems have become available.

At the moment, there are many niches of society that are not (and cannot be) populated with software systems. These potential application domains are currently viewed as inappropriate for a number of different (but interrelated) reasons: the problem is too ill-defined, the domain is too changeable, acceptable solutions are highly context dependent and open to debate - there are not enough clear 'rights' and 'wrongs'. Examples of such currently intractable domains are management decision-making, house-cleaning and natural-language communication. The production of useful working systems in these areas, which are currently viewed as closed to software technology, would again signal an advance in software power.

What's required to effect this sort of qualitative leap in the technology?

A lack of clear right and wrong answers in the problem domain would seem to require a change in software system validation techniques, as simple testability to ascertain correct or incorrect behaviour would no longer always apply. Highly changeable, or dynamic, applications suggest a need for sophisticated self-adaptivity, and we have little idea how to achieve this in a robust and reliable way.

1.8   Responsiveness to dynamic usage environments

This feature actually forms part of both of the previous ones, but it is, I believe, sufficiently important to merit a subsection all to itself. A major block to many aspects of increasing the power of software systems is the fact that all eventualities have to be figured out in advance and the software designed to cope with them. In many new domains, and for more ambitious software systems in everyday applications, there appears to be no possibility of foreseeing (and thus designing the software to accommodate) all of the possible outcomes of the problem solving strategy within the particular problem situation. In fact, I can make a much stronger statement than this: we cannot foresee (and thus design for) enough of the possible outcomes to enable us to implement self-adaptive software systems except at an extremely crude level. We must either avoid applying software systems in highly dynamic domains or we must content ourselves with dealing with only the static core of the problem, and perhaps a few major variants.

Take the house-cleaning robot as an example: such a robot will never clean the same house twice, not because it makes such a mess the first time that it is never used again (I am assuming that a mature and appropriate technology has been developed!), but because at the level of cleaning details such as furniture in certain positions, the scattering of dirt and debris, etc., every house is constantly changing, never to return to the exact configuration that it has just left.

Good house-cleaning requires almost continual creative problem solving on the part of the cleaner, not high-level creativity perhaps, but creative problem-solving that is way beyond the current state of the art in computer software technology.

1.9   Software systems with self-maintenance capabilities

This fourth aspect of software power is unique in this list because it is not really tied to the other three, although it is likely to become a necessity if significant advances are made towards realizing any of the other three features of software power. Quite simply, if software systems could monitor their own performance, report problems, suggest solutions, and even implement them (once they had been confirmed by some trusted human), we would have a minor miracle on our hands. However, software that embodies almost any part of this list of desiderata would be software that is qualitatively more powerful than any which exists today.

Self-explanation capabilities, which exist in a crude form in some expert systems, is a first step in this direction in practical software systems. It is possible to ask, say, a diagnostic system "how did you arrive at that diagnosis?", and it will respond with a trace of the reasoning process employed to get from the symptoms given to the diagnosis generated. It is then usually possible to further query the particular reasoning chain generated by asking "why did you conclude that X was true?" where X is some intermediate conclusion within the diagnosis presented. This feature is, in reality, little more than an automatic trace of the execution path, but it is,nevertheless, a first step in the direction of a self-maintenance capability. There are other, more ambitious examples, such as the TEIRESIAS system that assisted a domain expert in automatically debugging itself, but it was, and it remains, no more than a demonstration system in AI research.

1.10 A need for AI systems

This last point finally makes explicit a general theme that has been running under the last few subsections, but has been left unsaid. Now is the time to say it: each of these advances in software power will need to draw heavily on the field of AI before it will succeed. If we want to upgrade the power of software systems in the ways that I've been suggesting, then we shall have to incorporate AI into practical software systems.

Hence this first chapter ends with the reasons why I believe that software engineers should be interested in adding AI to practical software systems. The next chapter will explore the extra problems that such a move to add AI might cause bearing in mind our earlier discussion of software engineering methodology and the software crisis.

2
AI Problems and Conventional SE Problems

2.1 What is an AI problem?

It's all very well to suggest that we need to incorporate some AI into practical software systems in order to boost their power, but what exactly is this AI stuff? Before I venture to answer this question, let me put to you a simpler question: at what height is a person tall? I imagine that you feel quite confident about the meaning of the word "tall" and about the concept of "tall people", but can you then give me a definition of "tall" such that I can apply the term only when appropriate? No, you can't do this, and similarly I cannot give you a definition of AI such that you will be able to clearly decide between AI software and non-AI software. This is unfortunate, and it causes a lot of problems. But what it does not mean is that the term AI has no useful meaning, any more than it means that the term "tall person" is devoid of useful content. Therefore, in order to gain the comfortable warm feeling that comes with knowledge of what important terms like AI mean, in a general sense at least, we must spend some time looking at example AI problems and noting their salient features. But first, for those readers who really do like a succinct definition, here's a popular one for AI:

> **Artificial Intelligence**: is that field of computer usage which attempts to construct computational mechanisms for activities that are considered to require intelligence when performed by humans.

This 'definition' is not way off-line, and it does provide a starting point for those readers who lack any preconceptions in this area. But just to quickly make the point that this definition is less than perfect: note that an ability to perform complicated mental calculations is a sign of human intelligence, but that this a straightforward and thoroughly conventional application of computer technology - there is no demand for the art and artifice of AI in most numerical computation.

This type of definition of AI is a behavioural one: it specifies the nature of AI in terms of what the system can do, rather than how it does it. As we shall see below, such performance-mode specification is an important feature of AI. Such a definition might be termed an external definition, the alternative is an internal or mechanistic definition. And there are a number of mechanistic definitions of AI. They are particularly popular in the subdomain of expert systems where part of the definition of an expert system typically mentions that the system's behaviour is generated by an inference engine and a knowledge base. On a broader front, the notion of AI systems typically implies the use of **heuristic** mechanisms - i.e. rules of thumb, practical strategies that are shown to work well most of the time but with no general guarantees. In Europe particularly, the term **Knowledge-Based System** is taken as virtually synonymous with AI system, and this, note, is a description of how the system works rather than what it can do.

In order to approach the notion of AI, let me present and discuss a tabularization that contrasts AI and non-AI problems.

AI Problems	Conventional software problems
1. incomplete, performance-mode definitions	complete, abstract definitions
2. solutions adequate/ inadequate	solutions testably correct/incorrect
3. poor static approximations	quite good static approximation
4. resistant to modular approximation	quite good modular approximations
5. poorly circumscribable	accurately circumscribable

Let's start with point (1), the problem specification issue.

2.2   Ill-defined specifications

My point (1), tabulated above, amounts to the statement that AI problems are ill-defined. They are typically defined (if that's the word) by aspects of the behaviour of the only intelligent systems known - i.e. you and me. This is a performance-mode definition in that it is only our problem-solving behaviour that is directly observable, the mechanisms by which we achieve our incredible performances can only be inferred by indirect means. You might now be tempted to point out that a performance-mode definition is just the RFS that we looked at in the last chapter - a functional, or input-output relationship, is the very thing that is directly observable in human problem-solving. This is true, but not very helpful because of the nature of the RFS obtained by the observation of humans using their intelligence to solve problems.

To start with, the functional specification is *not* rigorous, so it's not really an RFS anyway. But, more importantly, it is both incomplete and composed of enumerated instances (and/or approximate generalizations). A traditional RFS, by way of contrast, is complete and captured by an accurate generalization. As an example of this difference, consider the problem of finding the square roots of numbers. An AI-style definition would have to be based on observations of the human performance of this task: "What's the square root of 9?" response 3 - "What's the square root of 25?" response 5 - and so on. I'll not bore you with the details (you can probably construct some more of them yourself). What sort of functional specification do we end up with? It's a partial enumeration of input-output pairs that are part of the square root function. They are, incidentally, part of many other functions as well, e.g. in the above case the specific examples also fit the function that computes the square root of odd numbers greater than 8, and the function that just takes odd numbers to odd numbers.

A proper RFS for this problem would be:

    square_root(x) is y such that $y*y=x$, and $x>0$

and this is very different from the AI-type functional specification:

    square_root(9) --> 3 and **square_root**(25) --> 5

This is in fact a caricature that makes the specification problem in AI seem less of a problem than it actually is. For in a real AI application both the input and the output information may be ill-defined, i.e. we may be unsure of the scope of the necessary input information as well as how best to represent it, and the related output may be similarly hard to pin down accurately. For example, in the area of medical diagnosis, the input-output pairs elicited from the expert diagnostician will be a collection of symptoms yielding a diagnosis of a specific disease. Looking at the input: do we have all the relevant symptoms? Are the ones that we have represented accurately? For example, is blood pressure really the relevant symptom, or is it something else that happens to affect blood pressure? There is no suggestion here that the human diagnostician may be trying to mislead us, but rather the question: can we be sure that he or she hasn't inadvertently misarticulated what is something of an innate skill? The diagnostician may not realize that he or she is taking body-language clues, for example, into account when diagnosing a patient. On the output side: different diagnosticians may come up with differing diagnoses for the same set of symptoms, and it may be difficult to single out any one diagnosis as the correct one. What exactly is a diagnosis? It is surely more than just the general name of a disease, like bacterial meningitis? But how much more? Merely degrees of severity and more specificity within the particular disease class? Or does a diagnosis need to take into account information about the patient - age, general physical condition, etc.?

Even this expert-system-type example is relatively benign, for a specification (however ill-defined) can be based upon overt input-output pairs, and ones moreover in which both the input and the output are (fairly) directly observable. Consider now the problem of natural-language processing (NLP). The input may be directly observable (i.e. a sentence, say, in English - although the real scope of the input needed to support 'understanding' is open to debate again), but what about the output? The meaning extracted exists only in the head of the processor. Answers to the questions of what is represented, and how it is represented, clearly cannot be based on direct observation. So, in this case, we don't even have much clear idea of what sort of output should contribute to any individual input-output mapping.

As a slightly more concrete example, consider the problem of generating summaries of stories written in English. You and I, and most of our friends can do this quite reasonably - so it's clearly 'doable'. But given exactly the same input story, we would all generate different summaries: some might be judged wrong (or, more likely, inaccurate) and others might be judged as essentially the same. Nevertheless, it is hard to imagine that we could reduce the variety of observed input-output pairs to a clean and well-defined set - which would be, of course, still only a partial characterization of the function that we seek.

The summarization of stories is, perhaps, an extreme example, but it does illustrate the difficulties associated with specifying AI problems. And, of course, these difficulties don't disappear when we tackle more tractable AI problems. They just become somewhat less obvious.

So now you know what's meant by an incomplete performance-mode definition - a partial non-RFS, might be another way to describe it- and that's the sort of specification that we must deal with in AI. Before we leave this subtopic I should draw your attention to the use of inductive generalization in expert systems' technology (described in Chapter 7). This approach to knowledge elicitation can be viewed as the production of a generalized 'specification' from a partial performance-mode one.

2.3   Correct versus 'good enough' solutions

The example just given can also be used to illustrate the second point of distinction tabulated above. Irrespective of how you do it, let's suppose that you produce a program that is meant to implement the square_root function. "Is this a correct implementation?" is a reasonable question to ask. And, although it cannot be answered with certainty (despite the fact that the underlying algorithm might be formally verified), we can test the program and decide quite categorically whether it is correct for the actual input values tested. We enter "9", and we get the answer "3". We enter "25", and we get the answer "5". Quite elated by these two instances of correct behaviour, we go for something more ambitious: we enter "16", and to our unbounded joy the answer is "4". All of these answers are correct(I leave the proof of this bald assertion as an exercise for the reader).

So now we know that the implementation is correct for the particular instances tested at least. We know nothing at all about its correctness with respect to the vast majority of the potential computations that it has been designed to be capable of performing. And this is the very problem that the advocates of verification quite rightly point out when confronted by a tested software system. This is then bad enough, but consider the plight of the designer of the story-summarizing system. How is it to be tested?

We input a story of the sort that the system was designed to summarize, and out comes a summary. Is the summary correct? Well, most likely, there is no single correct summary nor even a set of alternative correct summaries. There might well be some clearly incorrect summaries, but, in general, the straightforward notion of decidably correct or incorrect system behaviour even for specific inputs is difficult to pin down for many AI problems. Outputs are more likely to be judged as adequate, or 'as good as our resident expert would have done', etc. With AI problems we typically find that for a given input there is a multiplicity of 'good enough' solutions rather than solutions which are clearly correct or incorrect. So, for AI problems, we often find that the relatively simple property of decidably correct or incorrect input-output pairs is absent. Thus the basis even for testing is missing.

This sort of revelation about the nature of AI systems should appal all self-respecting software engineers, but, unfortunately, justified dismay makes the realization no less true. It just means that the actual problems to be tackled are worse than you thought.

2.4   It's the HOW not the WHAT

One significant objection to the characteristic features of AI problems that I am advocating here, which any but the totally AI-naive should be wanting to challenge me with, is that some AI problems are both completely and precisely specifiable in a thoroughly conventional way - the problem of playing chess is a case in point. Chess has long been considered to be an AI problem, and although I would maintain that it does not typify the nature of AI, it is an AI problem. But the problem of playing chess is completely specifiable, and in a formal abstract way. Have we then completely undermined the significance of this supposedly salient feature of AI problems? Not at all, you'll be pleased to learn. Chess is representative of a sub-class of AI problems: the sub-class that are AI problems in practice but not in principle. This is, in fact, not a major sub-class, but it has had more than its fair share of exposure because it is one of the more tractable sub-classes. And it is, of course, eminently sensible to explore the more tractable sub-classes before we turn our attention to their more difficult brethren - hence the attention and exposure AI problems like chess have received. But we must, at the same time, be careful to recognize that certain features of this sub-class are not general features of AI problems. This means that solution strategies which exploit the non-characteristic sub-class features may not be applicable within the general class of AI problems.

So why is chess an AI problem? Not only is chess a formally specifiable problem, but there is also a well-known, simple algorithm to play perfect chess. The point is that this algorithm is computationally intractable - i.e. it cannot be used in practice because its space and time requirements far exceed any conceivable resources. In addition, the best human experts do not play perfect chess, which suggests (but does not prove) that they employ heuristic strategies in their play. So chess is an AI problem in practice, but not in principle. Chess has a curious RFS: two different input states (i.e. the initial board configuration and whether the system is black or white) mapping to a win (or perhaps a draw) situation.The input and output structures are well defined, as are all the possible ways of transforming input to output (i.e. the legal moves of chess). Nevertheless, we have an AI problem, and this is a consequence of quite simple, but overwhelming complexity - the various options are quite easy to work out, it's just the sheer number of possibilities that defeats the analytical approach (for any conceivable computer). A point of significance for us here is that such problems are not typical AI problems, but formal games and puzzles are often used as the exemplars of AI techniques. So you must beware of such examples. To have validity in AI in general, the technique demonstrated must not rely on the non-AI characteristics of the example problem - they often do.

This sub-class of AI problems illuminates a further useful, and quite general, feature of AI software development. We can view most (perhaps all) AI problems as completely specifiable in principle. So, for example, forecasting the future of the economy might be considered a completely specifiable problem if we're prepared to specify all of the contextual features - i.e. full details of the current state of the economy, similar details of all other national economies, details of the current trends in public opinion, a detailed knowledge of global weather patterns, etc. Clearly, we could never get all the necessary information, but in principle it's possible (it all depends on your principles).

If you'll suspend disbelief for a moment and accept that AI problems are completely specifiable in principle, we can then see AI programming (or system development if you prefer) as:

> the search for an adequate approximation to a well-specified, but formally intractable, problem

and cast in terms of hows and whats:

> **AI system development** is a process a discovering an adequate **HOW** to approximate an impossible **WHAT**.

In other words, we can contrast conventional programming with AI programming in terms of reversing the significance of **HOW**s (the algorithms) and **WHAT**s (the specifications). Given that these two processes, both called programming or system development, are fundamentally different we can then begin to appreciate that adding AI to practical software systems may demand a radical change in system development strategies.

2.5   The problem of dynamics

Point (3) relates back to our earlier discussion of the problems caused by dynamic usage environments for software systems. Many AI problems are inherently dynamic - i.e. they change with time. "Many aspects of the world we inhabit have these properties. Nevertheless, we have software systems performing quite well in dynamic niches - so what's the big deal with AI?" you might demand.

The point is that current software does operate in dynamic niches but it tackles only a static approximation to the fundamentally dynamic problem. Hence, such software is sometimes severely limited in power (i.e. what it can actually do in the niche it occupies), and is nearly always in need of an upgrade - partly because some features of the original problem structure have changed. The very fact that there is a software system operating adequately in some niche is indicative of the fact that there is a quite good static approximation to the problem. The niches where we don't yet see computer software, e.g. management decision making, are characterized, in part, by being dynamic and resistant to reasonable static approximations.

2.6 The quality of modular approximations

A key strategy for coping with complex systems is to modularize them- i.e. break the total system into a collection of more-or-less independent and simpler subsystems. And, like the previous feature, modularization implies approximation, but in this case the degree of approximation involved can be completely counterbalanced by the exchange of information between the modules. So, complex problems are made more intellectually manageable by breaking them into independent subproblems, and then adding the inter-module interaction necessary to yield an accurate reconstruction of the original problem.

As a trivial example, consider once again our sorting problem. Our RFS of the problem did, in fact, break it into two modules: a subproblem of permutation, and another of order checking. The interaction between these two modules was primarily the passing of a list of values from one module to the other (although, as our crude design for an algorithm shows, the necessary interaction is a little more complicated). It is then quite possible, even easy, to accurately modularize the sorting problem, and this is the case with most problems to which conventional software engineering is applied.

Another aspect of similarity with the previous distinctive feature is that it is not the problems as such which are accurately modularizable, but that only readily modularizable versions of the problems are tackled in conventional software engineering. So, as with the static-dynamic dimension of problems, we may well see AI applied to seemingly quite conventional problems but the AI version will be more ambitious and realistic - it will be a manifestation of the problem to which we would like to apply software technology, but whose component subfunctions are too tightly inter-coupled to permit veridical modularization using conventional software technology.

A more realistic example is natural-language processing. There are now many commercially available software systems that boast natural- language interfaces of one sort or another. The obvious, but wrong, conclusion is that natural-language processing (NLP) is a solved problem. The correct inference is that certain highly-simplified manifestations of the NLP problem are accurately modularizable, and are thus amenable to solution by conventional software technology. In fact, a reasonable argument to make is that these commercial systems embody such a gross simplification of the NLP problem that it is no longer an NLP problem - it is a small, formal language with some English-like syntax.

A more ambitious attempt to develop an NLP system was the HEARSAY project of the 70s. The goal was to develop a computer system to "understand" (i.e. extract meaning, not just words and syntax, from) spoken English. The obvious, but simplistic, modularization scheme involves a module for analysis of the speech signal in terms of phonemes, then a module to extract words from the phonetic information, next a syntactic module would generate a syntactic interpretation of the wordstrings, and finally a semantic module could generate a meaning representation with the output of each module feeding successively into the input of the next. This modularization (which was in actuality a good deal more sophisticated than I have suggested) could not be made to work (although the project "met its goals", but that's another story) because the modularization destroyed too much of the essential structure of the original problem. If phonetic, syntactic, semantic, etc. modules are used then they are so tightly-intercoupled that they can't realistically be treated as independent modules. One interesting spin-off from this project was the "blackboard architecture" - a strategy for supporting modularization of highly-intercoupled modules, and one that is found in a number of expert systems shells.

We should note here that, as with skinning cats, there is more than one way to modularize a problem. And I don't just mean that we can often modularize a given problem in several alternative ways, I mean that there are alternative *bases* for determining what a module should embrace. What this can lead to is fundamentally different, alternative modularizations of a given problem. In particular, 'object-based' modules stemming from the **object-oriented** paradigm, will be quite different from the more traditional modules derived from the **structured** methodologies of the 70s and 80s which placed enormous emphasis on modelling of functions, and de-emphasized the modelling of data. One way to characterize an object-based module is that it encapsulates both behaviour and state - i.e. both function and data - whereas in the more traditional modularization schemes these two aspects of computation are kept well separate and data is usually a secondary consideration. Object-oriented analysis and design were introduced in Chapter 1.

2.7 Context-free problems

The final point of difference tabulated (point 5) refers to yet another aspect of approximation - roughly, how well a self-contained approximation to the problem can be formulated independent of its context. Elsewhere (Partridge, 1986), I have discussed this point at length and characterized AI problems as exhibiting tightly coupled context-sensitivity, while more conventional software engineering problems exhibit only loosely coupled context-sensitivity.

It is easily illustrated with the square-root problem and the story summarizer. Abstract mathematical problems, like square root, are at an extreme of the context-sensitivity continuum - in fact, they are largely context free. The problem of square root can be specified independent of all aspects of the real world. The only context necessary is that of mathematics. Thus a program to compute square roots can be written and used as a context-free function. The correctness of this program is independent of the context of its use - e.g. it is not affected by the source of the numbers that it receives as input, nor by the various uses to which its output may be applied.

Consider now the story summarizing system. We already know that there is no reasonable notion of a correct summary, but, in addition, the adequacy of the range of potential summaries will vary drastically dependent upon who is assessing it. The merit of the individual summaries (or the 'correctness' of the program, if you prefer) will depend upon the source of the input story (e.g. who wrote it, and why), the intended use of the summary (e.g. to support a particular line of argument, or to be indexed as an abstract of the original), and finally on the biases and prejudices of the human expert doing the judging.

Natural language, to take the extreme example, cannot be accurately represented as a set of sentences - there is no set of meaningful sentences, and there is no set even of grammatical sentences, under any normal interpretation of the notion of a set. Natural language is just not that sort of phenomenon. It is a thoroughly dynamic and open-ended phenomenon defined in a loose way by the population of its users and how they care to use it. How good a static, modular, and well-circumscribed approximation we can eventually develop remains an interesting open question. But there is every indication that it will have to be treated as an AI problem - perhaps open-ended and dynamic - before we'll see computers with anything like a sophisticated ability to process English.

In order to emphasize this important element of distinction, I'll provide you with examples from a totally different domain: the plant world. When wandering in the desert of New Mexico (to pick a location at random), the alert pedestrian will become aware of at least two rather different sorts of plants: certain more-or-less standard trees and bushes, such as the mesquite tree, together with a range of non-standard, solid, prickly rather than leafy, growing organisms, i.e. cacti. The mesquite tree is a system that is closely coupled to its context, while the cactus tends to be quite loosely coupled, almost context free. If you dig up a mesquite tree and transplant it immediately, it will die. If you rip up a cactus, and leave it sitting on a shelf in the garage, it will probably last for months, even years - it could even flower! A cactus deprived of soil, water and light (i.e. its normal context) is still a viable, self-contained system, a mesquite tree is not. AI problems tend to be like mesquite, and conventional computer science problems like cacti.

One of the conclusions the practising, or even just aspiring, software engineer should draw from the foregoing is that AI problems are just not the sort of problems for which we should be trying to engineer reliable software systems. It just doesn't seem sensible to pursue these largely chimerical phenomena with an intent to capture them in the framework of the explicit and precisely defined logic of a computer system. AI problems may be all very well as fodder for esoteric research projects, which have only to produce a fragile demonstration system, but to continue working on AI problems as a basis for practical software systems is tantamount to lunacy. Strong support for this view can easily be found, and it certainly has some merit, but for the moment let's put it on ice, and take a closer look at the fundamentals of what the software engineer does.

3
Software Engineering Methodology

A chapter on software engineering methodology may occasion some surprise in the alert reader who has read and remembers the contents of Chapter 1. In the first chapter, software engineering was explained by sketching out the task that software engineers perform, and the stages in a 'standard' software development life cycle. The sequence of stages presented comprises a methodology. In this chapter I want to focus attention on the ubiquitous skeletons that underlie the two major methodological variants (one osseous infrastructure for each). Just as the amazing diversity of mammals rests on but a single skeletal design, so the two basic bone structures of software methodology can, and are, fleshed out in many different ways. It is, however, useful to take a hard look at the essential elements of software methodology before we move on to consider the well-padded elaborations that software engineers and AI people actually use, or reject. In this way we can obtain a clear view of the range of problems that AI software introduces into the conventional life cycle: a view unobscured by the various embellishments that each practical methodology carries with it. With a clear appreciation of these problems in mind, we will then be in a position to explore the classical AI-system development life cycle, and see why, despite its problems, it may provide the best basis for engineering AI software.

3.1 Specify and verify - the SAV methodology

Let us start out by trying to do things properly. The keystones of the best (some might say, the only acceptable) way to develop reliable software systems are:

1. complete, prior specification of the problem, and

2. subsequent verification of the claim that the algorithm designed correctly implements the specification.

There are, of course, many detailed frameworks that will accommodate these two key ideas, but I shall lump them all together as the **Specify-And-Verify** or **SAV** approach to software system construction.

Advocates of the SAV methodology have to face a number of problems even if they are concerned only with the implementation of conventional software systems. First, problem specifications can seldom be complete. I am very tempted to replace "seldom" in the preceding sentence by "never", but am restrained by the fact that the sub-class of problems, which, one might reasonably argue, can be completely specified, are a collection of problems that add weight to my general argument - so I shall single this sub-class out for attention.

The sub-class of (perhaps) completely specifiable problems is the collection of abstract formal problems, such as factorization of integers, computing prime numbers, greatest common divisors, eight-queens problem, etc. Another way to characterize this sub-class (or at least pick out some simple exemplars of the sub-class) is that it is typified by the collection of example problems to be found in presentations of the power of the SAV methodology - I'll call it the set of **model computer science problems**. I believe that this sub-class differs significantly from typical software engineering problems, and that failure to appreciate the essential differences has always plagued (and continues to aggravate) the search for a solution to the software crisis. For when the arguments and strategies are developed using the model computer science problems as examples, and the results then have to be applied to practical software problems, that's a sure recipe for repeated disappointment - unless the crucial differences between these two classes of problems are taken into account.

In order to support my contention that there are crucial differences, here's another tabulation of essential differences which can be compared with the one in Chapter 2. It will provide a basis for discussion of my claim that there are essential differences, even if you find this tabulation falls short of being indisputable evidence that I'm right.

Practical software problems	**Model computer science problems**
1. fairly complete, abstract definitions	complete, abstract definition
2. solutions testably correct/ incorrect	solutions provably correct/ incorrect
3. quite good static approximations	perfect static approximations
4. quite good modular approximations	perfect modular approximations
5. accurately circumscribable	completely circumscribable

I would hope that this table is quite meaningful without much additional information. I've already given examples of model computer science problems. Examples of practical software problems are inventory management, payroll production, process-control problems, and so on - i.e. problems without an AI flavour, but real-world problems rather than simple elements of a grand abstraction like mathematics.

To press home the fundamental nature of this new category of problem, let me take you back to my earlier analogy with life in the desert. If mesquite trees are AI problems, and cacti are conventional software engineering problems, then what are the model computer science problems? The answer is: they are the smooth pebbles which are strewn along each and every arroyo (or dry gulch). A pebble exhibits a remarkable detachment from its context. It will typically continue to thrive in the complete and permanent absence of air, water, nutrients and light. In actuality, it's a radically different category of object, and it would be considered to be the height of foolishness to develop techniques for dealing with pebbles and expect to apply these techniques to plants.This analogy may contain a dash of exaggeration, but perhaps no more than that.

3.2   The myth of complete specification

The first column in this table is very like the second column in the previous tabulation of problem-class differences (in Chapter 2). I have changed the column heading, but there's nothing significant in that. But what you may be suspicious about is that I have made a small change to the first entry - I've added the word "fairly". Why did I do this? I did it because "fairly complete" is a more accurate characterization of the sort of specification available to practical software system designers. The notion of a "complete specification" is a convenient fiction that we could live with in Chapter 2, but now that your appreciation of the software engineer's task has matured I can tell it like it really is (and, of course, model computer science problems had not been separated off in Chapter 2 either).

The myth about complete specification of software problems has been discussed at length by Waters (1989), and I can do no better than quote at length from his argument. He begins by saying that the purpose of a specification "is to state the minimally acceptable behaviour of a program completely and exactly. The implementor is allowed to create any program that satisfies the specification." It is often said that a specification functions like a contract between the two, but, as Waters points out, "contracts only work well when both parties are making a good faith effort to work toward a common end. If good faith breaks down, it is always possible for one party to cheat the other without violating the contract."

The problem with specifications (and contracts) is that it is not possible for them to be complete. This is true, because no matter how trivial the program in question, there is essentially no limit to what you have to say. You do not just want some particular input/output relationship. You want a certain level of space and time efficiency. You want reasonable treatment of erroneous input. You want compatibility with other programs you have. You want documentation and other collateral work products. You want modifiability of the program in the face of change. You want the implementation process to be completed at a reasonable cost. You want feedback from the implementor about the contradictions in what you want.

The only way to deal with the impossibility of consistently nailing down everything you want is to assign specifications a different role in the programming process. Instead of setting them up as a defensive measure between adversaries, use them as a tool for communication between colleagues. Under the assumption that the implementor will make a good faith effort to create a quality program, many of the points outlined above can go unsaid. In addition, things should be set up to encourage the implementor to help evolve the specification into a good one.

There are several points of particular interest for us here. First, the complete-specification notion, which is clearly violated by most AI problems, may be a non-starter even for conventional software problems. If this is true, then there is nothing special about AI; it is just an extreme, in this respect. This is, I think, quite important for such a change of viewpoint (i.e. from AI as something rather different from conventional SE, to AI and conventional SE being similar and yet rather different from model CS problem solving), if justified, provides a radical new perspective on the problems of engineering AI software. I shall thus probe this issue a little more before moving on to consider the notion of verifiability.

And second, there is the very general point about complete precision when dealing with computers. There is a deep-seated and widespread belief in the computer world that we must specify completely and precisely whatever it is that we wish a computer system to do for us. Sloppiness is not to be encouraged in the arena of high technology. The upshot of this philosophy is that, most of the time, communicating with computer systems is a pedantic chore that only the most dedicated of humans are willing to tackle. Now, there are certainly occasions when high-precision communication is absolutely essential: take, for example, safety critical applications of computer technology (although I might add that the pedantry of the interface bears no necessary relation to the correctness or appropriateness of the instructions accepted by the system). However, there are also many applications of computer technology in which a 'forgiving' or tolerant computer system, with appropriate safeguards, would be most beneficial. Recent years, with, for example, the Macintosh computers, have given us a glimpse of a viable alternative. But it is taking a long time for the technologists to make computers generally available to those of us who are unwilling to learn the fine details of some pedantic communication protocol. It is possible that commitment to complete and precise specification may be the root cause of this obstacle to more general usage of computers.

As an example of the impossibility of specification completeness, consider the earlier RFS for sorting a list of values:

> **SORT(x)** gives **y**,
>   where the list **y** is a *permutation* of the list **x**,
>   and the list **y** is *ordered*

Suppose that the elements of list **x** happen to be strings of characters: what does an *ordered* list mean exactly? Dictionary order, then whose dictionary? And dictionaries typically only deal with alphabetic characters, how shall we treat non-alphabetic symbols in our list of objects to be *ordered*? In more general terms, the notion of ordering is not well defined for many types of objects. So are there unspecified restrictions on the sorts of objects that can constitute the list **x** ? Or is the order-checking module actually more complex that we might at first have thought?

What are the biggest lists that the resultant program is expected to deal with? Will they cause storage problems in main memory? What sort of efficiency is required before the program can be used effectively? and so on. There are, as Waters points out, an endless stream of further questions that might need to be answered before the implementor can guarantee that the program produced will effectively satisfy the need which originally gave rise to the specification.

You may find my short list of 'incompletenesses' unconvincing, but remember that it came from a problem that is both quite trivial and relatively well defined (compared to most AI problems). Is it hard to believe that a realistically large and less abstract problem would give rise to an endless supply of such unaddressed issues, however extensive the specification? Is it conceivable that this wouldn't be the case?

Requirements analysis can, and should, go a long way towards uncovering and resolving the hidden features of proposed software systems, but it can never be exhaustive. In fact, Rich and Waters (1988) argue at length for the "Myth: Requirements can be complete". They choose the example of withdrawing money from a bank teller machine; the initial requirements might be:

> After the customer has inserted the bank card, entered the correct password, and specified how much is to be withdrawn, the correct account must be identified, debited by the specified amount and the cash dispensed to the customer, etc.

This is, of course, nowhere near complete, but could it ever be?

> To start with, a lot of details are missing regarding the user interface: What kinds of directions are displayed to the customer? How is the customer to select among various accounts? What kind of acknowledgement is produced? To be complete, these details must include the layout of every screen and printout, or at least a set of criteria for judging acceptability of these layouts. Even after the interface details are all specified, the requirement is still far from complete. For example, consider just the operation of checking the customer's password. What are passwords to be compared against? If this involves a central repository of password information, how is this to be protected against potential fraud within the bank? What kind of response time is required? Is anything to be done to prevent possible tampering with bank cards? Looking deeper, a truly complete requirement would have to list every possible error that could occur - in the customer's input, the teller machine, the central bank computer, the communication lines - and state exactly how each error should be handled. (Rich and Waters, 1988, p.42)

For Rich and Waters, "At best, requirements are only approximations", and the subsequent specifications cannot be expected to fill in the holes by merely a move to more formal precision. This viewpoint causes them to see software development as a process in which the developer must be oriented towards making reasonable assumptions about unspecified properties, rather than trying to minimally satisfy specified properties.

A closely related point is whether specification can be completed before implementation begins, for the model that requires complete specification prior to implementation clearly implies that complete specification is possible. "This model," write Swartout and Balzer(1982), "is overly naive, and does not match reality. Specification and implementation are, in fact, intimately intertwined because they are, respectively, the already-fixed and the yet-to-be-done portions of a multi-step system development ... It was then natural [i.e. when multi-step methodologies were accepted], though naive, to partition this multi-step development process into two disjoint partitions: specification and implementation. But this partitioning is entirely arbitrary. Every specification is an implementation at some other higher level specification" (p. 26 in Agresti, 1986, reprint).

Swartout and Balzer emphasize that it is still of the utmost importance to keep unnecessary implementation decisions out of specifications and to perform maintenance by "modifying the specification and reoptimizing the altered definition. These observations should indicate that the specification process is more complex and evolutionary than previously believed and they raise the question of the viability of the pervasive view of a specification as a fixed contract between a client and an implementer." (p. 27)

There are clearly some grounds for challenging the key notion of complete specification; it is thus all the more surprising that so little debate and discussion surrounds this central question. I've nailed my colours to the mast with the heading to this subsection, but the question merits more than expressions of belief or disbelief, and efforts to implement practical AI software will force the necessary further discussion upon the software community.

One often hears of the plea for more "formal methods" in software design and development (the general notion was introduced in Chapter 1). The origin of this advocacy for a more formal approach was perhaps the general, and quite justified, dissatisfaction with software specifications couched in natural-language. There are several good critiques that expose the weaknesses of specifications resting on the inherent informality of say, English, however assiduous the specifiers are in their vain attempts to chase away errors of omission, ambiguities, contradictions, etc. - see Hill (1972) or Meyer(1985). Meyer (1985) lists the following "seven sins of the specifier" and uses them to highlight the weaknesses of natural-language specification and then the strengths of formal specification.

The Seven Sins of the Specifier

noise	an element that does not carry information relevant to any feature of the problem; variants: redundancy, remorse
silence	a feature of the problem that is not covered by any element of the text
overspecification	an element that corresponds not to a feature of

	the problem but to a feature of a possible solution
contradiction	two or more elements that define a feature of the system in an incompatible way
ambiguity	an element that makes it possible to interpret a feature of the problem in at least two different ways
forward reference	an element that uses features of the problem not defined until later in the text
wishful thinking	an element that defines a feature of the problem in such a way that a candidate solution cannot realistically be validated with respect to this feature

It is generally agreed that a move to more formal specification of software systems should contribute to the goal of more reliable software products. A number of formal languages, known as **specification languages**, are now available. The Vienna Development Method (VDM), originally designed for programming language specification by the IBM laboratory in Vienna, is one such specification language (see Andrews, 1990, for a short tutorial and Jones, 1986, for a more exhaustive treatment). Another popular specification language is **Z** developed by The Programming Research Group at Oxford University (see Ince, 1990, for a short tutorial, and Ince, 1988, for an extensive one).

And, as we have seen, the move to make software development an engineering science is sometimes viewed as a substantial shift into the realms of formal logic. In recent years, we have witnessed the blossoming of the logic programming movement, and within this general area there is advocacy of logic as a formal specification language (and also as a formal requirements-specification language as we shall see in Chapter 5). The significance of this movement, from our current perspective, is that, as its advocates point out, a specification couched in (an appropriate subset of) logic is also an executable program - a Prolog program. Hence the whole spectrum of knotty problems occasioned by the need to design algorithms to meet specifications collapses to nought.

As you might guess, this sort of good news is just too good to be true. For a start, a logically correct specification may be a computationally intractable algorithm. As an example, consider our specification of the **SORT** problem. The algorithm embodied in the logical specification, i.e. a permutation generator followed by an order-checker, is much too inefficient to use. So a correct specification is only part of the problem, and it may be only a small part. But we might note at this point (for it is addressed more fully before the end of this chapter) that although an executable logic-based specification may constitute an impractically inefficient program, it may, nevertheless, serve quite admirably as a prototype of the final system. The practical constraints (of, say, excessive running time for large data sets) that must be accommodated by the final product may be avoidable without penalty within a precursory prototyping exercise.

A second hitch in the logic programmer's world-view becomes apparent when we are contemplating AI programming rather than conventional programming. A quote from Kowalski (1984), illustrates this misconception neatly. He says: "Good programmers start with rigid, or at least formal, software specifications and then implement them correctly first time round" (p. 95). In fairness I ought to add that Kowalski is not focusing on AI software, but it is clearly meant to be within the compass of his comments. As you will see in Chapter 5, Kowalski feels that although some trial and error (i.e. exploratory activity) is unavoidable, it can be packed neatly away in requirements analysis once we use an executable requirements specification language such as Prolog. As you will realize from our earlier characterizations of conventional as distinct from AI system development, his somewhat bald assertion (quoted above) may be a little over the top with respect to conventional notions of programming, but for AI programming it misses the point completely: the construction of AI software centres on finding an adequate tractable approximation to an intractable problem. Subsequent to the task of finding this adequate approximation, a more conventional specification may be forthcoming, but this is merely the tidying up after the difficult work has been done.

Hogger(1988) tries to build in a realization that AI system development is fundamentally exploratory by noting that the current version of a system may well be an approximation to what we are aiming at, but it is, nevertheless, a specification of a particular computation. Then we should separate the correctness of our approximation from its aptness as an adequate solution to the problem. And, moreover, a logic-based analysis of our current approximation will enable us to formally comprehend the implications of exploratory changes introduced. Interesting as it is, there are a number of threads of reasoning in this proposal which invite discussion. But let me just point out that even if a logic-based analysis of a large program is possible, it will tell us only about "the logical impact" of our updates. Is there any necessary relation between "logical impact" and intended meaning - i.e. (to use Hogger's terms) can the logical correctness of the representation of the current approximation be expected to have any significant bearing on the central problem, the aptness of the approximation? Whilst the correctness of the representation would be a nice thing to know about, and constitute a real advance, it probably goes only a little way towards solving the fundamental problems of exploratory software development.

So, movements like logic programming are not to be dismissed out of hand, but neither are they to be taken on board, especially in an AI context, in the spirit that any move to a more formal basis must be an advance - they are sometimes an advance up a cul de sac, a long one perhaps, but not one with the goals that we have in mind at the end of it.

3.3 What is verifiable?

Verification is the second key point in the SAV methodology. In Chapter 1 we explored this notion a little and saw that a wide spectrum of opinions are available: from program verification being a totally misguided idea right through to it being our only real hope for elimination of the software crisis. At this point I want to emphasize what this positive hope is and why it may be seen as the only route to reliable software systems.

Verification is the process of constructing a logical proof that a given algorithm is functionally equivalent to a specification, and hence that the algorithm correctly implements the specification. Formal verification will provide us with a general assurance that our algorithm will always deliver output as characterized by the specification. It is this *general* assurance that testing can never deliver (as will be made clear below).

Logic is a syntactic exercise. It can be used to determine whether two structures are equivalent, or whether a given structure is deducible from another structure. It is an abstract formalism whose guarantees are necessarily limited to abstract symbol structures. Real programs running on real computers cannot be verified. Nevertheless, verification of the underlying algorithm might be very good start towards eliminating the software crisis. When (or if) large-scale algorithms become verifiable, we may have won a major battle, if not the war.

There are many sophisticated arguments about the sagacity of the urge to verify in computer software development (in Chapter 1, I briefly reviewed them and provided pointers to the major contributions). Fortunately, we can sidestep all these deep and devious arguments and just work from the standpoint that today, and for the foreseeable future, formal verification techniques are not available to deal with large software systems. So SAV, whether desirable or not, or impossible or not, is just not an option that we have. We must, for the time being at least, employ another methodological framework.

3.4   Specify and test - the SAT methodology

Given than we can't completely specify programs, but we can go as far along that road as we wish to, we'll stick with specifying our problems, deciding what we want the computer system to do before we launch into how we might get it to do what we want. And given that we can't even come close to verifying our algorithms, we'll reluctantly abandon that key notion and settle (only temporarily) for the stopgap technique of testing for program correctness. This sort of argument leads us to the essence of the fundamental methodology embraced by the vast majority of the software world - **Specify-And-Test**, the **SAT** methodology.

To some software engineers it is the correct foundation upon which to build more fancy structures for the development of robust and reliable software systems. To others it is a weakened version of SAV, and is used with distaste, to be abandoned just as soon as something more SAV-like becomes available.

So, the two anchor points of the methodology for practising software engineers are: first, specify exactly what is wanted and, finally, test that the system delivers what was specified. Specification, in particular, has been explored immediately above. But the notion of testing software in order to ascertain its reliability has only been mentioned in passing here and there. At this point, we can collect what we know about testing, and consolidate our views on this critical aspect of the software development process.

3.5   Testing for reliability

Perhaps the most famous comment about software testing, as we've already noted, is that of Dijkstra:

Testing shows the presence, not the absence of bugs
in Buxton and Randell (1970) p. 21.

This sort of observation is generally taken to mean that testing is a no-hope process, that is perhaps better than nothing - but not much better. So testing finds its way into the practice of software engineering only because verification techniques are not up to scratch.

I think that testing is generally being sold short. Testing is not a perfect solution but then there are no perfect solutions for guaranteeing the correctness of real-world artefacts. The software engineers might do better to cease gazing wistfully into the realms of logical proof, and to concentrate on improving testing strategies - as indeed many of them do.

The best that can be said of a tested software system is that it is free from known error, but if you've been through a sophisticated search for errors then "free from known error" can be a strong statement to make. Good testing regimes have been developed, and the programs that survive them are robust and reliable systems.

The strategies for constructing sophisticated test data are wide-ranging and comprehensive - and have been outlined in Chapter 1. The tests should, you may remember, probe all the limits of the data values - thus for our sorting problem we should include input that is a maximum-length list, a list just under maximum length, and a list just over. Tests should exercise all control paths in the program - thus sorted and reverse-sorted test lists would check for correct functioning of both branches of the IF-statement in our algorithm, and so on.

Testing, despite its much-maligned basis, is *the* foundation upon which software reliability is built. So much time and effort goes into this feature of the software development process.

3.6   The strengths

I have spent a considerable amount of space on criticizing the fundamentals of conventional software engineering, especially when these are applied, without due thought, to AI system building. But specification, testing and even verification have their roles to play when AI is countenanced - in fact, they need to be exploited to the full, but not mindlessly in the belief that they must be a good thing. We must not waste the accumulated wisdom of several decades of experience and research, but wastage may occur from misuse as well as underuse.

AI systems need to be specified as fully as possible before we embark on designing the system, but certain features of the problem will be identified as exploratory ones. It is no help to over-specify a feature just for the sake of having a precise specification to implement, because an important requirement of AI designs is that they are easily modifiable. Such a characteristic is nice to have in conventional software systems (it makes the maintenance and inevitable changes that much easier), but it is not a prime requirement - in AI it is, because change (in response to behavioural feedback) is an integral part of the development of an adequate system.

Testing as a component of system development methodology is, I have argued, typically undervalued. It is not a perfect solution, but it's the best we have, and, as long as we are aware of its weaknesses, it will continue to be a valuable foundation for robust and reliable software products. Testing is not a weak substitute for verification, but a valid procedure in its own right, that can be used to great effect provided it is used within its limitations (just like any scheme).

This brings me to verification: I've portrayed myself as an anti-verificationist thus far, but nothing's all bad, not even verification. The formal verification of components of software systems has its part to play in the overall quest for robust and reliable software products, but it is certainly not the key strategy and it may not even be of major importance. In attempting to maximize the use of both research and past experience in building software systems, we are well advised to formally specify and verify, whenever possible, the algorithms that comprise as much as possible of our AI systems. This might be possible for large portions of the framework for the AI components, a framework which can be formally specified at the outset. In addition, it might be possible for subfunctions of the adequate system once an incremental procedure has converged on a good enough approximation to the AI problem being tackled.

3.7   The weaknesses

So, despite my derogatory remarks, there are certain strengths associated with conventional software development that can, and must, be exploited in AI system development. But what are the weaknesses? We need to know these so that we can circumvent them, or formulate more appropriate substitutes.

A general source of weakness in software system development strategies stems from having too much faith in dubious assumptions, mostly ones associated with guarantees of correct software systems - complete specifications, formally verified systems, system design as a series of correctness-preserving transformations, software systems as abstract formal objects independent of user context, etc. These sorts of approaches seem to offer the very best of all worlds: software that is guaranteed correct. The temptation is thus to push to achieve practical viability with these techniques, and to leave less ambitious strategies without the benefit of serious and sustained development effort. These less promising techniques, such as testing, are used as stopgaps to be replaced by, in this case, formal verification methods just as soon as possible. But, if it should turn out that the golden promises (or at least, glittering hopes) of formal methodologists cannot, in fact, be cashed out in practice, then software technology will have been held back by the years of neglect of the 'lesser' techniques.

Testing is quite a good example here because it has been extensively developed by the commercial sector as their prime software validation tool, yet it has been hardly considered by the academics for it is unnecessary if the software can be verified. For example, the word "testing" doesn't even occur in the index (let alone as a section of the text) of either Jones (1980) *Software Development: a rigorous approach* or Gries (1981) *The Science of Programming*, and both are prestigious works in the area of software science. Ince (1989), in his tutorial guide *Software Engineering*, makes the point in his preface that his book includes testing "a task often omitted from other books".

This failure to give first-class status to tasks such as testing produces not only a weakness within the developing science of software construction but, in addition, spills over into poor system-design practice. If you think that your design will be correct then it is a waste of time and effort to design in checks and error traps (other than for incorrect input data). Once you realize that your design is not correct, it may be quite awkward (even impossible) to retro-fit the necessary checks and traps. Within a perfect technology redundancy is a negative term, but within an imperfect technology, it is essential: it can be the saviour of systems.

This last example also serves as a rejoinder to the charge that although formal methods may never achieve their ultimate goal, we may, by plugging away at them, go considerably further along the road than currently seems possible. So we must keep pushing on with these formal methods as that's the only way to learn what their real limitations are. And this is all well and good, provided that the informal methods don't suffer as a consequence. If we develop program design methods as if redundancy is a bad (or pointless) thing, then that may mean that we close the door on some good ways to introduce redundancy when we finally find that it is needed.

That's enough of the general weaknesses that spring from excessive zeal with respect to a desire for perfection. It's time to look more closely at the anchor points of practical software science: specification and testing, and since we've been discussing testing, I'll consider that first.

3.8 What are the requirements for testing?

Some less-than-serious readers might be tempted to answer this question with "an inability to do things right" - meaning failure to verify software is the reason for falling back on a testing regime.This is not the sort of answer that I have in mind. I dealt with the general grounds for testing as opposed to verification, what I want to focus your attention on here is the question of what is necessary before we can test a piece of software.

The answer is not tricky but it has serious consequences. Testing requires that the behaviour of the software can be clearly judged to be either correct or incorrect with respect to the specific test data. When you run some test data through a software system you must be able to decide whether the resultant behaviour of the system is correct or not. This is obvious (I hope), and not much of a requirement you might think. After all if you can't even judge the correctness of your system with respect to a set of specific data values then what hope is there for attaining general correctness?

Now consider an AI-ish software system: let's say an expert system for medical diagnosis. We present the system with a set of symptoms, and, many logical inferences later, out comes a diagnosis. Is it the correct one? We show the output to a human expert diagnostician, and she responds: "Yes, this is exactly what I would have diagnosed." (And let's be charitable and assume that a poll of all other experts in this domain supports her positive response). So our software performed correctly on this test, or did it? It clearly did as well as we could have hoped, but was it correct in some abstract sense?The answer is, no, because there is not an abstract sense of correctness in many parts of this domain, and this is itself characteristic of many AI problems (recall the table of differences between AI and conventional software engineering problems given in Chapter 2). In the medical domain much totally consensual decision making is viewed as an agreement on what seems to be best given the current state of knowledge; it is not seen as correct in some absolute and timeless sense. An abstract notion of correctness is typically patchy in its applicability to AI problems - i.e. there are often some clearly correct and incorrect behaviours of an AI software system but there are also behaviours that defy such a simple binary labelling scheme.

Referring once more to the table of differences in Chapter 2, you will see that the difference in typical problem definition is crucial here. Most AI problems are defined (if that's the word) by the behaviour of the only intelligent systems known - i.e. you, me, and a few other specimens of homo sapiens. And this sort of problem definition can quite easily exclude any comprehensive notion of correctness in an absolute sense.

What's the correct meaning of the sentence "I saw you looking"? It all depends on who said it, who they said it to, what the circumstances were, what the speaker's goals were, what the speaker believed that the hearer believed, and so on. The potentially relevant contextual information is endless, and so the original question can, with some justification, be classed as not very meaningful (I hesitate to write simply meaningless, because that is not the only alternative to entirely meaningful). There is no correct meaning (nor set of correct meanings) for a given sentence. Application of a binary decision procedure to program output in this domain (as in many other AI domains) just doesn't seem to be appropriate.

Sparck Jones (1990), for example, raises just this awkward issue with respect to her research on developing software for summarizing stories. There is no correct summary. There are many incorrect summaries, but there are also similarly many different, but adequate, summaries. She states that "we have no clear functional basis for evaluation." (p. 280) They are systems designed to meet some need and "this implies a performance measure related to the system's purpose, which may be more or less easy to find. But it is a measure of acceptability, not of truth".(p. 281)

So the basis for testing software systems, in the classical sense, cannot be assumed when we move to AI software. The weak notion of testing is further weakened by the patchiness of the abstract notion of correctness. This news, although not to be applauded, is also not to be taken as a reason for abandoning all hope of practical AI software systems. There are other approaches to evaluation, as implied by Sparck Jones in the previous paragraph, and we shall explore some of them in later chapters of this book.

The point for the moment is that with AI software the unitary, abstract notion of a traditional testing stage at the bottom of the waterfall (i.e. correct/incorrect decisions on all program output) in software development is unlikely to be usable in its conventional form.

3.9   What's in a specification?

We've already spent considerable time on various aspects of software specification - whether it can ever be complete, why it should be formal, etc. - but it is a very important element of the software design process, so we need to go further.

Ince (1990, p. 261) lists the following properties that, in general, a software system specification should exhibit:

- it should be unambiguous
- it should be free of design and implementation directives
- it should enable the developer to reason about the properties of the system it describes
- it should be free of extraneous detail
- it should be partitioned
- it should be understandable by the customer

This is something of a wish list: it is a list of features that we would like our specifications to exhibit, and we should strive to construct them in accordance with this list. It is a list of tendencies whose presence within a specification we should attempt to maximize rather than a list of clear goals to be achieved. Thus, we have already seen how specifications and implementations tend to intertwine. So the second of the above-listed desiderata is not achievable in an absolute sense, but (all other things being equal) the fewer implementation directives that we have in a specification the better.

What I want to concentrate upon in this section is not the technical issues of formal specification, but issues that stem from the necessary interrelationships between a formal specification and the relevant humans - system designers and users.

A specification for a large software system is a large and complex document, and it is, moreover, a document that contains many implicit consequences - i.e. a specification will specify many problem features implicitly. Thus in our trivial sorting problem, the specification implies that there is a well-defined order relation for list elements. This is nowhere explicitly said in the specification, but is implicitly specified in the specification by the stipulation that the resultant list be an ordered permutation of the original list.

In a large and complex specification it is difficult enough to comprehend all that is specified explicitly, and it is, of course, much more difficult to gain full knowledge of all that is specified implicitly. So, there is a big difference between having a precise specification of a problem, and having a full grasp of all that is in fact specified.

Compounding the problem is the fact that a specification typically specifies only what is true - or, put another way, it specifies what the eventual system will do, and says nothing about what it won't do. So our specification for sorting doesn't specify that it won't sort tree structures, and that it won't sort lists of images, etc. There are clearly many more things that a given software system won't do than it will do. Hence, it would make little sense to attempt to explicitly specify what the system will not do, as well as what it will do. But, having said that, there are some aspects of what a specification excludes that may be worth explicitly stating, perhaps because they may be loosely implied by the specification, or perhaps because it would be particularly damaging to wrongly assume them, etc. Our specification for sorting, for example, is not expected to cover the possibility of infinite lists. We have not explicitly excluded this possibility, but its exclusion is implicit in, for example, the exhaustive check for ordering. If exclusion of infinite lists is an intended constraint (and one suspects that it is) then maybe it should be explicitly excluded in the specification. On the other hand, if this exclusion is thought too obvious (in that it makes no sense to include infinite lists), then explicit inclusion of this list-length constraint within the specification might be viewed as unnecessary clutter. Unfortunately, one person's unnecessary clutter is another's essential detail - this is a rider on the fourth-listed desideratum given above.

The third of the desirable properties listed - i.e. the one concerning facilitation of reasoning about the properties of the specified system - addresses yet another point of communication between specification and the interested human parties. In this case we are concerned to provide the system developer with the facility to link by reasoned argument the specification (which is the developer's major interest and responsibility) with the behavioural properties of the desired system (the customer's major interest). This sort of linkage is necessary in order to check that the system specified is indeed the system that the customer ordered.

Now, we can extend our statement, about the difference between having a specification and having a full grasp of all that is specified, to encompass also full knowledge of what has been excluded from the desired system's behaviour. In sum, we have to avoid equating the possession of a specification (formal or not) with knowing what has, and what hasn't, been specified. This might sound like really bad news, and in truth it's nothing to rejoice about. But is it a special problem for software systems developers? No, and yes, are the answers (in that order).

No, it's a problem that occurs with the development of any complex system. The specification (if I can use that word in this context) of a building or a bridge will similarly embody unforeseen implications in the resultant artefact. What do they do about it? In part, the engineer tackles this problem by building models, prototypes, in order to explore the implicit features of the specification, and we shall discuss this strategy in the following subsection.

But first, I still have to tell you about the "yes" answer. The problem of system features and limitations hidden within the folds of the specification is much worse for the software engineer than for the real engineer - in general. And this aggravation of the problem is due to the tight constraints on acceptable functionality typically found in software systems but not in, say, buildings (we dealt with this point of difference in Chapter 1). The upshot of this crucial difference is that the engineer has considerable freedom to make adjustments to his building while it is being built - i.e. as the implicit features of the specification are elaborated, by the act of construction, and thus become manifest as specific problems. In the world of tight and highly interrelated constraints to be found in software systems, the software engineer dabbles with individual, specific problems as they arise in the implementation at his peril. Such a procedure is a recipe for chaos.

So how is the software engineer to explore the hidden features of a specification? He or she builds prototype systems.

3.10 Prototyping as a link

A prototype is a small-scale version of the desired system, one that facilitates the exploration of a maximum of the implications of the specification with a minimum of resource commitment. As you can see, the name is something of a misnomer in the software context.

Floyd (1984) sees prototyping as consisting of foursteps:

1. functional selection
2. construction
3. evaluation
4. further use

Step 1, functional selection, refers to the choice of functions (or range of features) that the prototype will exhibit - this will be some subset of the functionality of the final product. The difference in functional scope between the prototype and the final system can be delimited by two extremes:

"the system functions implemented are offered in their intended final form but only selected functions are included" - this is **vertical prototyping**

"the functions are not implemented in detail as required in the final system; thus they can be used for demonstration, part of their effect being omitted or simulated" - this is **horizontal prototyping** (Floyd, 1984, p. 4).

Thus a vertical prototype of the sorting problem would an implementation of the order-checking module without the permutation function preceding it. This prototype could be used to explore the accuracy and efficiency of, say, various order-checking strategies. Whereas, if we implemented both modules such that they could deal with, say, lists of integers of length ten, then we would have a horizontal prototype. And, of course, all intermediate mixes are possible. The second feature, construction, refers to the time and effort needed to put the prototype together. Clearly, the amount of effort needed should be much less than for the final system, and this is achievable by judicious use of functional selection as well as use of prototyping tools. In prototyping, with respect to conventional software engineering, the emphasis is on the intended evaluation (what you are expecting to learn that will result in a better specification of the final system), it is not on long-term use - this may be obvious, but it's not true when AI enters the picture.

The evaluation step is the crucial one, for the whole point of the prototype is to gather information that will improve the development of the final system. What information is being sought from the prototype and how it will be gathered (e.g. by providing the necessary resources in terms of personnel and time) should all be clearly set out before the prototype is built. It should not be the case that we build a quick and dirty version of the proposed system and see what we can learn from it.

Further use of the prototype leads us into the domain of incremental system development methodologies. At one extreme, the prototype is a learning vehicle, and having learned all that we can from it, it is thrown away. There is not much choice about this in real engineering. The model building or model bridge can be broken up and discarded, or it can be put on display to gather dust, but what cannot be done with it is to use it as part of the actual building or bridge for which it was a prototype. But the software engineer has this option. A software prototype is exactly the same sort of thing as a software product: they are both software systems, programmed artefacts (a point that we mentioned in Chapter 1).

In fact, it can take a considerable act of will-power for the software designer to throw away the prototype. However little time and effort was expended on the prototype, it was by no means negligible, so why waste it? The overriding temptation is to make maximal use of the prototype in the final system, and this is not necessarily a bad thing. It all depends on the sort of prototyping that you have embarked upon.

Three broad classes of prototyping are sometimes distinguished:

- **prototyping for exploration**, where the emphasis is on clarifying requirements and desirable features of the target system and where alternative possibilities for solutions are discussed

- **prototyping for experimentation**, where the emphasis is on determining the adequacy of a proposed solution before investing in large-scale implementation of the target system

- **prototyping for evolution**, where the emphasis is on adapting the system gradually to changing requirements, which cannot reliably be determined in one early phase (Floyd, 1984, p. 6).

These three classes of prototyping are fuzzy, let's not try to hide that fact. But they are, nevertheless, a useful starting point. Exploratory prototyping is directed towards elucidating the system users' vision of the final product for the software engineer. It contributes primarily towards the construction of the specification. Experimental prototyping is the form that accords most closely with my introduction to the need for prototyping to uncover implicit features of a specification. It focuses on the behaviour of the specified system, and allows a user to determine if the proposed system will in fact do what was envisaged and will not exhibit any undesired behaviours. The third class, evolutionary prototyping, is the one that will lead us onto the incremental development methodologies of AI. It is not, in fact, prototyping at all in a strict sense, and it is sometimes referred to as **versioning**. An evolutionary prototype is not built, evaluated and discarded; it is built, evaluated, modified, and re-evaluated, which leads us to a **Run-Understand-Debug-Edit** (or more memorably **RUDE** cycle) as a possible basis for system development.

One can quite easily accept prototyping as a legitimate component of the software life cycle, and yet utterly reject the incremental notion encapsulated in the RUDE cycle. Consider the case of the wax bell as it was once put to me: if you want to make a bell, do you take a block of metal and carve away at it until it's a bell? No. You make a prototype out of wax. It is quick, cheap and easy to model with a wax prototype. But it also has some disadvantages: it will droop in hot weather, it goes "phlub" instead of "ding-dong", it's a fire hazard, bees will tend to nibble at it, etc. However, this is all beside the point, which is that when you are happy with your prototype you can take it to a foundry where they will make a metal bell out of it using various proven techniques. So, if you want a piece of AI software you don't want to hack it directly out of LISP (carving out a metal bell). It makes more sense to explore and model with a more humanly understandable, malleable, mathematical medium (the wax). Then conventional computer science can use established techniques to turn the mathematical description into a machine-executable form (the foundry). The RUDE approach, when exposed as the metal carving exercise, looks to be clearly the wrong option to go for.

However, there is a response to this argument. Although it certainly appears to be eminently sensible to model with a wax bell rather than start carving away at a lump of metal from the outset, despite the disadvantages of wax as a medium for bells, certain disadvantages may be crucial. Take, for example, the tone disadvantage: a wax bell doesn't ring like a bell, in fact, it doesn't ring at all. Now, the main reason for making a bell is usually to obtain an object that can produce a ringing sound. So exploration of the space of potential bells using wax models may well allow us to find a pleasing-looking bell shape that is also within the technical and budgetary constraints. But the resultant metal bell may not ring with a pleasing sound. Indeed, it may not ring at all, in which case the project could hardly be counted as a success. The point here is that a prototype in a different (more convenient modelling) medium - i.e. a conventional engineering prototype -- may necessarily lack, by virtue of the prototyping medium used, one or more crucial features of the desired final product. This inadequacy of the modelling medium may be obvious, and therefore not a real problem, in the case of the wax bell, but will it always be so obvious when the goal is a large software system?

When we increase the complexity of what we are trying to build by several orders of magnitude over and above that exhibited by the bell problem, there may be aspects of the desired system that are not addressed by any conceivable prototype (partly because we cannot know all of the implications of a large and complex system before we have such a system). Thus prototyping in the more conventional engineering sense certainly has its advantages, but it also has its limitations. The ultimate prototype is some crude version of the final system that will itself become the final system as a result of evolutionary development. To take us solidly back to the world of software systems, I can draw your attention to Turski and Maibaum (1987) who consider a range of possible formalisms as candidates for the modelling medium for software development. They review the advantages and disadvantages of each as well as their applicability to various software domains.

One can argue the toss about the virtues of various modelling mediums as vehicles to support a prototyping expedition (as we can similarly argue about so many of the claims in this field). There is, however, some empirical data available pertaining to the implications of prototyping as opposed to specifying. The existence of real data is a rare occurrence in this area and thus we should not ignore it. Boehm, Gray and Seewaldt (1984) conducted an experiment to compare prototyping and specifying as techniques for software development. Seven teams each tackled the same 2-4K source-code lines project.The specifying teams were constrained to produce a requirements specification and a design specification before any implementation. And the prototyping teams had to produce and exercise a prototype by week five (the midpoint of the overall project). The seven versions of the final system were compared both quantitatively (e.g. lines of code and pages of documentation) and qualitatively (e.g. maintainability and ease of use). Because of the small number of (small) teams involved and the use of limited subjective evaluation, the results should be thought of as no more than suggestive, certainly not definitive. But with this disclaimer in mind, it may be useful to see the major conclusions.

1. Prototyping tended to produce a smaller product, with roughly equivalent performance, using less effort - almost half the size from almost half the effort. The specifiers often found themselves overcommitted by their specifications. "Words are cheap," they ruefully remarked.

2. Prototyping did not tend to produce higher "productivity" (measured as delivered source-code instructions per man hour). However, when "productivity" was measured in equivalent user satisfaction per man hour, prototyping was superior.

3. Prototyping did tend to provide expected benefits such as:
   * better human-machine interfaces
   * always having something that works
   * a reduced deadline effect at the end of the project

4. Prototyping tended to create several negative effects such as:
   * less planning and designing, and more testing and fixing
   * more difficult integration due to lack of interface specification
   * a less coherent design

The authors comment that these last negative effects from prototyping will become particularly critical on larger products. In summary, they say that both prototyping and specifying have valuable advantages that complement each other, and that for most large projects a mix of these two approaches is the best strategy. This last point fits in nicely with Boehm's (1988) "spiral model" of software development which we shall discuss in the next chapter (it is illustrated in Figure 4.7).

I wish to present prototyping as the link which can take us smoothly from the thoroughly respectable procedure of building a small-scale, throwaway model of a proposed system in order to gain useful information before a major commitment is made, to the highly dubious process of continually re-modelling successive, inadequate versions of a system in the hope that a system with the desired characteristics will be forthcoming. The first procedure is prototyping in its strictest sense and the other is software system development at its worst, but it is also prototyping in which a large number of prototypes are built and maximum use is made of each 'prototype' in the final system. All intermediate positions in this spectrum of possibilities provide us with possible strategies for software system development. An interesting question is: at what point do we leave behind the strategies that can give us robust and reliable software and enter the realms of no-hope methodologies? As I shall demonstrate in the next chapter, AI software system development seems to demand a strategy somewhere towards the undesirable end of this range of possibilities. Let's hope that it doesn't necessitate that we cross the 'no-hope' threshold (if there is one).

4
An Incremental and Exploratory Methodology

4.1   Classical methodology and AI problems

Within the previous chapters we have seen mention of a number of different ways in which AI does not mesh well with conventional software engineering both theory and practice. In general, the notion of a more or less linear progression from problem specification to tested software system does not look as though it will be readily applicable to AI software systems. In AI we usually have no abstract specification of the problem which is even close to complete or comprehensive, and the basis for comprehensive testing (let alone verification) also seems to be missing on many occasions.

It is at this point that we can clearly see the sense behind the dismissive view of AI disseminated by Dijkstra, Hoare, and many other Computer Scientists. They habitually talk of problems "that admit nicely factored solutions" as being "the only problems that we can really solve in a satisfactory manner" (Dijkstra, 1972). And that the only way to significantly increase the level of confidence in our programs is to give a convincing proof of correctness.

Does this mean that we must abandon the idea of robust and reliable (and therefore practical) AI software? Or does it mean that we must find a way to curb the worst of AI's excesses and constrain the problems to fit with the SAV (or SAT) methodology? Or does it mean that we must generate a new software system development methodology, one that is tailored to the idiosyncrasies of AI problems? It is, of course,this last option that I shall concentrate on in the remainder of this book. But the reader should realize that to tread this path we have little more than blind faith to sustain us. The eminently sensible alternative takes us away from AI and back to a more concerted study of model computer science problems.

AI software systems have been built and demonstrated, sometimes to great acclaim, within the last three decades. So, it is possible to build AI software, but it has been primarily demonstration systems. There is a world of difference between software that will be judged successful if it performs impressively on a few well-chosen examples administered by a doting parent, and software that needs to run the gauntlet of disinterested, or even downright hostile, users day after day. Nevertheless, we might learn something from a study of the way that AI demonstration systems are typically constructed.

4.2   The RUDE cycle

When we come to study the strategies actually used for building AI demonstrations, we find (not too surprisingly) that these somewhat ad hoc systems are built in similarly ad hoc ways, but some general features are discernible. In particular, AI systems tend to be built incrementally - an evolutionary paradigm is used. The essence of these incremental methodologies is captured in the notion of the RUDE cycle.

The fundamental elements of all incremental system development procedures are:

1. **Run** the current version of the system

2. **Understand** the behaviour observed

3. **Debug** the underlying algorithm to eliminate undesired behavioural characteristics and introduce missing, but desired, ones

4. **Edit** the program to introduce the modifications decided upon.

An illustration of this general procedure is provided in Figure 4.1.

The RUDE cycle as a basis for software development has its problems. That much should be obvious from our earlier discussion of the problems that beset all software development together with an inspection of the RUDE cycle itself - lack of a clear initial specification and criterion for success, and its iterative framework containing no guarantee of termination. But is there any hope that it might form the core of a methodology for developing robust and reliable AI software? Can we develop a discipline of incremental software development? First, we need to look more closely at the problems associated with this process.

4.3   How do we start?

The first question, which I glossed over in my brief introduction to the RUDE cycle, is where do we get the first version of our system from? How do we start this process of incremental development?

What we need is a runnable prototype. Hence, the first link-up with the last section of the previous chapter. We can construct a first version of the proposed AI software in much the same way as we construct prototype systems in conventional software engineering. But the AI context does introduce some salient differences in the prototyping strategy.

To begin with, in AI we have no illusions about our specification: it is either incomplete, or the specification of an intractable problem, or both. We are aiming only for a software system that is an adequate approximation to the initial problem, and adequacy is primarily a behavioural characteristic. And, if this isn't bad enough, behavioural adequacy is not a readily decidable property like behavioural correctness, such as conventional testing strategies enjoy. Faint-hearted readers, and those who were never too convinced that AI software was a good idea in first place, can, at this point and with the strength of conviction born of sure knowledge, abandon all hope for practical

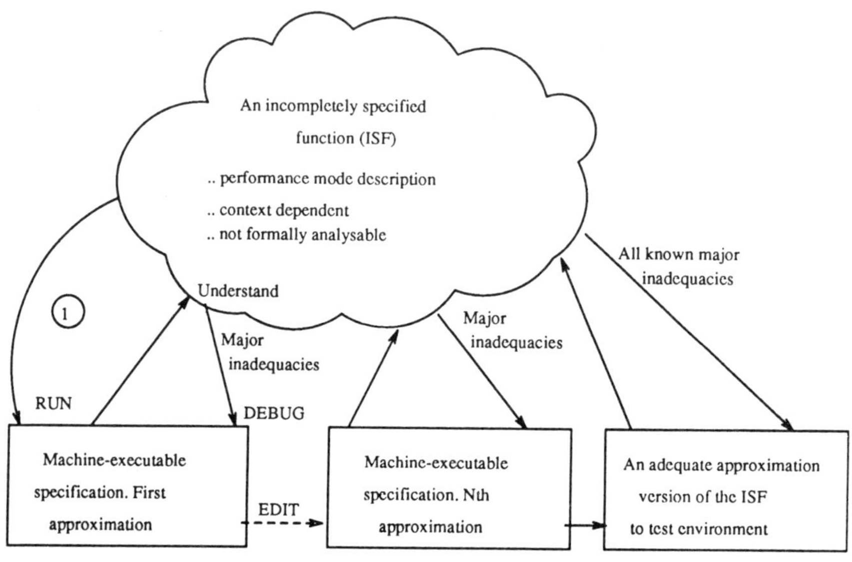

Fig 4.1 "The RUDE cycle"

AI software - and join the confirmed non-believers led by Dijkstra. But the rest of us will push on to see what can be done with this seemingly hopeless state of affairs.

Our AI-system prototype is thus not a prototype at all (in the strict sense of a throwaway experiment): it is a first version (hopefully) of what will subsequently become an adequate, practical AI system. In this respect it is quite like the notion of evolutionary prototyping as described at the end of the previous chapter. The main difference is that we are not versioning in order to adapt the system to changing requirements, but versioning in order to find an adequate approximation to the requirements.

This first version is a probe into the vast space of behaviours that surround the ideal (but impossible) solution to the problem. The point is that the probe is not a disposable one to be discarded after we have learnt all we can about a particular locality of solution space. It is to be an evolving probe, and like a ferret in a rabbit warren it should work its way around the space until it finds an adequate solution. Unfortunately, this cute simile breaks down when we observe that the ferret will actively explore the potential rabbit-space of the warren, while our first version of a software system will do nothing of the sort in its problem space - it will just sit there, reporting on its immediate locality, but making absolutely no effort to look elsewhere. It is, of course, the AI-software engineer who does the ferreting (as it were) on the basis of the information gained from the passive probe.

The AI-software engineer must gather behavioural data from this first version of the software, analyse its import, and then devise a second version of the software to probe in a potentially more-adequate part of the space. And this is, of course, just another rendering of the RUDE cycle. All this should make it very clear that a major requirement of the first version system is that it should be readily modifiable - such a requirement has no force if the version is a throwaway prototype. A second crucial requirement is that it does run, and the further the better (see the Wizard-of-Oz approach later in this chapter).

4.4   Malleable software

Software that is readily modifiable is malleable software; it should exhibit a maximum of functional flexibility. The reader with a good memory for details will recall that malleability with respect to software systems received a mention at the very beginning of this book. In that context, I was contrasting bridges and buildings with software systems and making the point that software systems are highly malleable objects. But at that point the emphasis was simply on how easy it is to alter software systems, at this juncture we have the extra constraint that they must be alterable to achieve some predefined behavioural goal (i.e. introduce new behaviours, modify in specific ways existing behaviours, and eliminate undesired behaviours). So now we are discussing malleability as a reshaping to achieve some desired form (modelling in its basic sense, re-modelling would be more accurate if interior designers had not hijacked the term). And there is still an extra complication to add in: we want to change the structure of a program not to achieve a new structure, but primarily to achieve a new behaviour - this discontinuity between means and ends is not at all helpful. What does all this amount to in practice?

Modularity, as always when we are called upon to manage complexity, is an obvious strategy to support malleability. Malleability, as a characteristic of software systems, has two main aspects: we must be able to understand the working of the system - and hence make good judgements about what changes to introduce; and the system must exhibit a maximum of functional decoupling - so that the identified change can be introduced with minimal effect on other subfunctions that we do not wish to modify. These two aspects are both supported by a modular approach to system design.

The rather nasty phenomenon shift that occurs when we must reason from function (system behaviour) to form (how to modify that behaviour by changing the program), and from form to function, is a considerable hindrance to the versioning process. This leads to another guideline for version construction: minimize this discontinuity by choosing a form that accurately reflects function.

Every programmer is familiar with this strategy. You can see it at work when you compare a high-level language program (in say FORTRAN or COBOL) with its compiled equivalent. They both have the same content and exhibit the same behaviours, but the difference in discontinuity between form and function is vast. In fact, this discontinuity for the compiled version is so devastating for attempts to reason between form and function that it proves to be an effective block on such ventures. Hence, a software vendor will typically sell only the object code of the software, and refuse you access to the source code knowing that this is a foolproof way to prevent you from working out how it does what it does, and from meddling effectively with the system. Compiling is a fairly easy technical exercise, decompiling is not. To some extent, it is a decompiling exercise that is demanded in incremental system development that is driven by behavioural inadequacies.

I have discussed this problem previously (Partridge, 1986), and so can terminate this presentation with a couple of further examples and a summarizing illustration, all from the earlier work.

Most people who have had the good fortune to program a computer will probably have come across the formal notation called Backus-Naur Form (BNF). It is used to define the syntax of programming languages, and does so most successfully. BNF is particularly successful, I believe, because it is a representation scheme that clearly displays (rather than masks) the content of what it is defining - i.e. the form of BNF is transparent to its function. This may be an easy example in that the content of what BNF defines is syntactic structure, but it is far superior to, say, English as a representation scheme in this particular role.

MacLennan (1987, p. 160-165) is, it seems, making this very point about BNF. He presents the following precise definition (assuming a prior definition of *digit*) of a number.

1. An *unsigned integer* is a sequence of one or more *digits*.

2. An *integer* has one of the following three forms: it is either a positive sign ('+') followed by an *unsigned integer*, or a negative sign ('-') followed by an *unsigned integer*, or an *unsigned integer* preceded by no sign.

3. A *decimal fraction* is a decimal ('.') immediately followed by an *unsigned integer*.

4. An *exponent part* is a sub-ten symbol ('10') immediately followed by an *integer*.

5. A *decimal number* has one of three forms: It is either an *unsigned integer*, or *decimal fraction*, or an *unsigned integer* followed by a *decimal fraction*.

6. A *unsigned number* has one of three forms: It is either *decimal number*, or an *exponent part*, or a *decimal number* followed by an *exponent part*.

7. Finally, a *number* can have any one of these three forms: It can be a positive sign ('+') followed by an *unsigned number*, or a negative sign ('-') followed by an *unsigned number*, or an *unsigned number* preceded by no sign.

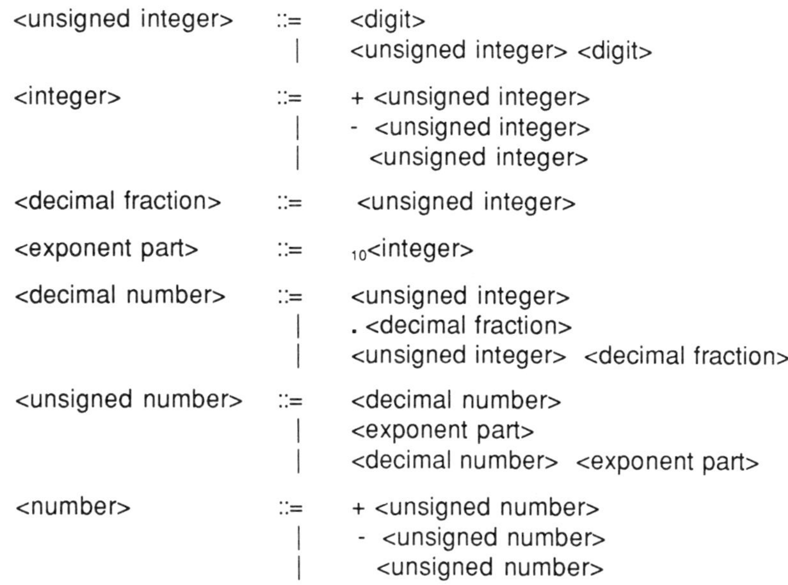

Fig 4.2 A BNF definition of 'number'

As MacLennan says, "We have a feeling that we have read a very precise specification of what a number is without having a very clear idea of what they look like." At this point one typically starts making up examples in order to understand what has been defined. The above definition can be contrasted with the BNF one given in Figure 4.2.

Given some brief tutoring on how to interpret the BNF symbols (such as'|' which means 'or', and '::=' which means 'is defined as'), and a certain familiarity with recursive definitions, the BNF definition exhibits a much smaller distance (distance of representation in Figure 4.3) between form and function than does the English definition. The BNF definition would be much easier to modify as one can 'see' how changes in the structure will yield changes in the function (i.e. what structures it defines) much more easily than with the English definition.

Figure 4.3 (derived from Figure 4.5 in Partridge, 1986) provides a schematic summary of this notion of discontinuity (or distance of representation) together with the distance of successive approximations (or versions of the system) from a position of adequacy within the problem space.

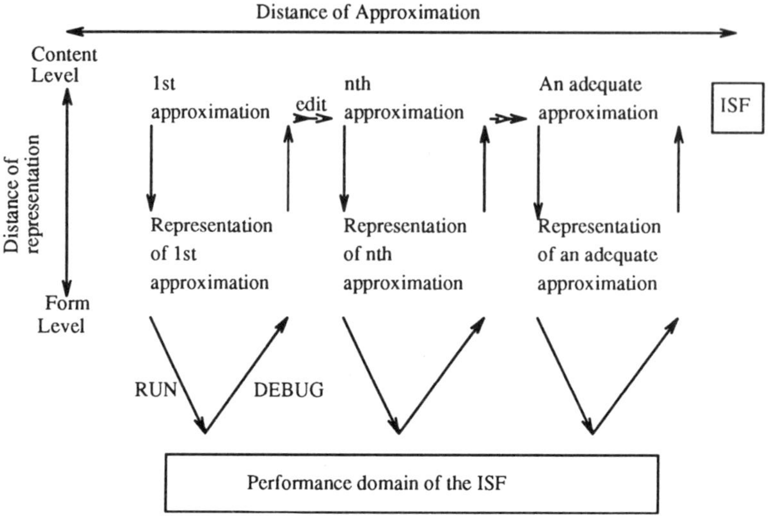

Fig 4.3 A schematic illustration of form-content distance and adequacy distance for successive versions of a system

4.5   AI muscles on a conventional skeleton

In accord with the earlier exhortations to exploit conventional software engineering wisdom as completely as possible, a first version of the AI system should be structured so as to separate out and localize the effects of the AI as much as is possible within the system. The essential metaphor here is one of a body: the rigid and robust bones provide a firm basis for the muscles to operate from and together great power can be produced. To stretch this metaphor to the limit: huge increases in body power (usually called muscle power) can be obtained by building up the muscles on the rigid, fixed skeleton.

For our first version of an AI system we want it to be mostly a robust, reliable, and well-defined skeleton of conventional software. To this framework we can then attach the AI muscles that will provide greater power to the overall system but need to be closely confined and controlled if they are to be developed effectively.

An echo of this strategy is found in conventional software system design strategies: a proposed software system can be tested top-down(i.e. general design decisions before implementation details) by constructing the framework of the system with dummy functions and procedures. These dummy structures, sometimes called stubs, either do nothing or simply return a fixed value, or whatever is necessary to test the general system structure before commitment is made to a detailed design of these stubs.

Clearly, the suggested AI muscles are just such stubs, although how to elaborate the essential details is no longer a clear-cut procedure. In conventional software engineering, once you've tested and are happy with the general framework it is then a fairly straightforward task to design and implement a mechanism to realize each of the well-defined stub functions. In the AI analogue we are faced with the more demanding task of exploring (typically heuristic) designs and implementations that represent an acceptable compromise between adequacy and cost in terms of time and space.

A recent proposal takes this methodological strategy one step further: as part of the Wizard-of-Oz enhancement of the RUDE cycle, Mc Kevitt and Partridge (1991) propose that in the interests of getting prototypes working to the full as early as possible (and thereby gaining a maximum of informative feedback) the system stubs should be active rather than passive. An undeveloped AI muscle can be replaced by a 'hidden' human who supplies, on demand, appropriate, intelligent information. More mature readers will recall the hidden human who was in fact the 'brains' of the Wizard of Oz and hence the name of this approach (younger readers for whom this attempted explanation is still a mystery may want to read the book or see the classic film in order to attain enlightenment). As understanding of the problem develops (and it is expected to develop more quickly as a result of feedback from experimentation with a comprehensive and robust working system), computational alternatives to the Wizard will begin to emerge, and so the role of the Wizard atrophies. The point of the 'hidden' Wizard is so that the behaviour of the hybrid prototype can be under normal conditions -i.e. without system users reacting unnaturally to the knowledge that there is another human 'in the loop'.

This proposal has yet to be evaluated comprehensively, but has been employed with success in the development of the OSCON interface to UNIX (Mc Kevitt, 1990). Clearly, there are some restrictions on its scope of applicability, but it would appear to be a useful technique whenever the system under development (AI software or not, incidentally) is one that interacts directly with human users.

We see the general strategy of isolating AI muscles at work in the current plague of knowledge-based systems. To a first approximation the AI, in the sense of the heuristics to be developed, is encapsulated in individual rules, and the rule-base as a whole is separated off from the processing mechanism (inference engine, if you will). First versions of the system can employ very basic, non-heuristic rules in order to facilitate the construction of a strong skeleton within which heuristic rules and even heuristic reasoning mechanisms can later be introduced.

Finally, Bader, Edwards, Harris-Jones and Hannaford (1988) criticize the basic RUDE cycle for just this reason, as well as the lack of control in the iterative process of version development which, as it happens, is the next subtopic to be addressed. We'll see the details of the methodology of Bader et al. in the next chapter. Incidentally, it's called the POLITE methodology - decompile that acronym if you can.

4.6   How do we proceed?

Let's be kind and assume that we have a first version of our software up and running on a computer system. The task now is to see how it behaves (test it, in more classical language), understand the observed behaviour, and modify the current version so as to give a more adequate subsequent version. This is a

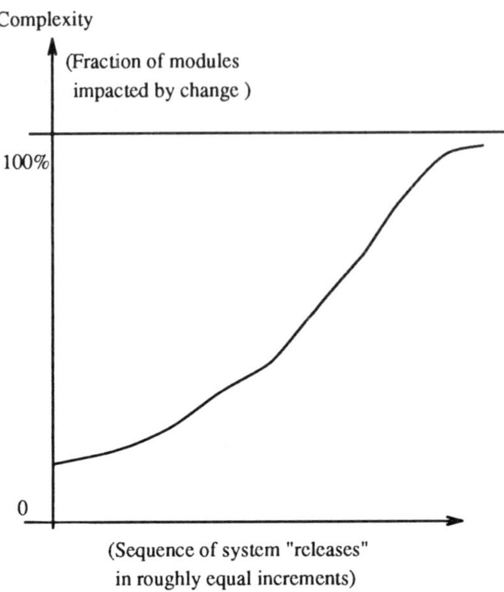

Fig 4.4 Software system complexity as a function of successive modification from Lehman and Belady, 1985, p. 357

procedure that is fraught with danger - why?

"Things are always best at the beginning," said Pascal, apparently (in French one suspects). It is not clear what he was referring to - choux creme, marriage, who knows? - it certainly wasn't the working week, nor was it software systems, but it just goes to show how a universal truth is timeless: computer software wasn't around in the time of Pascal (even FORTRAN hadn't been invented), but his observation encompasses this new phenomenon quite comfortably.

Brooks (1975), who gives the quotation from Pascal, goes on to elaborate: "Systems program building is an entropy-decreasing process, hence inherently metastable. Program maintenance is an entropy-increasing process, and even its most skillful execution only delays the subsistence of the system into unfixable obsolescence" (p. 123).

This is not good news for the incremental system development methodology; it seems to indicate that, starting with an inadequate software system, we can, after a long sequence of modifications, expect to arrive, with some certainty, at only the heat death of our project - i.e. unmanageable chaos. Lehman and Belady (1985) have edited a complete book entitled *Program Evolution*, and they provide general support for Brooks's pessimistic outlook. Figure 4.4 is an empirically determined curve which shows that system complexity seems to rise inexorably with each successive modification.

They have even formulated five laws of program evolution, of which the second is particularly pertinent to our current concerns:

The second law of program evolution

As a large program is continuously changed, its complexity, which reflects deteriorating structure, increases unless work is done to maintain or reduce it. (p. 253)

They point out that the concepts of structure and complexity are imprecisely defined (in this context), and, in particular, complexity (as referred to above) is not the computer science concept of algorithmic complexity. They say, "from the engineering point of view complexity relates strongly to the macro and micro structures of a program. The programmer and the user must be able to visualise and understand the linkages between the various parts of the program and its code ... in a software engineering context the term complexity is used to express the degree to which a program is intelligible ... and we claim that this depends ... primarily ... on the extent and pattern of program interconenctivity [*sic.*] of program structure" (p. 253).

As the notion of program complexity is important for us we might do well to follow up on Lehman and Belady's further explication of the notion. They state:

- Program complexity is *relative*. An absolute measure of understandability cannot be formulated.

- Program complexity is relative to a *level of perception*. A program may be studied at, say, functional, subsystem, component, module and instruction levels. The topology or pattern of interconnections at each level will be largely formed from a subset of the interconnections at the next lower level. Each will be a representation of system complexity. Which one is selected will depend on the objective of the study.

- Program complexity is relative to prior *knowledge* about the program and its use. In particular we may distinguish between the *internal, intrinsic* and *external* complexity of a program. The former we define as that which reflects only the structural attributes of the code. It expresses inversely the relative ease with which a program may, without prior knowledge, be understood directly from the object text. A formal definition would add the assumption that comprehension of the semantic intent of individual statements requires no effort.

For a well-structured program the internal complexity will be related to an intrinsic complexity that reflects the variety, extent and interconnectedness of the various aspects of the application parts of the problem addressed by the program.

External complexity is seen as an inverse measure of the ease with which a program text may be understood when read in conjunction with its documentation. In the limit it would measure the difficulty of understanding the code when accessible, complete and consistent documentation that describes the intent of individual code sections and their joint action in unambiguous terms, is readily available. External complexity really measures the remnant difficulty of understanding when

> the program and its documentation are read and absorbed sequentially. With well structured documentation, however, the external complexity measure at one level is likely to be closely related to the internal complexity at a (the next) higher level.   (Lehman and Belady, 1985, pp. 254-5, authors' emphasis)

They go on to note that directives about software system modification often contain statements of objectives (in addition to the raw functional requirement) like achievement at minimum cost and by a certain date, etc., but there is seldom one requiring minimization of structural degradation. They ask: why is this?

The answer, they suggest, is not because structural degradation cannot be quantified, but because the ultimate purpose of the modification is economic gain, and that is assessed on completion of the change in terms of cost-effectiveness. The value of good structure, however, is long term. It's a property whose benefits are apparent only in a negative sense, in that the system does not deteriorate, or that there is a comparative absence of subsequent problems when the system is changed.

In the context of the RUDE cycle the emphases might be quite different. For any modification (except the last) will have to result in a modifiable system, and this property is likely to be exercised fairly immediately by the same person who did the previous modification. Any modification is thus part of a sequence; it is not a one-off process whose undesirable consequences will only come home to roost at some much later date and to the discomfiture (most likely) of somebody else.

The prognostication for evolving software systems is not good, but it is not as bad as a superficial inspection might lead us to conclude.In particular, the second law of thermodynamics (i.e. that entropy always tends to increase) is true of the universe when taken as a whole - it's true on average if you like. This means that there can be local phenomena for which entropy is steadily decreasing over any period of time, and indeed such islands of entropic decrease do exist - you and I are just two such islands standing up and defying the second law of thermodynamics. The not so good (one might almost say, bad) news is that it will, most likely, get us in the end, but then software system don't have to last forever either. So, some things, things like you and me, are not "always best at the beginning". (I certainly wasn't if my mother is to be believed.) It's true that we're generally not best at the end either, but the point is that complex systems can and do improve over time with successive modifications.

At this point, you might feel obliged to dampen the current buoyancy of the narrative by noting that you and I are organic systems that actively adapt and modify ourselves. Programmed systems are not organic: modifications must be explicitly introduced by some external force. This might suggest that my examples of entropy-defying system development lose some of their validity in the context of software development. But, to return to the familiar domain of bridges and buildings: all major engineering is an entropy-decreasing exercise, and bridges and buildings tend to continue to perform adequately overlong periods of time despite continual modification. So why not software systems? As we know, they are more complex and have tighter functional constraints. Nevertheless, it ought to be possible. We just have to be more sophisticated about how the successive modifications are introduced. The point is that incremental development towards an adequate system performance is not flying in the face of a fundamental law of the physical world. This means it might be possible; it does not mean that it will be easy.

A key to locking out the bad influence of the second law of program evolution is to introduce modifications at the highest level possible in the design structure of the system. This is the conventional wisdom from software engineering. When you have analysed a problem and understood the fault in the current version, you do not dive into the code and modify it (unless the fault is a trivial code-level fault). What you should do is go back to the design documentation and determine where this fault was first introduced into the system - it may be a basic design fault, it may be a fault in the detailed design, or (as I noted above) it may be simply a coding fault. When you have located the origin of the fault, you modify the system to remove it *at the source* - this might mean modifying a modular design document, or it might mean modifying a detailed structural design document. Having corrected the problem at its origin you must then re-elaborate the changed design to determine the actual code changes that it specifies. So, the program code does, of course, become changed, but only as a result of a systematic redesign of the modified system.

Such a scheme of systematic redesign, or controlled modification (as detailed in Chapter 6), would seem to be a necessary basis for a discipline of incremental system development. The reader who has entered properly into the spirit of this text will now be expecting to read about why AI takes us two steps back after this confident step forward towards practical AI software. Surely AI introduces a few extra problems?

To begin with, in AI we lay no claim to a complete specification of the original problem. Do we have design documents that can form a basis for systematic redesign? We are going to develop an adequate implementation as a result of successive modifications of a first version. So, do we cobble together something that may have potential and dive into a long-term commitment with the RUDE cycle? Sometimes we do, but this has got to stop. We must design a first version bearing in mind both malleability and exploitation of conventional aspects of the problem.Then conventional design documents will be available, and thus systematic redesign is an approach to modification that we can use.

Some more unqualified good news is that decompiling (i.e. inferring form from function) is not impossible in the context of the RUDE cycle. This is primarily because we have to modify not a monolithic function but a highly structured, and hierarchically functional object. We thus have access to form-function correspondences at various levels in the system, as you will see when you get to Chapter 6.

4.7   How do we finish?

Having a procedure for successive modification that does not lead us inexorably to a state of high-entropy software systems is a good thing, but it is by no means a complete answer to our overall problem. We now have some inkling of how to proceed sensibly, but how do we know when to stop? Remember that there is no precise specification (at least not one that describes a tractable problem) to measure the performance of the current version against.

This is a nagging problem in AI, but not one that has yet been faced squarely. The PhD demo AI systems have a fairly clear stopping point: it's when your money has run out and you've manage to get the system to do some impressive tricks on a few selected examples. For practical AI software, this will not do. Everyone knows this, but it has not occupied too much of anyone's time as there is no point in learning how to recognize the finish line before you have much idea of which direction it's in and how you might approach it.

We are now beginning to see a growing concern with essentially this problem; it is typically addressed in the guise of 'validating expert systems'. The relative success of expert systems technology - the first major practical exploitation of AI - has forced this halting problem into general awareness.

An expert system has to be validated (and sometimes verified according to the more ambitious practitioners - hence V&V) before it is fit for public use, or any real use, even an in-house application. Validation is a process that determines that a particular version of the software system has attained (or has not attained) an adequate level of performance with a reliability and efficiency that is satisfactory for the proposed application. We shall concentrate on adequate level of performance but we should not lose sight of the fact that a useful practical system must simultaneously satisfy a web of constraints.

So, validation is a stopping test. Successful validation is not necessarily the cue for a full stop on the versioning cycle, it is more the sanctioning of a move from experimental to real-world application.The incremental development of the system may well continue within the system's application niche (in fact, it almost has to), for AI software is never finished: it is always possible to evolve a more adequate system from the current version.

The reason that incremental development is almost certain to continue within the application niche is that validation cannot be a one-step procedure: it must be a long-term in-use procedure. So we can't expect to validate our AI system completely in an abstract test harness. We need cautious use of the system, and then validation will be attained as we build confidence in the system by assessing its performance repeatedly in the work environment. As is sometimes pointed out, this is exactly the way that we assess a human candidate for expert qualification.

There are, at least, two rather different views of the notion of validation with respect to AI software systems. The view presented above expresses the idea that validation and verification are two different processes. The latter is usually associated with the formal notions of proof of correctness, leaving the former term to cover the more down-to-earth, workman-like activities of checking that the system satisfies the operational need. This view is summed up neatly as:

verification confirms "we have built the system right"

validation confirms "we have built the right system"

Verification is used to determine that the system is composed of modules correctly implementing the desired functionality. If, for example, you have determined that a sorting procedure is needed, then the implementation of that sort can be verified (in some sense). Thus you can be assured that the sorting function does indeed sort correctly. Validation is concerned with the problem of whether a sorting function applied in this particular context will contribute to an adequate solution to the problem - i.e. is sorting the right thing to be doing?

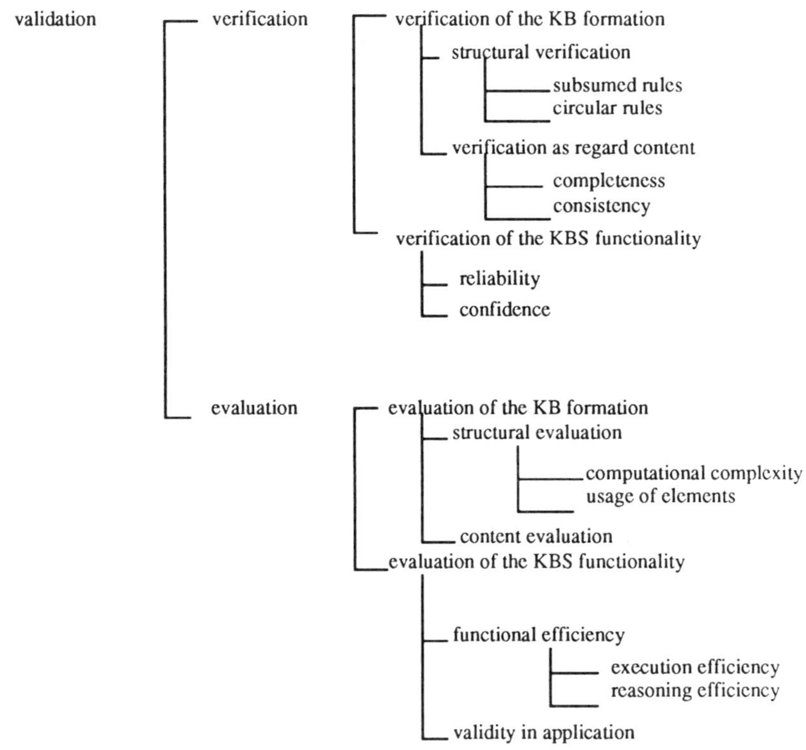

Fig 4.5   "The validation structure used in the VALID project" from Vaudet and Kerdiles, 1989, p.4

Another view of the relationship between validation and verification is found in the VALID project (Vaudet and Kerdiles, 1989) which aims to produce generic validation tools for knowledge-based systems. They have designed VETA a metalanguage for validation. Figure 4.5 illustrates their validation taxonomy.

As you can see, verification is no longer seen as a different sort of checking procedure to validation, but as a component of the validation process - a major subdivision contrasted with *evaluation*. They describe their two major kinds of validation as follows:

By **verification** is meant "proving that the KB or the KBS is in accordance with specifications or expectations".

By **evaluation** is meant "judging or measuring the KB or the KBS characteristics". (Vaudet and Kerdiles, 1989, p.4)

These two views can be brought together if we call validation in the first scheme evaluation. Then given this renaming, you can see that determining that we have built the right system (i.e. validation in the first scheme) seems to closely fit judging the KBS characteristics (i.e. evaluation in the second scheme - the one illustrated).

An important validity-checking technique that has arisen in AI is that of the self-explanation by the system of the reasoning behind its behaviour. Using this technique, which we shall see in detail in Chapter 8, the software system actually presents to the observer a rationale - a justification for the validity - of its specific output. This is a technique that has been pioneered in expert systems (hence the examination of it in Chapter 8) because it is particularly easy to implement in conjunction with the basic architecture of an expert system - i.e. a set of facts and rules together with a mechanism of logical inference. Nevertheless, it is an idea that has potential in all types of software systems, but it is yet to be thoroughly exploited outside (or inside for that matter) the domain of expert systems.

An objection to this approach to software validation is that just because a software system tells us this is how it is computing a result that is no reason to believe it. The point is not that software systems tell lies (mostly they don't), but that any programmmer will tell you how easy it is to tailor a system to output totally misleading information. So can we put any credence in the system's explanation of its behaviour? Clearly, we must be careful, but, given safeguards about the generality of the underlying mechanism and the independent random checking of some explanations, this technique can be reliable and useful. We can't guarantee that the explanation-generating module is correct and never generates spurious explanations, but then this sort of guarantee is never possible in the real world anyway. How do we verify the verifying system? The answer is: we can't, but we can generate sufficient confidence and use the results in conjunction with other information to minimize reliance on any one source.

Interestingly, Michie and Johnston (1984) elevate this feature of AI (often viewed as no more than a minor spin-off from expert systems' technology) to *a* (perhaps *the*) fundamental goal. They see the rise of technology as increasing the complexity of the environment which the human race must learn to comprehend and control if it is to continue to develop and prosper. From the software viewpoint, they believe that we must strive to construct programs which are understandable, and this means that the programs must be built "in the image of the human mind" (p.60). "No longer can they be built with the central aim of maximizing performance and making the best of machine resources. Instead they will have to be ... designed to be anthropocentric" (p. 60). So, for Michie and Jonhston, the important question seems to be not whether the algorithm is a correct implementation of the specification but whether an applied software system is transparent to its users - i.e. can the user readily 'see' why and how the system is doing what it is observed to be doing. As examples of this problem, they cite the Three Mile Island nuclear power station disaster as well as numerous other instances of problems caused by the inscrutability of high-technology systems. As a path to the solution of this problem, they offer us AI. "What AI is about is ... making machines *more* fathomable and *more* under the control of human beings, not less" (p. 214, authors' emphasis). And what they mean is that we need "rule-based systems" for they "are specifically designed to operate with human concepts, both accepting them from the domain specialist and displaying them to the user as explanations" (p. 72). We shall take a look at this technology in

Chapter 8, but for the moment just note this novel angle on software validation, which is fairly radical although quite widespread among the expert systems' technologists.

So far, I have concentrated on the nature of individual elements of a validation strategy, but what about the overall strategy? Testing for correctness has its problems as we noted in the earlier chapters. But a given software system either succeeds on a suite of test data or it doesn't - there's no two ways about it (or perhaps, there's only two ways about it!). Adequacy, as opposed to correctness, is a very different phenomenon. Experts will argue about adequacy of system performance with respect to a suite of test data, and there is no well-defined way to adjudicate.

This raises a question more properly considered earlier (perhaps) of how should we best proceed from one inadequate version of the system to the next. If the system is clearly in error then we know that the error is to be removed in order to progress to the next version, but if the system is fairly adequate, what should we do to generate a more adequate version?

The scheme that I like to invoke in this awkward situation first came to my attention through the architectural design work of Alexander in his influential little book *Notes on the Synthesis of Form* (1964). There has been much subsequent research on design methodology, and his simple linear scheme is undoubtedly much too simple. Nevertheless, his basic idea is still valid and can be used to seed systems development in the AI domain.

His core idea is to approach adequacy through the elimination of major inadequacies. We don't say 'Is this system adequate?', but 'Does it exhibit any major inadequacies?' If so, it is not adequate. This may seem like a trivial shuffling of the words that leaves the problem much the same. It is not. If you can say that a system contains no major inadequacies, that system is adequate.

The implication of this approach to the problem of incremental system development is that the direction of successive modifications of the system should be towards eliminating major behavioural inadequacies of the system. This may be a non-trivial strategy, but it is by no means a solution to the fundamental problem either. In fact, I will leave this topic as a largely unsolved problem, which is what it is in reality, but we shall return to see various approaches to it in the next two chapters.

Bad solutions, based on thoughtlessness or a misguided belief that a sufficient input of energy can cancel out a lack of planning, abound, and form the central topic of the final section in this chapter.

4.8   The question of hacking

By 'hacking' I mean the thoughtless, more or less random, changing of system code in the hope that the problems or system inadequacies will go away. My use of the adjective "thoughtless" needs a little explaining, as hackers might want to object that they sometimes spend long hours hunched over the keyboard thinking out the next fix to try on the system - the changes are far from thoughtlessly introduced. But my use of "thoughtless" refers to the lack of consideration of the system specification and design documents when generating a modification to the system code. You can spend as much time as you like wading back and forth through the program code itself, but you'll seldom see the wood because of all the trees in the way - less metaphorically: an overall view of the system will be obscured by the mass of code details. The resultant, local fixes, will seldom prove to be globally satisfactory in the long run. The preferred alternative is, as we have seen above, a procedure of systematic redesign.

Boehm (1988) dignifies this hacking with the status of a software development model and calls it the **code-and-fix model**. This was, as he says, the basic model used in the earliest days of software development; it contained two steps:

1. write some code,
   and
2. fix the problems in the code.

Boehm sees three primary difficulties with this model:

a. system quickly becomes excessively expensive to maintain,

b. initial system is such a poor match to user's needs that it is either rejected outright or expensively redeveloped,

c. lack of preparation for testing and modification of system means code fixes are expensive.

This view of code hacking is clearly a commercial perspective, with its continual reiteration of the high costs associated with the code-and-fix model. Boehm uses this critique to motivate the emergence of the waterfall model, and then he goes on to explain the subsequent spiral model; we shall also look at both of these models in the final section of this chapter.

But even today, when we can no longer plead ignorance of the real consequences, why is code hacking so prevalent? There are several reasons. The first is the malleability of software systems, as I stressed in the opening chapter of this book. Making unthought-out changes to the code is quick, easy, cheap (in terms of immediate cost) and therefore difficult to resist. Lack of resistance is also due, I think, to the almost inextinguishable optimism of computer programmers, and a refusal to countenance the possibility that any given problem with the system is a fundamental problem in the design rather than a trivial slip in the coding. I'm sure that the psychological factors are complex, and so in order not to trivialize this aspect, I'll say no more, except to record my belief that this is an important factor in the overall problem.

Another important reason for the ubiquity of code hacking in software system's development is to be found in the nature of the tools of the trade. Software tools and software development environments tend to make code hacking even quicker, cheaper, easier and thus less resistible than it already is, and AI-software development which, I shall argue, requires sophisticated support systems has an unfortunate tendency to fuel the problem. A state-of-the-art AI-programming support environment can all too easily be a code hacker's paradise. This may then be a problem that is endemic to AI-software system development - we shall see. But it's not at all obvious how to provide the necessary support for a discipline of incremental system development without at the same time also providing most of the goodies on the code hacker's Christmas wish list. Most powerful tools can be misused, but with the detailed specificity available with software support tools it is tempting to think that we may be able to provide power that is not easily abused.

Finally, code hacking sometimes works. And it nearly always works for really good hackers working on small systems from which no great longevity is expected. Such work is necessarily the norm in educational situations, hence many software engineers enter the world of commercial software development with the firm (but erroneous) conviction that, irrespective of the principles of good practice, they will be able to hack any system into shape. It's viewed as a puzzle,and a challenge to their problem solving abilities at the keyboard.

The ancient programming proverb:

The sooner you start coding, the longer it takes to finish.
(adapted from Ledgard, 1975, p. 10)

can be reconditioned for the incremental context:

The less you consider the design documents, the less chance that you'll ever finish.

or:

The more you concentrate on the code, the less likely that you'll ever finish.

Traditionally, consulting the design documents requires breaking away from the keyboard and leafing through stacks of diagrams and charts. It is part of this breaking away from the keyboard that is so hard to do when you are concentrating on an awkward problem in the system. As we shall see, part of the move to support an effective process of incremental development involves building and maintaining the system designs within the computer system itself. If this were the case, it might be both easier to persuade system developers to consult the designs as well as easier to enforce the stipulation that all modifications must come through the system designs. Interest in such construction and maintenance of system designs within the computer system is now quite intense, not only as part of the general move towards online everything but also as a definite aid to incremental system development methodologies. We shall look at some of there search in this direction in Chapter 6.

4.9 Conventional paradigms

The single, most widely acknowledged (although now somewhat dated) software development paradigm is based upon **the waterfall model**; it is illustrated in Figure 4.6.

Boehm (1988), who devised the waterfall model, presents it as a refinement of a stagewise model that emerged from the problems inherent in the code-and-fix model which we have examined above. According to Boehm, the stagewise model stipulated that software be developed in successive stages such that some planning and design preceded coding and that a proper testing and evaluation stage followed it. The waterfall model was a 1970 refinement that provided two primary enhancements to the stagewise model:

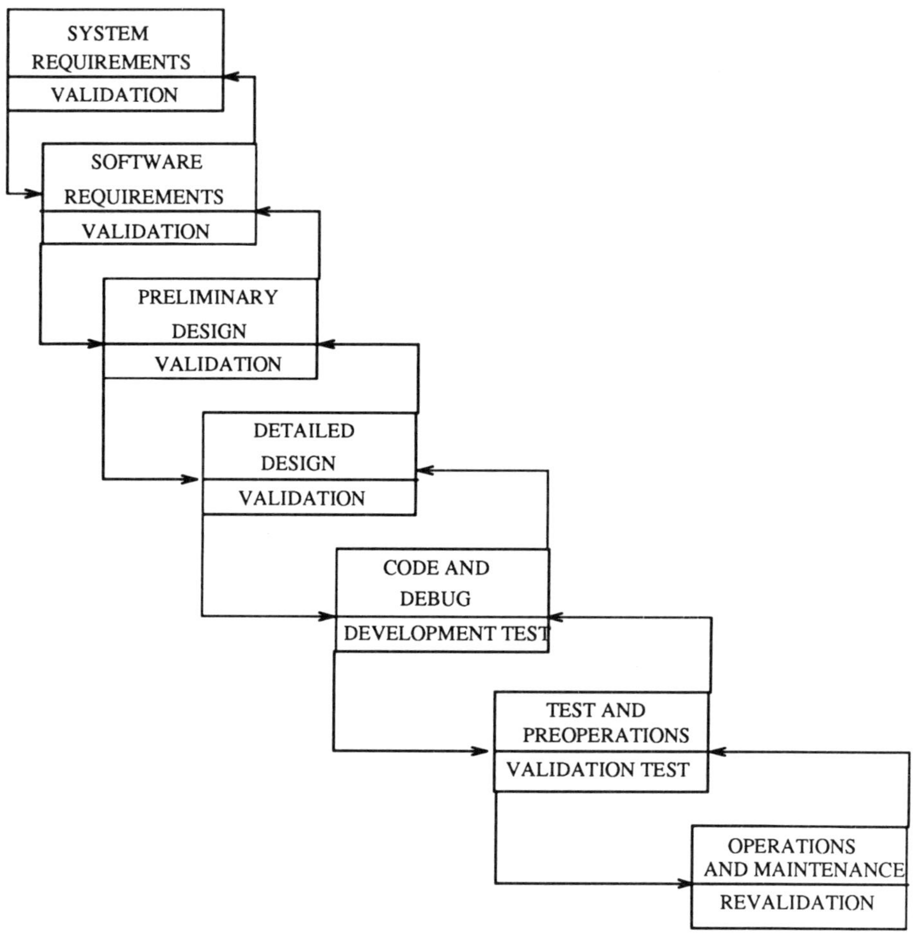

Fig 4.6   The "waterfall" model of software development

(1) Recognition of the feedback loops between stages, and a guideline to confine the feedback loops to successive stages to minimize the expensive rework involved in feedback across many stages.

(2) An initial incorporation of prototyping in the software life cycle, via a "build it twice" step running in parallel with requirements analysis and design.   Boehm, 1988, p. 63

Fundamental difficulties with the waterfall model "have led to the formulation of alternative process models. A primary source of difficulty with the waterfall model has been its emphasis on fully elaborated documents as

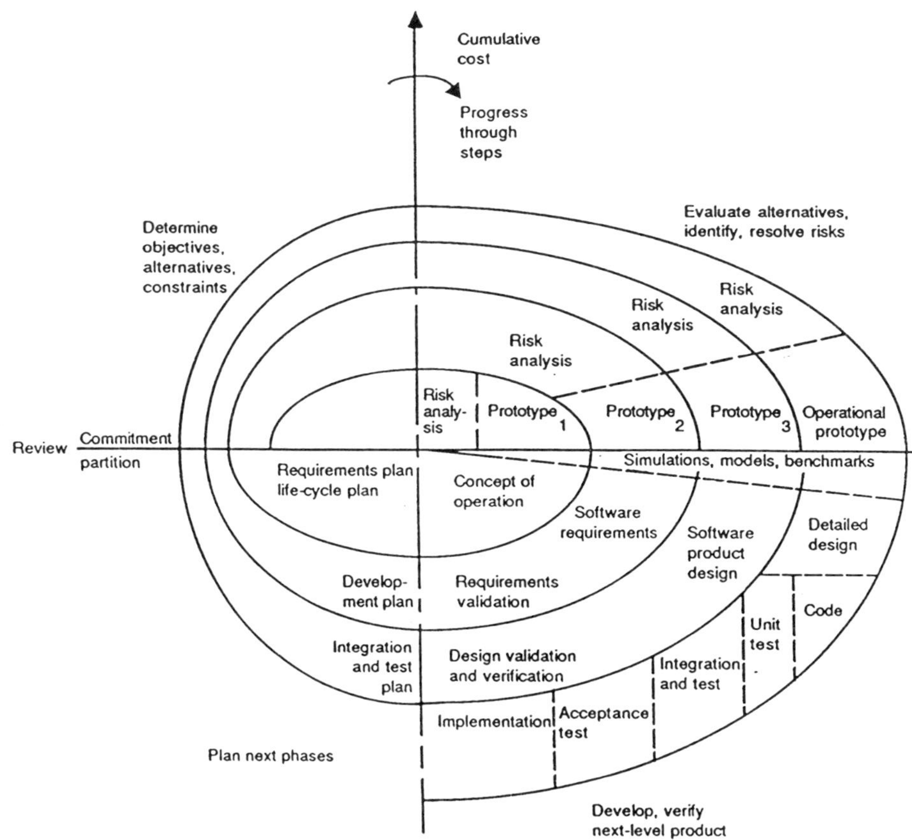

Fig 4.7 The spiral model of the software process

completion criteria for early requirements and design phases." (Boehm, 1988, p.63). For some classes of software(e.g. compilers) this may still be the most effective way to proceed, but for others (e.g. interactive end-user applications) it does not work well.

Boehm offers us three classes of model that have been proposed as improvements over the waterfall - the evolutionary development model, the transform model, and the spiral model. As the first two are dealt at length in subsequent chapters, we'll just look at the spiral model for the moment which is, in fact, also the one that Boehm focuses on.

The spiral model (illustrated in Figure 4.7) reflects the underlying concept that each cycle involves a progression that addresses the same sequence of steps, for each portion of the product and for each of its levels of elaboration ... each cycle of the spiral begins with the identification of

- the objectives of the portion of the product being elaborated (performance, functionality, ability to accommodate change, etc.);

- the alternative means of implementing this portion of the product (design A, design B, reuse, buy, etc.); and

- the constraints imposed on the application of the alternatives (cost, schedule, interface, etc.). p. 65

Boehm terms the spiral "a risk-driven approach", which he contrasts with the "primarily document-driven or code-driven process" portrayed in the earlier models (p. 61). Having identified the alternatives relative to the objectives and constraints, the next step is to evaluate them. "Frequently, this process will identify areas of uncertainty that are significant sources of project risk. If so, the next step should involve the formulation of a cost-effective strategy for resolving the sources of risk. This may involve prototyping, simulation, benchmarking" etc.

Boehm sees the spiral model as accommodating the previous and supposedly alternative (e.g. evolutionary or transforms models) schemes as special cases. For example, if performance risks strongly dominate then the next step may be an evolutionary development one.Whereas, once prototyping efforts have resolved all the performance or user-interface risks, the next step may follow the basic waterfall approach. So, using Boehm's terminology, we might view AI software as software within which performance risks predominate, and reach extremes. Thus the question: is there an adequate approximation to this impossible problem? may be rephrased as: is there an achievable performance level which is both adequate and within acceptable constraints? And dependent upon whether this performance risk refers to overall behaviour (with many component performance risks) or can be contained within specific, non-dominant aspects of system functionality, we can expect overall system development to be primarily RUDE. It will become conventional once the necessary RUDE development steps have been employed to resolve the performance-risk elements of the problem, respectively. But in either case (and in all intermediate ones) Boehm sees the spiral, risk-driven framework as applicable.

Before leaving the spiral model we should see Boehm's answers to four fundamental questions:

1. How does the spiral ever get started?

2. How do you get off the spiral when it is appropriate to terminate a project early?

3. Why does the spiral end so abruptly?

4. What happens to software enhancement (or maintenance)?

To begin with this model is meant to apply equally well to development or enhancement efforts. The model is started by a hypothesis that a software system is needed in some role. The spiral process then involves a test of this hypothesis, and failure of the test terminates the spiral. The alternative to failure is termination by installation of new or modified software. This leads to tests of operational effectiveness which can then lead to further hypotheses about software improvements and a new (maintenance) spiral is initiated.

In his very-readable book on *The Principles of Software Engineering Management*, Gilb (1988) deals with totally conventional software and the management and organizational problems not the programming ones. Of particular interest are his "moves away from the 'Waterfall Model' to the Evolutionary Delivery model" (p. ix). The **evolutionary delivery method** (evo method) is based on the following principle:

Deliver something to a real end-user.
Measure the added-value to the user in all critical dimensions.
Adjust both design and objectives based on observed realities.

(p. 84)

As Gilb explains it the evo method is used to build systems that are "real and evolving. Users can modify design, coding detail and even their final objectives" (p.84). He sees this method as rooted in engineering literature and practice: "It is time the software community recognized the potential of the method and exploited it fully" (p.84). He contrasts the evo method with the dominant 'Waterfall Model' in which there is little or no formal feedback and learning because of the necessity to freeze the system requirements and design specification at an unrealistically early stage of knowledge and experience.

The evo method is not radically new (IBM Federal Systems Division, for example, has been using it since about 1970), but it is, Gilb claims, "still the least understood of all the methods", and this despite the fact that it is "the most impressive method for ensuring dramatic productivity in software products" (p. 260). He then devotes a whole chapter to various sources of commentary on the idea of evolutionary delivery. It is composed of quotations, from both inside and outside software engineering, and (sometimes) his own commentary on them. Within the quotations from engineering, he gives us from B.V. Koen:

Engineering is a risk-taking activity. To control these risks, engineers have many heuristics.

1. They make only small changes in what has worked in the past, but they also
2. try to arrange matters so that if they are wrong they can retreat, and
3. they feed back past results in order to improve future performance.

(Gilb, 1988, p. 301)

This viewpoint is of particular interest because it links back to our Chapter 1 discussion of what exactly is the nature of engineering practice, and what are its implications for development of robust and reliable software products.

Gilb also consider Boehm's spiral model within his chapter on the evo method. He comments that the spiral model is not in any sense identical to the evo method but more of a framework within which evolutionary delivery could be chosen as a strategy. Gilb claims that the evo method, together with the tools and principles supplied in his book, constitutes a complete mechanism for making decisions about risk in software development. He does not see the spiral model as adding any necessary ingredient. It's just another perspective, and one that may be particularly useful in the context within which Boehm finds himself - i.e. where there is a need to find a "politically viable way to convert from a waterfall model dominated environment into a more evolutionary environment, without having to make a major formal shift of direction" (p. 270).

Quite apart from the possibility of these political considerations, the spiral model is far broader in scope than other models we shall look at. This broad perspective in software development is sorely needed but largely neglected (as you will see in the most of the subsequent chapters). The reason for this seems to be that purely technical issues already provide us with more than enough problems, and that when these technical problems (such as specification-implementation correspondence) are solved we will be ready to raise our sights to consider the broader questions of, for example, the societal niche within which the system operates. It is not clear that such a partitioning of the total problem is a workable one, and although the spiral model is far-ranging, it still leaves many issues unaddressed. We shall return to explore some of these societal issues of software development in the last chapter of this book, but for the moment we must focus again on the purely technical questions.

5
New Paradigms for Software Engineering

We are now at the point where we can fully appreciate the inadequacies of conventional software engineering methodology when confronted with AI-ish problems - not to mention its inadequacies *tout court*. And those of us who have not given up on the possibility of practical AI software will probably concede the need for significant changes in the way that software systems are developed - perhaps changes so radical that, in effect, we are looking for a whole new way to go about building software systems, in a phrase, a new paradigm for engineering AI software.

In the last chapter we explored the nature of the incremental scheme that is at root the way that most AI systems are developed. And we saw only too clearly that the RUDE cycle, as a basis for the construction of robust, reliable and maintainable software systems, is also rife with problems. On the positive side however, we saw that there is in fact substantial practical activity with evolutionary schemes in the software-systems world: primarily a strategy of evolutionary software delivery which shadows our desired incremental system development paradigm in a non-trivial way. Before I go on, in Chapter 6 to sketch out the possibilities for a discipline of exploratory programming based on the RUDE cycle, it might be wise to invest one chapter in trying to convince you that the problem has not yet been solved. Then I can't be accused of reinventing the cycle (as it were).

Activity within the software world has not been totally focused on improving specifications, verification techniques, and testing regimes: there have, of course, been attempts to appreciate 'the big picture' and set the software world aright by presenting new paradigms for software-system development. In this chapter we shall examine some of these proposals. Most are not engendered by an appreciation of the extra problems that AI brings to the software engineer, although a number of them do propose the use of AI technology as a crucial element of their paradigm. The majority of these new models for the software development process are a response to the unsolved difficulties of large-scale, but totally conventional, software engineering - the continued presence of undesirable phenomena, legacies of the software crisis, if not the good old software crisis itself.

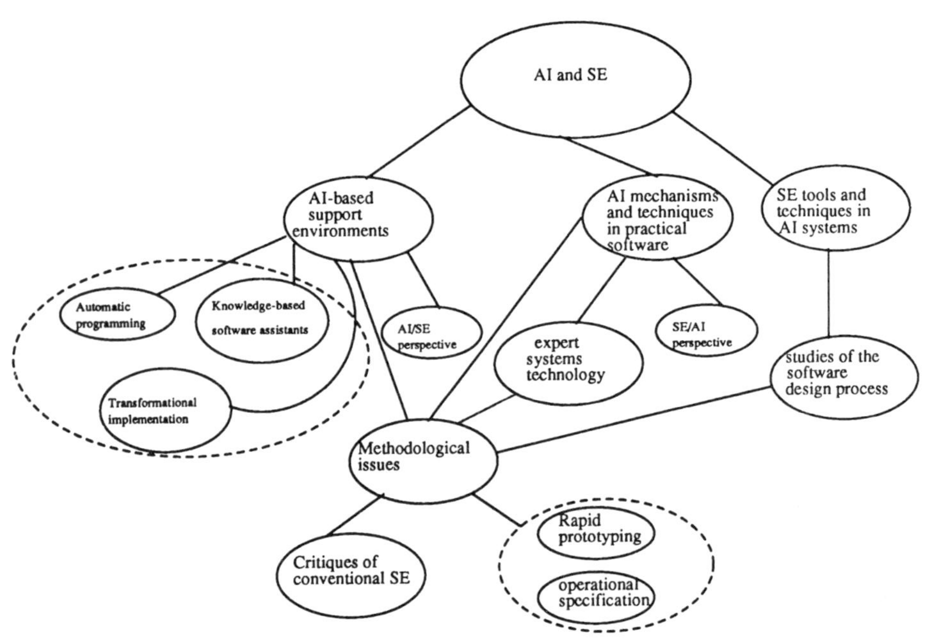

Fig 5.1 "A taxonomy of AI and Software Engineering"

In Figure 5.1 we have a taxonomy of AI and software engineering. The node labelled methodology is the centre of interest for us. You will notice that it is directly connected to a number of other nodes. We can interpret the upward links as providing three perspectives on methodology within this broad domain of AI and software engineering overlap. It is the central perspective - "AI mechanisms and techniques in practical software" - that is of central concern to us, but achievement of this goal will require that we also devote some considerable attention to both of the other two perspectives: sophisticated support environments (probably containing AI-ish features) are needed to help us manage the development of practical AI-software, and, although we might reject the basic framework of conventional software engineering, we should reuse and exploit as much as possible of the conventional wisdom.

We can begin by looking at the possibility that the programming task is (or should be if done properly) quite well defined: we have a formal specification and the task amounts to transforming it into a different sort of formalism, an operational one, a program. Perhaps this transformation from one formalism to another can be done automatically, thereby removing the human from this essentially mechanical process and probably gaining confidence that the transformation is a correctness-preserving one to boot. Automatic programming is the subdiscipline (traditionally of AI) that takes roughly this line of attack on the problem.

5.1 Automatic programming

Within the short span of computer science history, research in automatic programming has had a long run. It was there almost at the outset.With creative problem solving finished once an acceptable specification was developed, it seemed not too unreasonable that a correct operational equivalent could be generated automatically - i.e. that a program could be automatically (logically) deduced from a specification. The temptation to view programming in this theorem-proving manner is yet another legacy of the fact that a program (and in this case the specification as well) is a statement in a formal language and so the power of logic ought to be applicable, etc.

If automatic programming were possible then the bulk of the programmer's headaches would vanish and the software crisis would be a thing of the past, a quaint old phenomenon (like say, phlogiston) to be chuckled over as we wait for the automatic-programming system to churn out the latest, guaranteed correct, implementation of our specification for a desired piece of software. But, sadly, it does not appear to be possible. In fact, it is more likely that we will be chuckling over the early proposals for automatic programming systems as we take a break from the demands for creative input made by the software development environment that we are piloting through a software design sequence. Rich and Waters (1988) provide a comprehensive review of automatic programming, presenting what they see as both its myths and its prospects. They see the simplistic view (outlined above) as describing an unachievable goal because it is based on false assumptions (such as the one we surveyed earlier, that requirements and hence a specification can be complete). But they also see work in automatic programming as making continual progress and thus yielding many benefits which have resulted in (and will continue to produce) dramatic improvements in programmer productivity and in further reduction of the distance between programmers and end users.

Automatic programming, in its extreme manifestation and as the answer to the software engineer's problems, is clearly a pipe dream, but it may have a useful role to play in the future of software engineering. It is an AI topic because, just like straightforward theorem proving, the logical deduction is only a minor part of the problem. There is a practical necessity for heuristics to choose effectively between alternative proof paths, proof strategies, when there are far too many to consider them all, and no well-defined way to choose the best (or even guaranteed adequate choices). There is also a need to represent and efficiently employ domain knowledge. Application-domain expertise is required for software development, and this requirement lands us squarely in the middle of another AI sub-area.

For the reader who would like to delve further into the current state of the art with respect to formal synthesis of programs (particularly the logic-programming approaches), Kodratoff, Franova, and Partridge (1990) give a critical appraisal in *The why and how of program synthesis* as well as provide some positive contributions to the problem. Of special interest to our general concern in this book (i.e. engineering AI software) is the authors' introduction of a formal reverse transformation to give a complete cycle - i.e. specification to algorithm and algorithm to specification. Clearly,we might expect such formalized support for the transition from program behaviour to specification to be most useful in the context of exploratory, evolutionary programming. And as we shall see below, the new paradigms may be iterative and evolutionary but they all pivot on the notion of specification *without ever saying how we draw implications for the specification from observed behavioural inadequacies.* It is one thing to say that changes should be made to the specification and not the implementation, and quite another to determine what those specification changes should be on the basis of observation of the behaviour of an implementation. The failure to address this crucial question is a major reason why the proposed new paradigms fall way short of providing a methodology for the incremental development of AI software.

A useful compendium of the current wisdom on this topic is the collection (mis)titled *Readings in Artificial Intelligence and Software Engineering,* edited by Rich and Waters (1986); it might easily have be entitled *Readings in Automatic Programming.* In the introduction they make the claim that:

> The ultimate goal of artificial intelligence applied to software engineering is *automatic programming.*[!] In the limit, automatic programming would allow a user simply to say what is wanted and have a program produced completely automatically. However, it is unlikely that this sort of performance will be achieved soon. (p. xi, authors' emphasis)

But they note subsequently that "By itself, deductive synthesis is not likely to be a solution to the automatic programming problem. However, deductive methods ... will very likely be an important component of all future automatic programming systems." (p. 1)

This last view is much more in accord with the notions that I shall promote in this chapter. So, where and how will deductive methods fit into a methodology for engineering AI software?

Rich and Waters (1986) provide us with a useful framework within which to develop answers to this question. They explain their scheme with reference to Figure 5.2.

Working from the bottom up there are projects to develop so-called *very high level languages.* Coding (i.e. writing the program) is done with structures that are both human- and problem-oriented such that you almost don't realize that you are indeed programming when you cast your problem in terms of the a language provided. In this (somewhat strained, I admit) sense of automatic programming, the necessary techniques have

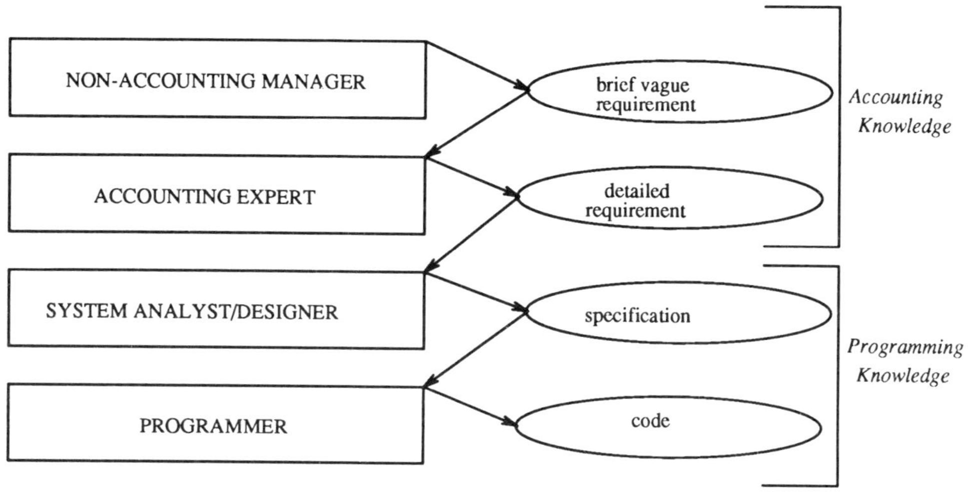

Fig 5.2 "A hierarchy of agents producing an accounting system" from Rich and Waters (1986) p. xii

been 'compiled' into the very high-level language, and the programmer is programming without knowing it (and the built-in constraints in the language ensure that a minimum of errors are introduced).

The complementary line of attack is to work top-down with respect to Figure 5.2. The research in this area centres on converting free-form English into formal requirements and also on the representation of knowledge in a requirements document. In this niche, automatic programming delivers a formal (and by implication reliable) requirements document, which is, of course, not a program, but it would, nevertheless,constitute a big advance towards the more lofty peaks of automatic programming dreams.

Two more ways to view the automatic programming problem are presented by Rich and Waters as "vertical slices" through Figure 5.2. One sort of vertical slice is obtained when we limit the domain so drastically that a complete automatic programming system can be constructed. Within this subdomain we do already find some practical systems in existence. Use of a special-purpose problem-oriented language and a special-purpose program generator makes completely automatic programming possible, but at the cost of a very narrow domain of applicability. Such systems exist for certain business and scientific applications and are called **Application Generators (AG)**.

Horowitz, Kemper and Narasimham (1985) survey the AG systems available. They provide evidence to support the contention that there is an urgent need for more productivity in software engineering - productivity increases in the field have been relatively small in the last decade whilst demand has grown alarmingly, and the qualified manpower available has similarly only increased relatively slightly. And, of course, automatic programming could help alleviate the worst impacts of this problem - the end-users would develop their own software systems given a suitable AG. Quite surprisingly, in this narrative packed with overambitious aspirations yet only lightly sprinkled with mentions of practical demonstrations, an impressive range of practical AG systems exist and perform a useful service in the real world of business systems. So here's a rare opportunity for me to provide you with some concrete details; I shall avail myself of it.

Horowitz et al. (1985) give Table 5.1 to contrast typical programming languages with their equivalent in AG systems. From this table it is quite easy to see why automatic programming is possible in certain domains and what characterizes those domains.

Programming Languages	**Application Generators**
Procedural; programs define computations step by step	Non-procedural; very high level programs that mainly state the required results
Usually non-data-intensive	Data-intensive
Explicit iteration and loops	Implicit iteration
Very wide range of application	Limited problem domains
Detailed documentation necessary	Mostly self-documenting
Prototyping is usually slow and error prone	Supports fast and correct prototyping
Difficult to maintain	Easier to maintain

Table 5.1 A comparison of programming languages and AGs [from Horowitz, Kemper, and Narasimhan, 1985, p. 50]

Automatic programming, in the form of AGs, is a viable technology in domains of data manipulation as opposed to what we might call computation (either numeric or pattern matching operations). This excluded domain is, of course, the major domain of good old-fashioned programming - detailed organizing of the primitive steps to achieve some desired computation. This might seem to limit the scope of AG technology rather severely, and it does, but in the business world especially many of their problems are ones of management, manipulation, retrieval, and presentation of data from large files or data bases. And this is the domain of AG technology. Figure 5.3 is an illustration of the sort of facility that an AG can offer.

As you can see from Figure 5.3, a report generator can really be an automatic programming system. But as you can also see, it's not really a programming problem, at least not one from the major class of programming problems - it's a data retrieval and presentation (or formatting) problem.

```
                              <open file EMPLOYEES>
    file EMPLOYERS            for i:=1 to maxNumOfEmpl do
    list NAME SALARY
    WHERE DEPT= "CSCI"            begin
                                     <retrieve ith data record using
                                       some existing retrieval path>
                                     <extract NAME and SALARY fields>
                                     if DEPT[i] = "CSCI" then

                                         begin

                                             writln(NAME[i],SALARY[i]

                                         end

                                 end
                              <close file EMPLOYEES>


        (a)                   (b)
```

Fig 5.3 Program fragments in (a) a report generator language, and (b) a conventional programming language from Horowitz, Kemper, and Narasimhan, 1985, p. 43

AGs are seen as a powerful technology within their rather limited niche, and so interest focuses on whether and how this technology maybe extended to broaden its scope of applicability. Horowitz *et al.* (1985) argue that the merger of AGs with conventional programming languages is both desirable and feasible as a route to extending their scope.

After that short excursion into the world of AGs, we can return to consider the last approach to the notion of automatic programming.The second slice through our diagram yields the approach in which we find partial automation at many levels. Work with this emphasis has given rise to systems that are termed assistants: The Designer/Verifier's Assistant, the Programmer's Apprentice, the Knowledge-Based Software Assistant, etc. This approach might be termed semi-automatic programming, as some of the programming burden is taken from the software engineer's shoulders - just as much as the current state of the art will permit.

In sum, the practising software engineer is not about to be made redundant by automatic programming systems, but he or she will probably experience one or more of these different manifestations of automatic programming helping to manage the complexity or increase the reliability of the software design and development task. Purely hand-crafted software is rapidly becoming a thing of the past. And as our automatic tools improve we'll see hand-made software, like certain hand-made artefacts, become the expensive and unreliable alternative. Old-fashioned software systems may possess the charms of individuality and the blemishes that a low-tech cottage industry engenders, but most users would willingly forego these niceties when grappling with a software product, as opposed to admiring the one-off features in an old Persian carpet.

5.2 Transformational implementation

This is an active, and therefore important, subfield of automatic programming. A **transformational implementation** scheme is typically based on the notion of achieving program correctness by converting programs in an easily readable, very high-level, wide-spectrum language into an efficient, directly executable form.

If the transformations were all automatic and the original statement of the problem (in that highly qualified language) was something more like a user specification than a conventional program, then we should be right back to the notion of fully automatic programming. Interest in this area stems from the realization that although there is little chance of fully automating tranformations there is a lot of scope for developing very useful, semi-automatic transformations. In other words, there is no requirement to solve the problem completely before anything of use will be forthcoming.

Agresti (1986) in his edited collection, *New Paradigms for Software Development*, distinguishes between the **operational paradigm** and the **transformational paradigm**. He illustrates the differences as shown in Figures 5.4 and 5.5.

Notice that both paradigms focus on the specification of the problem-i.e. they follow the conventional wisdom of SAV/SAT.

Advocates of the operational paradigm expose the fiction that specification and implementation (the **WHAT** and the **HOW**) of a problem can be separated and dealt with sequentially (**WHAT** before **HOW**). The reality is that we cannot discuss the **WHAT** of a system effectively without considerations of design and implementation intruding in our discussions.

A second major problem with the conventional wisdom is that it relegates too many important concerns to the later stage of design. According to Agresti (1986, p. 7), the designer needs to consider:

- Problem-oriented issues of decomposing high-level functions into successively lower levels

- Purely design issues such as information-hiding and abstraction

- Implementation issues such as system performance constraints and the feasibility of the design to be implemented in the target hardware-software environment

The operational paradigm employs a different basis for the separation of specification and implementation. In Agresti's (1986, p. 7) words: "The guiding principle is not to overwhelm system designers by requiring them to assess simultaneously the varied issues above. Instead, the separation is based on problem-oriented versus implementation-oriented concerns. The goal is to produce an operational specification that deals

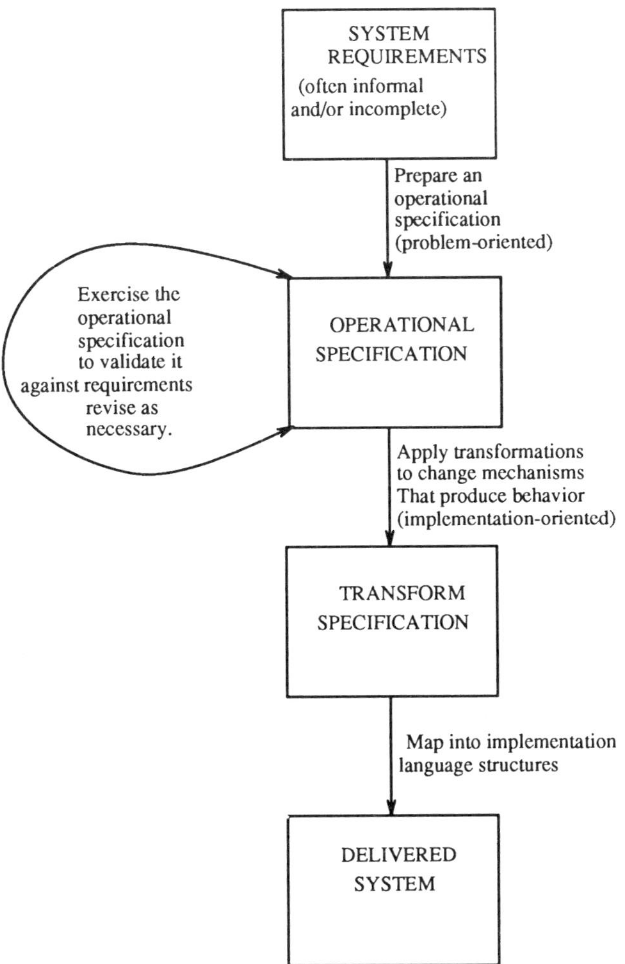

Fig 5.4 "The operational paradigm"

only with problem-oriented issues and to express it in some language or form that enables it to be executed, evaluated, or interpreted to reveal the behaviour of the system." The resulting specification, as Agresti also notes, is a kind of prototype.

According to Agresti (1986), the transformational paradigm "is an approach to software development that uses automated support to apply a series of transformations that change a specification into a concrete software system". This may not strike the reader as very different from

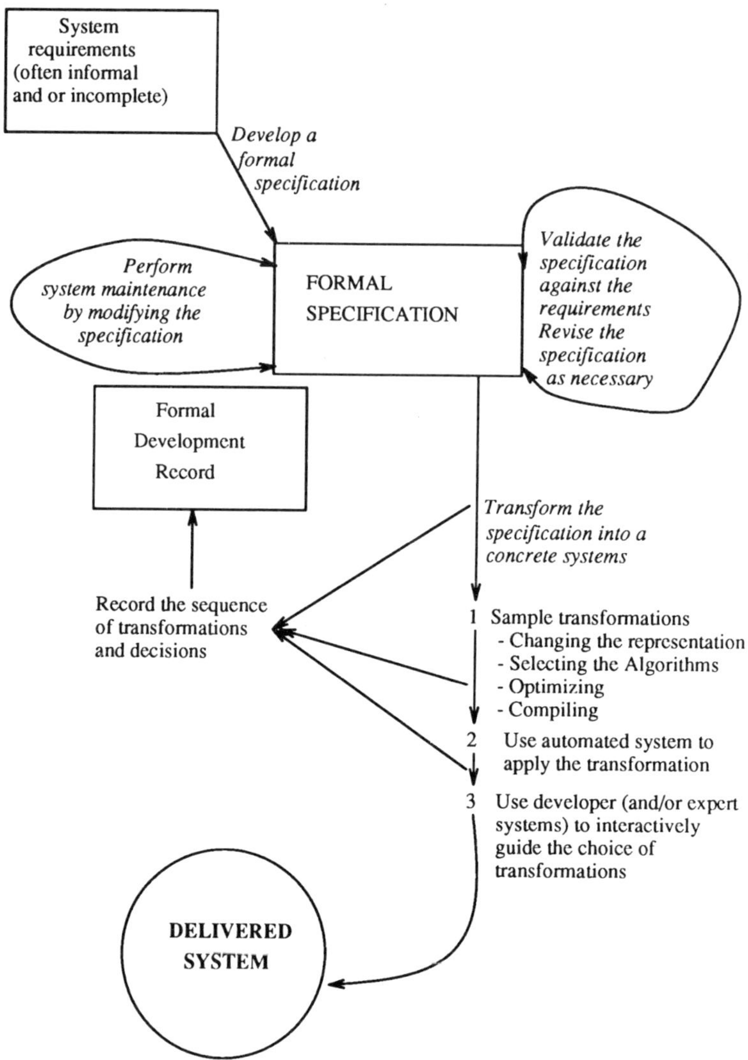

Fig 5.5 "The transformational paradigm" both from Agresti, 1986, p.8 and p.9

the operational paradigm, but the difference in emphasis comes out when he continues: "The transformational approach addresses the labor intensiveness of software development by using specialized computer software to transform successive versions of the developing system mechanically."(p. 8)

So, the operational paradigm focuses on developing an appropriate specification for your system, and the transformational paradigm then concentrates on how to transform most accurately and efficiently your specification into a usable implementation. But notice that both schemes give pride of place to the specification; it is still taken to be the lynch-pin of the software development process.

There are two classes of transformation, **vertical** and **lateral** (Rich and Waters, 1986, p.XV). Vertical transformations are between different levels of abstraction, as, say, from an abstract specification language to a more concrete operational representation. Lateral transformations are within a level of abstraction and are used to produce an alternative equivalent form, as, say, transforming X**2 to X*X. Lateral transformations can then be used to improve program efficiency.

An important spin-off from the transformational paradigm (as we shall see) is that it holds the possibility of recording and storing the essential details of a design and implementation sequence (perhaps a largely human-driven one) for subsequent reuse and replaying of the design and implementation process automatically. Why would you want to keep redesigning and reimplementing the same program? That's the obvious question, and the equally obvious answer is that you wouldn't. But you might well want to keep redesigning and reimplementing variations on the initial specification. And if so, it seems reasonable to expect that substantial portions of the earlier design and implementation sequence could be reused to automate significantly the implementation of successive versions of a system.

This notion has its problems. To begin with we have little idea what are the essential details of a design process, nor how to store them such that they are conveniently retrievable when we want to reuse the stored design knowledge. But clearly, if this concept is not totally impossible (and there's no reason to believe that it is) then it may well contribute to a discipline of incremental system development - this chimerical beast that I claim we need for engineering artificially intelligent software. But this is not generally the motivation for exploring the transformational paradigm, as we can see in the following manifestation of a transformational scheme.

5.3   The "new paradigm" of Balzer, Cheatham, and Green

A representative example of the work on transformational schemes can be found in *Software Technology in the 1990's: Using a New Paradigm*, by Balzer, Cheatham, and Green (1983). Figure 5.6 illustrates their new paradigm and contrasts it with a more conventional paradigm (SAT with prototyping).

If you half-close yours eyes and look at the two diagrams in Figure 5.6, you will gain a fairly accurate impression of the major innovation introduced in the new paradigm. It is that a bunch of the iterative loops back to an earlier stage have been shifted left in order to generate the new paradigm from the old - i.e. the bulk of the iterative system development has been moved from operating on the implemented system to become manipulation of the specification. The new paradigm thus

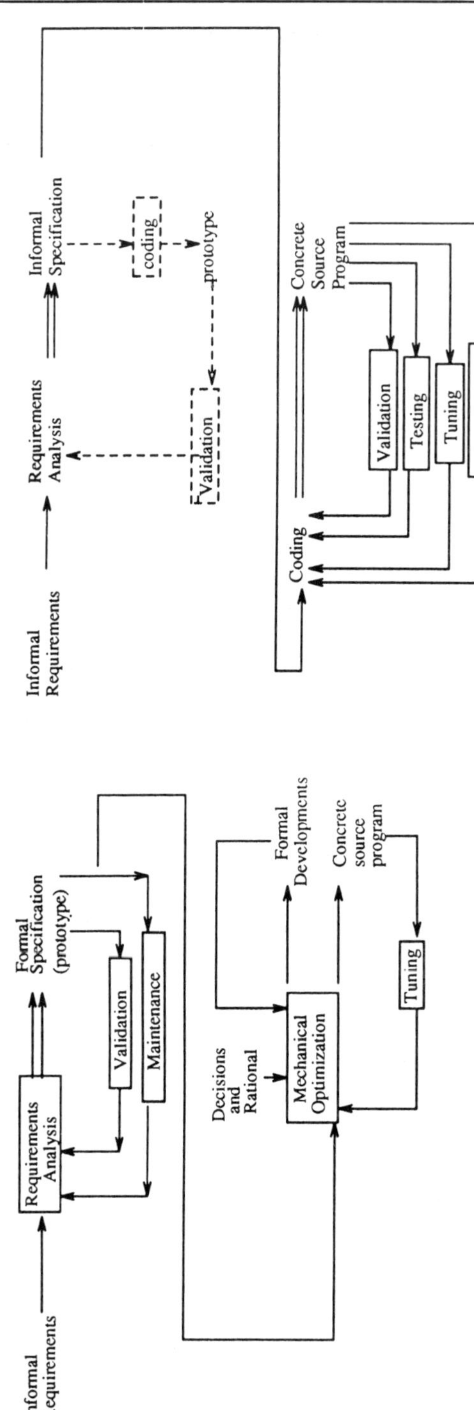

Fig 5.6   "A new paradigm and the conventional paradigm for software development" from Balzer, Cheatham, and Green, 1983

clearly embraces the notion of iterative development, but as development focused on the specification and system requirements.

This is precisely in accord with the oft-heard lament from the centre party of computer science when its members feel motivated to comment on the difficulties facing the AI programmer, to wit. the fundamental mistake is to work with the implementation when it's the specification that you must concentrate on.

The authors are again motivated, not by concerns for AI software, but by the problem of escalating demand for software unmatched by increasing productivity of thoroughly conventional software systems. Hence, they propose more automation of the software development process (and this implies, for them at least, more formalization). The foremost problem, as they see it, is maintainability - both correcting bugs and, more importantly, adding enhancements. From the perspective of AI-software building we might view their goal of tackling the successive-enhancements problem as quite similar to our one of evolutionary software development - but there is a critical difference in the 'well definedness' of the two sorts of enhancement, and we should not forget that either. However, for the moment, we can see that progress towards this maintainability goal may well contribute significantly to our overall goal of engineering AI software.

Balzer, Cheatham, and Green single out two major flaws in the conventional methodology for software development:

1. There is no technology for managing the knowledge-intensive activities that constitute software development processes. These processes, which convert requirements into a specification and then into an implementation, are informal, labor intensive, and largely undocumented. Information behind these processes and the rationale behind each of their steps is crucial for maintenance, but unavailable.

2. Maintenance is performed on source code, a representation that is cluttered with programming-language idiosyncrasies and is likely to be made even more opaque (with respect to attempted visualization of the underlying problem) by the introduction of optimization tricks and the like.

I'm sure that their second flaw actually exists, but the fact that it does so is perhaps more a denunciation of current practice than a criticism of the conventional methodology which (in its better manifestations) makes it quite clear that code-hacking is not the route to system enhancement. But the prime reason why code-hacking is the usual approach to system enhancement is because of the first of the two flaws listed: it is because the record of the prior processes is scanty, when it exists, usually out of date (i.e. it documents some earlier version of the system) and, even more usually, doesn't exist at all in the vicinity of the software. But if it was in the system and updated automatically as new enhancements are introduced, then both of the methodological flaws would have been repaired without recourse to a whole new paradigm. However, as mentioned earlier, we don't know what to store, how to store it, nor how or when to retrieve it, let alone how to make the process automatic (or compulsory) as each new modification to the system is implemented.

Deciding what information to store and how to best store it to constitute effective on-line documentation of a piece of software is, as I've said, an open problem (but see one solution in the Eiffel system in Chapter 9). But it's one that we can confidently expect to get to grips with by appropriate study of the problem. The associated subproblem of ensuring that the on-line documentation is entered and updated whenever necessary also needs to be addressed. For in just the same way as you can take a horse to water but can't make it drink, you can supply the software engineer with the tools but you can't make him or her use them - or can you?

As it happens we may be in a position to ensure that the horse drinks when it's supposed to drink, as it were; perhaps we can make an offer that can't be refused. By encapsulating the software development process in a comprehensive support environment we gain the power to virtually insist that the software developer follows almost any procedure that we care to specify - a carrot and stick strategy, metaphorically speaking of course. This point will be elaborated in Chapter 9, but I mention it here because Balzer, Cheatham and Green make a similar proposal.

They sketch out the possibilities for a **knowledge-based software assistant (KBSA)**; Figure 5.7 depicts their vision.

The KBSA supports the new paradigm by recording the development activities, performing some of them, analyzing their effects, and aiding their selection. By mediating in the development (using the new paradigm) of a particular piece of software the KBSA can record the human design decisions such that when the specification is modified this recorded history of the design process can be reused to more or less automate the reimplementation. This scenario removes much of the pain from the process of modifying a specification and thereby making reimplementation necessary. This makes specification modification less problematic (at least it would if it were possible), but by my reckoning code hacking is still the more tempting option. I believe that we must, in addition, actively eliminate the code hacking option (and we'll get to that in Chapter 9).

5.4   Operational requirements of Kowalski

Another example of a new approach to engineering software systems stems from the logic-programming movement. I shall use Kowalski's schemes as a representative sample from this active subfield.

With the advent of the programming language Prolog, something quite close to logic became a machine-executable notation - i.e. a programming language. This gives logic (I should write, almost gives logic, but I'll stop quibbling as long as you bear in mind that Prolog programming is *not* programming in logic) a new face - a procedural interpretation in fact. So, a statement in logic can take its usual stance in the world as a declarative statement, which may be either true of false, and is rather like the specification of a problem. But, in addition, as a Prolog program it can be executed - interpreted procedurally as a specification of a sequence of actions to be performed.   This raises the exciting possibility

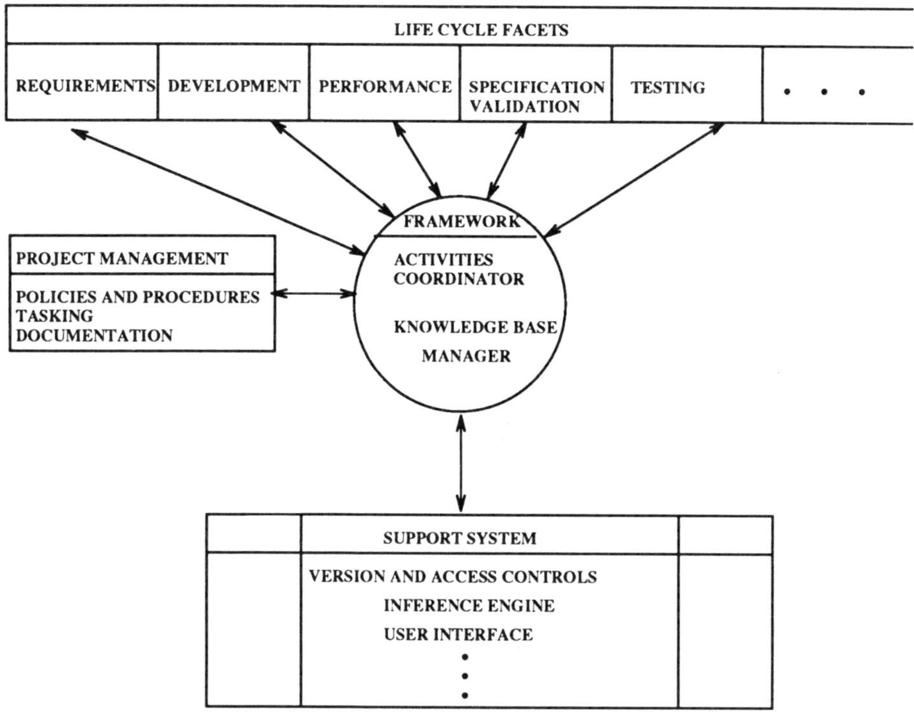

Fig 5.7 "A generalized knowledge-based software assistant structure" from Balzer, Cheatham, and Green, 1986

that logic can be an executable specification language, or even a representation of requirements, as we shall see.

Kowalski gave us the following observation about programs:

PROGRAM = DECLARATION + CONTROL

This slogan equation makes the point that there are two rather different features in a typical program, say, a FORTRAN, PASCAL, or COBOL program, and they are intermeshed. The programmer makes decisions about fixed relationships between objects in the computation, e.g. if one item in a list of numbers is greater than the following one then the list is not sorted in ascending order. The programmer also has to make detailed decisions about the flow of control in the program, e.g. how to exchange the places of two items in a list, and how to ensure that the last list item is not compared with a non-existent successor. And to make matters worse both sets of detailed decisions are tightly intermeshed and interrelated - no wonder programming is so difficult.

Logic programming, and hence Prolog, is just the right scheme to deal with this confused state of affairs. In logic programming we have a clear separation of declarative structure and control structure, and moreover the control-structure considerations are removed from the programmer's scope of concern - they are packed away in the language processor. So the programming task has been reduced to the simpler task of just specifying the relationships that must hold true if the desired computation is to be correct. I'm sure that this must all sound mysterious and quite dubious to the non-Prolog programmer. A healthy scepticism is to be encouraged, but, for once, it's almost unfounded. It is thus time for an illuminating example.

Consider the trivial problem of counting the number of items in a list, whose name is L. The conventional programmer, untainted by exposure to either LISP or Prolog, would immediately think of setting up a loop structure together with an accumulator initially set to zero. And then of starting at one end of the list and moving item-by-item through the list adding one to the total in the accumulator on each move until the end of the list is reached. The total number of items in the list will then be given by the final number in the accumulator.

This is classical mixed declarative and control-structure programming. The programmer has to worry about the declarative essentials of the problem, e.g. that the discovery of another list item means that one must added to the accumulator. And, at the same time, the programmer must be concerned about setting up a loop structure that starts at the first list item and finishes at the last whether the list has zero, one, or ten thousand items in it.

The logic programmer approaches the task totally differently. This person observes that the number of items in any list is one plus the number of items in the same list without its first item. And this is true for all lists except the empty list which contains zero items.

After this sort of statement one is very tempted to retort, "That is obviously true but not much help. It's just a less slick re-statement of the problem." If you feel this sort of temptation coming on, resist it vigorously, because we can rewrite that re-statement of the problem directly in Prolog and execute it to compute list lengths. As a Prolog program it would look like this:

```
listlength( [], 0 ).
listlength( [Head | Tail], Length ):-
                    listlength( Tail, Lengthtail),
                    Length is Lengthtail + 1.
```

The cryptic syntax of Prolog is no help, but I can transcribe this Prolog program into English. It consists of two clauses. The first one just states the (seemingly) trivial fact that the length of an empty list is zero. No quarrel with that I hope. The second clause states the similarly obvious fact (although not in such an obvious way, I admit) that the length of a non-empty list is the length of its tail (i.e. the original list without its first item) plus one. This second clause can be written out in a more Prology way: the length of a non-empty list is the value of variable **Length** if the value of **Lengthtail** is the length of the tail of the original list and the value of **Length** is equal to the value of **Lengthtail** plus one.

To claim that this last sentence is one from the set of obviously true statements may be stretching credulity a bit, but if you close your eyes and think about it step by step, there will be no doubting its veracity. This is taking us somewhat far afield, but it is worth the journey if we can use it to dispel some of the magic and mystery that often surrounds logic programming.

Hopefully, even those readers who suffer from Prolog-phobia have been able to stay with us for the requisite couple of paragraphs and thus now have a fairly firm idea what is being claimed about declarative programming. The above two clauses constitute an executable Prolog program that will compute the length of any list that it is given, and yet we did not have to bother ourselves with setting up a loop, or a counter variable and incrementing it to move from one list item to the next, and how to test for the end of the list, etc. In short, we wrote a program (I'm being overgenerous here, but I'm sure that you could have done it if this was a dynamic, on-line book) to compute list lengths without any of the normally necessary, petty concerns of control structure. But at least one aspect of conventional control structure did intrude.

The whole truth is that I did (I'll accept full blame) introduce just one control structure consideration. I plead guilty, but I had no choice. The offending feature is the ordering of the two parts that constitute the latter part of the second clause. The statement that the length of the tail of the original list is the value of **Lengthtail** *must precede* the statement that the value of **Length** is the value of **Lengthtail** plus one.

Why is this? As a declarative statement of logical truth the order has no significance. It's just a fact that if the value of **Length** is to be the length of a non-empty list then two things have to be true: the tail has to have a length (we called it **Lengthtail**) and the relationship between the two values has to be that the length of the tail is one less than the length of the original list. But in order to compute specific values with this structure, the computer cannot add one to the value of **Lengthtail** until it has computed a value for this variable. So we need to ensure that the computer finds the length of the tail of the list before it tries to add one to it in order to obtain the length of the original list. The commonly available (sequential) Prolog, which executes these subclauses in left-to-right order, forces the ordering that I gave upon us. The program would crash if the order was reversed.

So, there's an example of why Prolog is not quite logic programming, and why programming in Prolog does not quite allow you to forget control-structuring details. There are a few other reasons why the popular equation:

programming in Prolog = programming in logic

is not a true statement of equality. But just as long as you are aware of this popular misconception, and no longer view Prolog as a total mystery, then you will be in a better position to assess the merit of the software engineering proposals that emanate from the logic-programming world.

Having set the scene, I am now in a position to present and discuss the operational requirements approach to software engineering as advocated by Kowalski. In the proposals that I am about to present,he argues that "artificial intelligence technology [i.e. logic programming] [can] be applied to software engineering, and in particular to the systems analysis stage of software development" (Kowalski, 1984 ,p. 92). He credits the Japanese with drawing world attention to the potential for logic programming, especially when combined with parallel processing machines.

It is easy to appreciate the potential benefits that may accrue from a sensible marriage of parallel hardware and logic programming. It stems from the earlier point that logic is purely declarative, and so programming in logic banishes control flow concerns from the domain of the programmer. At a general level, we can appreciate that if programs are declarative objects (i.e. the traditional notion of specific sequence of control flow through the algorithm no longer exists) then there ought to be great opportunities for parallel processing of components of the algorithm - because the typically strict requirements on sequential processing have gone. Let me illustrate this with reference to the (much) earlier example (Chapter 1) of sorting a list. For the sorting program to be correct when it generates a list **y** from any input list **x**, two relationships must hold:

SORT(x) -----> **y** where,
   y is a *permutation* of **x**
  and
  y is *ordered*

As a statement in logic no notion of sequencing is involved. It is simply that if both relationships hold true (i.e. *permutation* and *ordered*), then the **SORT** procedure is correct. There is no implication that *permutation* must be checked before (or after) *ordered* - they just must both be true.

So, if this sort of logical statement were executable by a computer,we would expect a parallel-processing computer to be able to execute it more quickly as it could check the truth of the two relationships in parallel. Hence, the interest in parallel architectures together with logic programming.

We have seen how some control flow constraints do have to be observed in Prolog programming. Prolog is a sequential, logic-programming language (which is, of course, something of a contradiction in terms), but it's only a first cut at a tricky problem. There has been a great deal of work on the development of parallel Prologs (e.g. PARLOG) that should allow some exploitation of the promises of parallelism in logic programming, in the near future. As another example, in the Godel language of Burt, Hill and Lloyd (1990) every effort has been made to remedy the problems that the inter-tanglement of declarative logic and procedural interpretation cause in Prolog. A program in Godel will have a simple declarative meaning and the procedural interpretation is a deduction from it - i.e. the logical meaning is primary and the necessary computational procedures should not distort nor undermine it as they do in sequential Prolog.

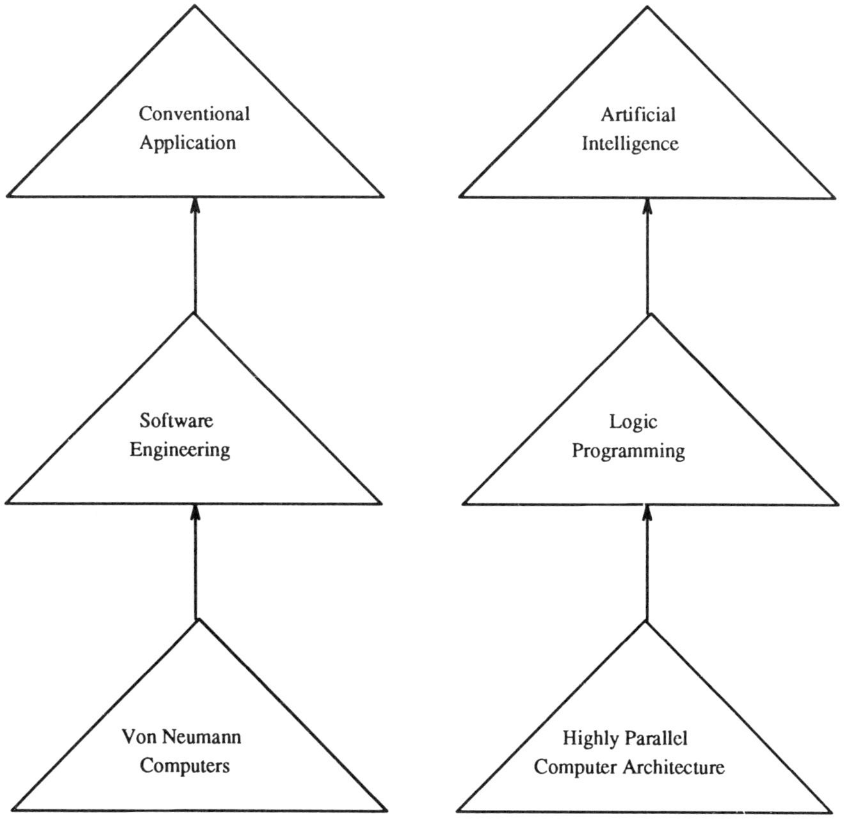

Fig 5.8 "The conventional view"   **Fig   5.9** "The Japanese view"

   Kowalski (1984) summarizes the general situation with the diagrams in Figures 5.8, 5.9, and 5.10. I trust that the first two are now completely self explanatory, and that 5.10 makes sense even it is not clear what this "new software technology" is exactly. We shall now see Kowalski's elaboration of the this "new software technology".

   "So what is this new software technology? The new technology allows knowledge to be represented explicitly. It disentangles what the computer knows from how the computer uses it." (Kowalski, 1984, p.92). And this is clearly a restatement of our earlier discussion of how logic programming allows the separation of declarative information (Kowalski's "what the computer knows" or "knowledge") from control structure information ("how the computer uses it").

   I don't like to keep throwing wet blankets on exciting notions, like the notion that programming in Prolog is programming in logic, but I

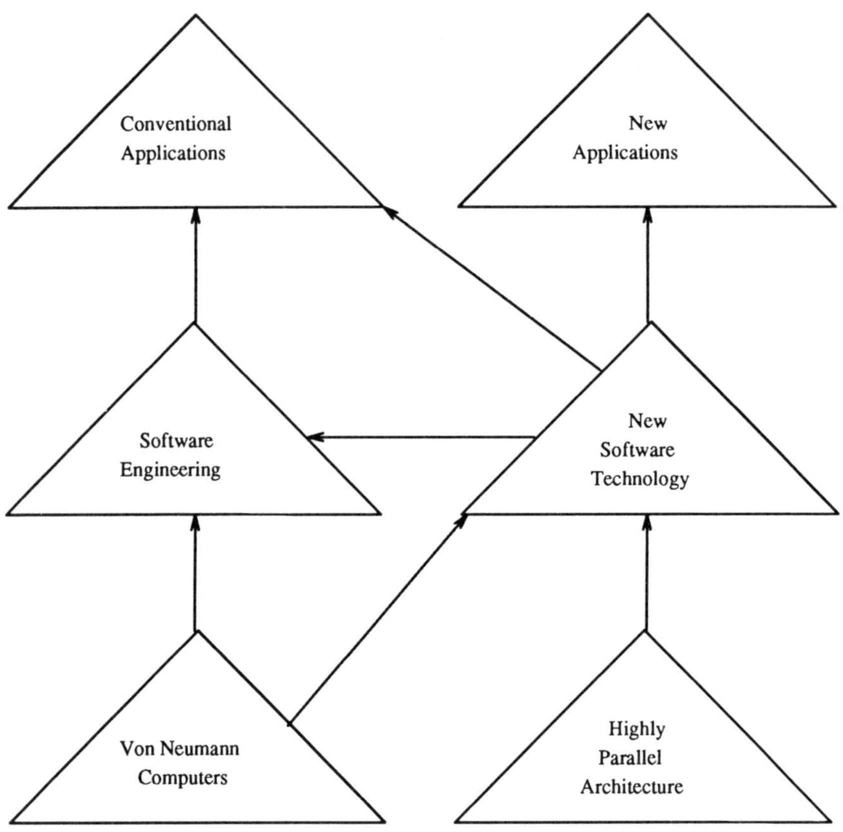

Fig 5.10 "The Kowalski view" all from Kowalski, 1984, AI and Software Engineering, *Datamation*, vol. 30. no. 10, pages 94 and 95

must interject just one more dampening observation. I refer to the widespread,almost universal, cavalier use of the word 'knowledge'. Modern computer technologists, expert systems enthusiasts in particular, have succeeded in stripping this word of most of the depth and richness of association that it used to possess, and indeed still possesses for that rapidly shrinking portion of humanity that has not heard of expert systems. In short, when 'knowledge' is mentioned, fight off the welter of rich and complex connotations that try to force themselves upon your consciousness, and keep telling yourself that it only means a set of facts and rules. And in the current context it means an axiom set in logic - i.e. facts and rules that specify only absolute truths in some timeless, abstract, closed world.

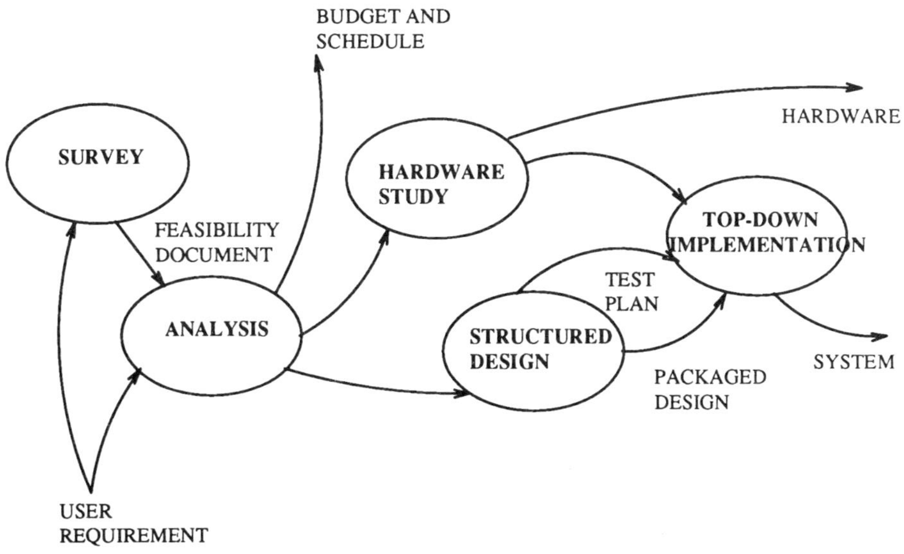

Fig 5.11 "The software development life cycle of DeMarco" from Kowalski, 1984, p.98

To continue: Kowalski mentions the structured analysis techniques that are typically employed in the development of large-scale, practical software systems. As an example, he gives the software development life cycle of DeMarco (1979) - Figure 5.11.

He draws our attention to the bottom half of the life cycle diagram - i.e. user requirements analysis, functional specification, design, and implementation. Systems analysts often clarify user requirements by recourse to data flow diagrams. A **data flow diagram (DFD)** is a graphical representation of information flow and the transformations that are applied to it as data is input, and moves through to the output of a program. A DFD representation of the **SORT** procedure is given in Figure 5.12.

Kowalski reminds us that DFDs are a particularly convenient way of communicating with the user. He then points out that DFDs can be interpreted as an alternative graphical syntax for logic programming. Thus the DFD, given above, is an alternative representation for the rule:

an ordered list **y** can be computed from a list **x** if **y** can be permuted from **x** and **y** is ordered

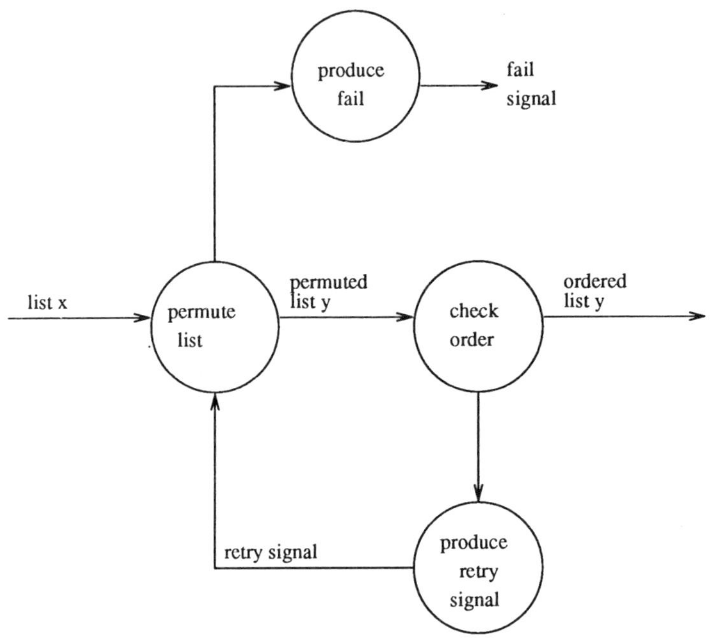

Fig 5.12 A DFD of the sorting problem

This sort of equivalence "shows that logic-based programming is not necessarily programming, or even formal specification ... logic-based programming is an executable analysis of the user requirement. Therefore it can assist the conventional software development life cycle at the earliest possible stage. The user requirement can be analysed and executed before we derive a functional specification, design, or program" (Kowalski, 1984, p. 94).

Clearly, Kowalski is claiming that logic-based programming allows us to strengthen the software design process right at the outset even before we reach the specification stage. The simple equivalence between DFDs (which experience has shown to be a good notation for sorting out user requirements) and logic-like rules has opened the possibility of mechanically executing, and thus checking and exploring, user requirements before they become transformed into a specification.

Kowalski goes on to elaborate on the benefits that accrue from the state of affairs in which logic is a programming language (if only it were! - but it's close). A major weakness of structured systems analysis is that "users don't know what they want; and often, when they do, they don't need what they want" (p. 94). But having an executable representation of the result of requirements analysis allows us to sort out the "wants" and "needs" of the user by prototyping. By running trial representations of what the user seems to want, the hidden (and missing) implications can be explicitly exposed, thereby speeding up the process of homing in on a statement of the necessary and sufficient requirements for the proposed system. And, on top of all this, because logic is the basic notation in use, we can expect to reap considerable benefits from the fact that logic is a well-defined and well-understood formal notation - e.g. we can expect to prove that the requirements satisfy certain criteria.

Kowalski sums up his "new logic-based software technology"(p. 94) as follows:

> I have concentrated attention on those applications of AI technology to software engineering that revolutionize the software life cycle, and which in many cases do away with program implementation, and even system specification (p. 100).

But, of course, you, the practising software engineer, are not about to witness a revolution as logic-based software technology sweeps across the world of software engineering. Why is this? It is because the technology has some problems, although they were not mentioned.

To run through just a few reasons why (apart from pig-headed resistance to new ideas) logic-based software technology is not about to take over: first, logic is not a programming language (and it's not totally clear that it ever can be) - Prolog is, but logic isn't. Secondly, there is always the awkward problem that comes with neat formal techniques of distinguishing what can be done in principle from what can be done in practice on realistically sized software. In this particular case there are questions of whether a rule-based representation of a large requirements DFD is too cumbersome or inefficient to actually execute. And whether a logical execution of it (basically a theorem-proving exercise) will yield the sort of information that is needed to properly explore the users wants and needs. Related to this question of whether the logical manipulation can really tell you what you need to know, there is the further question of how much of the essentials of requirements analysis will be missed in a rule-based representation of a DFD. A DFD may be the hard-copy representation that forms the basis for discussion between user and systems analyst, but how many of the problems are exposed and resolved by information explicitly in the DFD? Are none of the crucial exchanges being instigated and settled in terms of difficult-to-formally-represent use of English combined with impossible-to-formally-represent use of body language (particularly hand waves and head nods)? It seems unlikely, particularly if you subscribe to the Rich and Waters (1988) view that requirements can never be complete.

Suffice it to say that there are some neat ideas coming from the logic-based software technologists, but they are not yet solutions to the major problems of the practical software engineer. Use of a logic-like specification language which is also machine executable provides us with, for example, a useful scheme for rapid prototyping. This sort of benefit will be extended and others will surely emerge in the wake of Prolog's successors.

We have now looked at two representative examples of new methodologies for software development. They both explicitly recognize the need for prototyping in some guise or other to help sort out what the user really wants and how the software engineer is going to supply it.Gone from both methodologies is the simple linearity of more conventional methodologies - although they both try to hang on (especially the logic-based technology) to an exclusively left-to-right flow of system development - i.e. flow from specification through implementation to testing. The SAT core is still quite sound within both paradigms (although it is likely to be closer to SAV for the logic-based one).

Both schemes tacitly admit that there is much more to building a software system which accurately reflects user needs than having an agreed specification. For such a necessarily complex object will hide undesired features of system behaviour from, as well as falsely promise desired characteristics of the final system to, both the user and the analyst. Its implications must then be explicitly explored. But notice that both methodologies try to pack the exploratory features at the front end. Clearly, it is more cost effective to sort out the problems as early as possible. And it is traditional to take the specification as the keystone of the whole development process, so you can't really mess about after you've settled that. But the point that I want to make is, nice as it may be to do all the exploration at the front end,will it solve the essential problems for the development of practical AI software? I think not, because we are building a behaviourally-adequate approximation to some ideal and hence behavioural feedback is the primary force driving system evolution. But more on this anon.

For the moment, I'll complete this brief survey of responses to the perceived inadequacies of the conventional software development methodologies with a look at one more paradigm. This one, the POLITE methodology, is directly aimed at improving on the basic RUDE cycle (not hard to do, you might think).

5.5 The POLITE methodology

Bader, Edwards, Harris-Jones, and Hannaford (1988) maintain that "knowledge-based systems" (KBS) are not yet associated with an accepted software development life cycle (SDLC) or development methodology. And if KBSs are to become an established technology within the data processing industry an appropriate SDLC will be needed so that the standards expected in commercial and industrial software are met by future KBSs. They describe "a practical approach to building KBSs and, in particular, how the development of hybrid systems, containing both conventional and knowledge-based components, can be managed effectively" (abstract, p. 266).

They make the point that the major system development feature that KBSs bring to the fore is a necessity for iterative refinement, and so something like the RUDE cycle is a likely basis for the required methodology. Figure 5.13 is their simplified view of the RUDE cycle.

Two fundamental flaws are singled out for treatment: "an *engineering* methodology for KBSs needs to   provide a method for constructing an initial system from which the RUDE cycle can begin, as well as

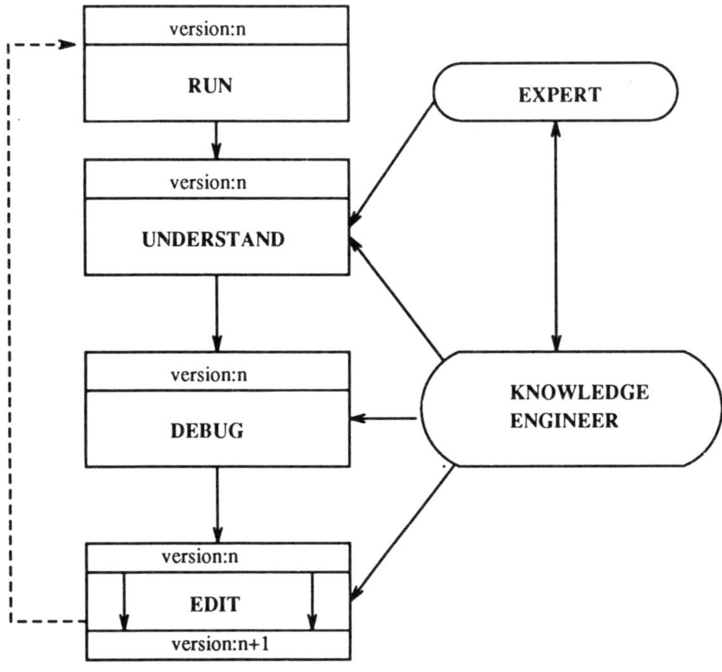

Fig 5.13 "A simplified view of the RUDE cycle" from Bader et al.1988, Figure 1, p. 270

encompassing some form of control of the iterative process of development" (p. 270, authors' emphasis). As it stands, RUDE development is likely to lead to problems of documentation, maintenance and testing, all of which must be easily accomplished in an engineering methodology.

Rather than generate a more disciplined version of the RUDE cycle, and thereby correct the two flaws, it is suggested that "the iterative features of the RUDE paradigm need to be incorporated within a structured and controllable framework" (p. 270). They select the waterfall model of software development (see Figure 4.6) as the "structured and controllable framework", and what was RUDE (plus waterfall) becomes POLITE, which is derived from:

Produce Objectives - Logical/physical design - Implement - Test - Edit

and, as we all know, POLITE is always preferable to RUDE. This is, of course, a slightly underhand way to introduce a possible enhancement. (But one that the RUDE paradigm seems to encourage - see, for a further example, Mostow's [1985] COURTEOUS alternative, and, as a counter-example, Trenouth's [1990b] VERY RUDE development.)

As much fun as it is to work on acronym derivation and development, we, in this thoroughly serious book, must look beneath the name. A schematic illustration of the POLITE life-cycle is given in Figure 5.14.

As you can see, this scheme is definitely waterfall based. The methodological enhancements come with elaboration of the infrastructure. To begin with: each step in the waterfall is now divided into two. "The left side is related to conventional components and the other side to the knowledge-based or cognitive elements of the system" (p. 270). For, as they state, the methodology was designed to deal "with the development of hybrid systems comprising both conventional and heuristic components" (p. 270). Personally, I would not separate off such "hybrid" systems as all systems are some sort of hybrid, it seems to me. (What would be a purely AI system?) The development of any AI system involves a large measure of totally conventional system development, and the lessons of conventional software engineering must be exploited to the full wherever appropriate. But Bader *et al.* do provide a useful three-way division of overall system structuring, and one that has application beyond the so-called "knowledge-based" systems. Their suggested trimorphism is illustrated in Figure 5.15.

They name these three structures:

- when the interaction is with the user only

- when the interaction is with other systems, such as company databases, as well as with the user

- when the KBS is buried within a larger system and thus the user only interacts with the KBS through the host system interface.

The second infrastructural addition is a RUDE cycle within each step of the process. So RUDE development is not the monolithic object that has to be disciplined; it has been broken down and distributed throughout the waterfall framework. This move is either an example of divide and conquer where the elemental RUDE cycles are sufficiently small and constrained to be manageable, or else it's the result of a hydra-like response in which the destruction of the one major RUDE cycle has spawned a sequence of six RUDE cycles, none of which is indisputably less troublesome than the original. Clearly, the authors view their rearrangement as fitting into the former category.

To return to the ways that the POLITE paradigm deals with the two fundamental flaws in the RUDE cycle: great stress is laid on the production of performance objectives at the start of a project. **Performance objectives** "are a statement, in the problem owner's terms, of how the KBS should operate in the chosen domain" (p. 270).The existence of such objectives, clearly stated, is essential for validation, and it provides a framework within which any RUDE development that is required can be controlled.

The authors view the production of performance objectives as part of the initial feasibility phase which, of course, directly addresses the problem of obtaining a first operational version of the system. Figure 5.16

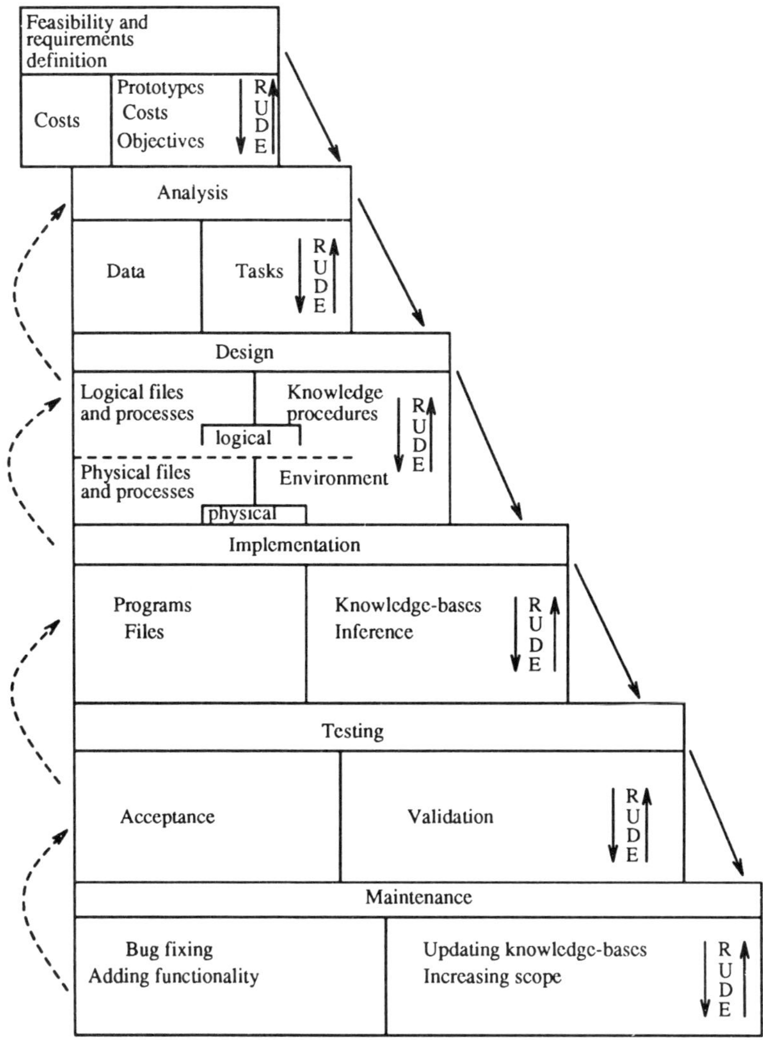

Fig 5.14 "The POLITE life-cycle" from Bader et al., 1988, Figure 2, p. 270

illustrates the POLITE view of this crucial initial stage of system development.

As you can see, management oversees the process of input from four information sources (the problem itself, the developers, the experts in the problem domain, and the eventual system users) and the generation of a number of outputs. In particular, we get the performance objectives and a prototype system.

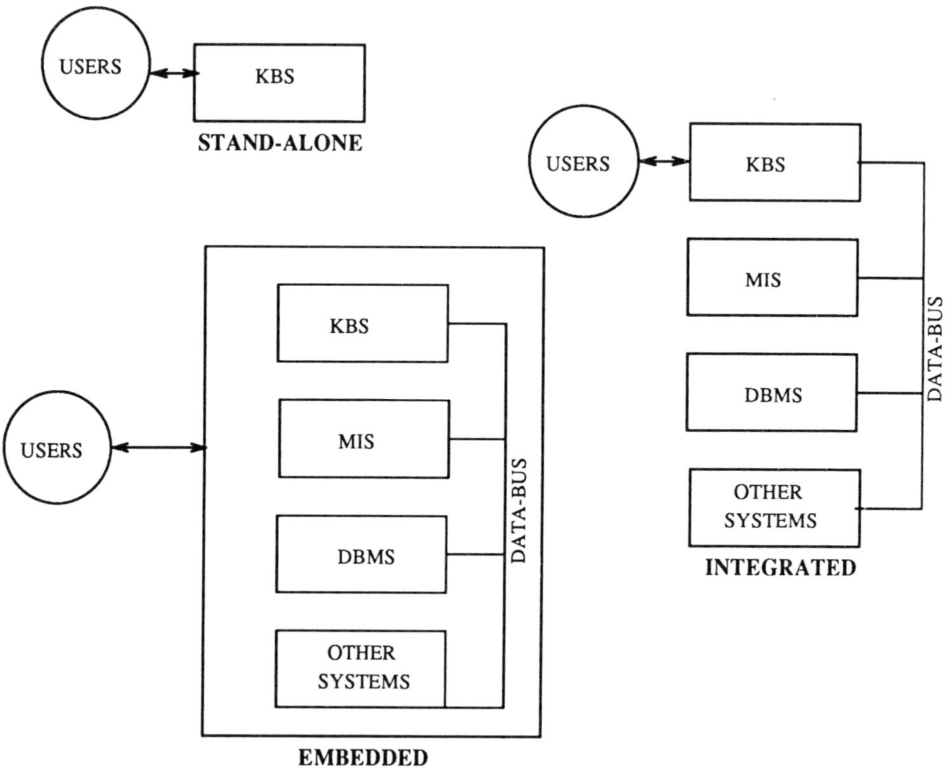

Fig 5.15 "Types of KBS interaction with other systems" from Bader et al., 1988, Fig. 4, p. 271

So, the POLITE paradigm can be summarized as an attempt to exploit the necessity for iterative system development but to keep it in check by allowing RUDE cycles only within steps of the conventional waterfall model. Clearly, one of the tests of this paradigm concerns the degree to which iterative development can indeed be modularized and encapsulated within the analysis step, or the design step. etc. It may be, as I tend to believe, that the iteration necessarily swings from end to end of the development paradigm - certainly the less the better, but some such multi-step, module-busting evolution seems inevitable. For example, as the need for prototyping tacitly admits, much useful information about the desirability of prior decisions (both explicit and implicit ones) is gained from the behaviour of an implementation. So information gained at the far end of the development process can feed back to impact on any earlier step - design, specification, or even requirements. It is difficult to imagine (however convenient it would be) that all such informational feedback can be neatly encapsulated in the modular steps of the waterfall

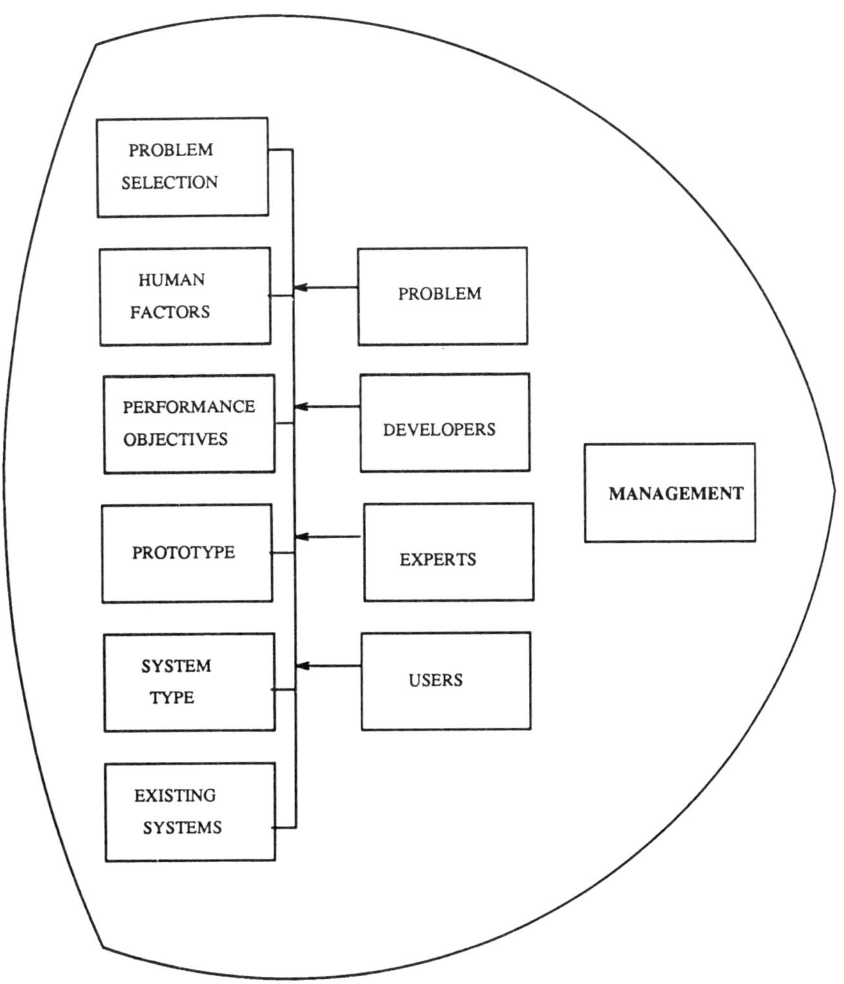

Fig 5.16 "Feasibility and requirements definition" from Bader et al., Figure 3, p. 271

model, or even that non-local feedback can be propagated back effectively through a series of such steps.

The POLITE paradigm is thus rather different from the two previous ones that we've considered, and a good deal less radical than either. But whether we can generate the necessary new paradigm by introducing perturbations to a thoroughly conventional scheme is an open question.

In his book *Building Knowledge-Based Systems*, Edwards(1991) gives a full presentation of the POLITE methodology as applied to "knowledge-based systems" which he sees "as different from 'conventional' computer systems, but not very different" (p.1).

This book is specifically aimed at exposing the problems peculiar to the task of engineering AI-software, and at presenting and discussing the alternative approaches to solution of these problems. In the current chapter we have seen a number of new paradigms for software development, but the new models are not always motivated by concerns for AI. If they are not interested in AI software then why are they devising radically new paradigms for software development - and incremental ones at that? This seems a reasonable question to ask.

If we ignore the possibility that our paradigm creators are motivated merely by a desire for novelty, we must assume that there is perceived to be a real need - i.e. that the conventional paradigms are unsatisfactory. And there is indeed a growing awareness in some sectors of the software engineering community that some sort of fundamentally incremental paradigm is required for *all* practical software development - AI-ish or not. Arango, Baxter and Freeman (in press), for example, report on their experiences at several workshops on software development. One recurring theme is that (as Brooks,1979, first made clear) there are no silver bullets - i.e. no simple answers. "A natural conclusion is that for the time being we must strive for incremental approaches. The questions are 'how can we identify opportunities for incremental advances?' and 'how can we achieve these advances?'" (p. 3, of draft).

It is time to move on and examine some of the likely components of a discipline of exploratory programming.

6
Towards a Discipline of Exploratory Programming

At this point in the book we've subjected the conventional software system development methodologies to scrutiny and exposed their weaknesses, especially with respect to the possibility of engineering AI software. We've also taken a brief look at a few proposals for schemes, or new paradigms, for overcoming certain of the weaknesses that are apparent; they do not solve, or circumvent, the fundamental problems, I hope that I've convinced you of that as well. And finally, I've been promoting the need for an iterative, evolutionary approach to engineering AI systems. The RUDE cycle was presented, but within it we could see even worse problems for the possibility of engineering robust, reliable and maintainable software systems. But in the absence of serious schemes that do solve the important problems, I propose to persist with the RUDE cycle and to examine its potential as a basis for AI-software development.

What we need is a discipline of exploratory programming, or, more grandly, a discipline of exploratory system design - a discipline of ESD. Now, in this life there are many wondrous things that it would be just terrific to get hold of for various purposes.Many of these things we just can't afford (personal chauffeured transport springs to my mind in this category of desiderata), some are excluded by local context (I, for example, would very much like a mango tree in the garden, but this is not possible in this sceptred but oft-times frosty isle wherein I live), and others simply refuse to exist anywhere in this particular world (for example, weightless solids, frictionless wheels). So, we may know what we need, but what we also need to know is that it is not in one of these unobtainable categories, particularly the last.

I can find no guarantees that the necessary discipline of ESD is not in the same category as the excluded middles of logic, nevertheless there is every reason to be optimistic. In this chapter I shall discuss some of the likely components of this hypothesized paradigm. This will stand us in good stead for consideration of a further source of problems (machine learning) and some possible cause for optimism (expert systems) before we attempt to frame a general superstructure for a discipline of ESD.

6.1   **Reverse engineering**

The term reverse engineering has, in the last few years, been boosted to the forefront of general concerns that occupy the time of software engineers. Most software engineering books merely mention it at best, but it's a term that now peppers the papers of the practical software engineering world.

As the name suggests, **reverse engineering** is a process of moving backwards from an engineered product (in our case a software system - a program) to extract the representations (such as specification, and general design) that would have been generated *en route* to the product had it been developed in accordance with a proper SDLC. In fact, my use of "would have been generated" really ought to be watered down to "might have been generated", for, as we shall later see, any given product will map comfortably back to any number of possible design schemes and specifications. The relationship of a program to possible design sequences is one-many: any given program could have been the final outcome from any one of a wide range of design sequences. This fact is important, as we shall subsequently see, because there can be a real need for a selection of alternative, roughly equivalent, but different representations of the possible 'designs' for a given program. I have put the word "designs" in qualifying quotes to emphasize the special usage here. It is not really potential alternative designs that we shall need to represent, but alternative, differently biased abstractions from the detailed complexity of the program. Such abstractions (of which the actual design is just one) provide the software developer or maintainer with a less complex and therefore more conceptually manageable representation of the program. And the need for alternatives arises from the fact that the software person will want to focus on different aspects of the program in order to pursue different software development or enhancement goals. Each specific software-modification task will emphasize and de-emphasize different aspects of a program, and a representation that reflects this pattern of emphasis can provide the best framework for reasoning about the program. Figures 6.5 and 6.6 provide concrete examples of alternative, rather different representations of program infrastructure - there is potentially much more underlying a given program that the actual design and specification.

We are now in a position to fully appreciate the lack of promotion that reverse engineering has received in the software world (especially the academic one), and why it can claim very little page space in treatises on software engineering. In a nutshell: reverse engineering is also the reverse of good practice. In addition, it is, I think, a less glamorous exercise for the scientist or technician - fiddling with a detailed mechanism in order to conjure up a possible design strategy is a challenge to the compulsive problem-solver, but can it be a formal science?

So, the need for reverse engineering (e.g. the boss has dumped a huge listing of uncommented code on your desk with orders to debug it, or to add a functional enhancement) arises only as a result of bad practice, and you are often better advised to redesign a comparable piece of software rather than waste endless days trying to work backwards from the (apparently, if not actually) tangled mess of code in front of you - unravelling an entangled mass of wool is no one's idea of fun. Thus, on two rather different counts, we can dismiss the need for serious consideration of reverse engineering: it can only arise as a result of thoroughly bad practice, and so the need should be avoidable; and when totally unavoidable, it is more productive to re-engineer than to reverse engineer.

Now, I'm clearly not spending all these words on something that is better dead and buried, so why am I doing it? The point is that as soon as we countenance the use of an evolutionary system development paradigm, and especially one that is driven by behavioural feedback, then reverse engineering is suddenly elevated to a position of both respectable and essential practice. This dramatic change in status (which we've seen emerging slowly from the world of software practitioners) occurs because reverse engineering is the key process behind transforming a behavioural observation into a specification change. Once we abandon the simple, linear SDLCs, and admit the necessity of prototyping, we are required to transform an observation of system behaviour into a modification of some earlier representation - we are required to reverse engineer.

As a specific example of a manifestation of reverse engineering, and one that was developed explicitly to support "the production of robust exploratory software", we can look at the "type flow analysis" of Johnson (1990). The classic AI programming languages, primarily LISP but Prolog too can now be so classified, offer the programmer a flexibility and freedom that facilitates the rapid evolution of software. Neither language requires, for example, an extensive definition of data types as do the more conventional languages such as Pascal and Ada. But freedom has its price, and in this case the absence of type declarations is paid for in terms of inability to guarantee type-level consistency in, say, a LISP program. As Johnson says: "This means that executing exploratory programs may contain an entire class of type-level errors that are absent from their non-exploratory counterparts. The inability to detect these errors automatically, compounded with the lack of explicit structural information and the high amount of structural change, is a principal cause of exploratory brittleness" p. 3.

Type flow analysis is used to generate from the LISP code a representation of the type-level structure implicit in the program. This technique, which has been implemented in a system called ESSIE, is based on the observation that, although it is impossible to verify the type-level consistency of any *arbitrary* LISP program, it *is possible* to assess the type-level consistency of an interesting and large subset of all possible LISP programs. Type-flow analysis thus provides us with a classic illustration of the sort of technique that we shall see occurring repeatedly in our survey of component elements for a discipline of ESD - i.e. a special-purpose, limited technique is substituted for a general impossibility without eliminating practical effectiveness.

The fundamental representation of type-flow analysis is the **braid** which represents the set of execution strands through a function at the type level. As an example, consider the following function "size" which exploits the ad-hoc polymorphism that is typically available in exploratory languages.

```
(defun size (obj)
   (cond ((listp obj)           (list-length obj))
         ((hash-table-p obj)    (hash-table-count obj))
         ((vectorp obj)         (array-length obj))
                                     ))
```

This function returns the length of different types of objects using a length function that is specific to the particular object type. Given this function, ESSIE will generate the braid Br1 which is composed of the three execution strands St11, St12 and St13. The resultant type-flow analysis can be illustrated as follows.

$$
Br1 \longrightarrow
\begin{cases}
St11 & \{FC: (listp\ obj) \\
& CE: obj:\ list[v1] \\
& RT:\ integer \\[6pt]
St12 & \{FC: (hash\text{-}table\text{-}p\ obj)(not(listp\ obj)) \\
& CE: obj:\ hashtable[v2] \\
& RT:\ integer \\[6pt]
St13 & \{FC: (vectorp\ obj)(not(hash\text{-}table\text{-}p\ obj))(not(listp\ obj)) \\
& CE: obj:\ vector[v3] \\
& RT:\ integer
\end{cases}
$$

The feasibility conditions (FC) represent the type-related constraints that must be satisfied in order for the execution path represented by the strand to be valid; they are normally produced from the presence of type predicates such as "listp". The constraint environment (CE) holds the type-level properties of variables that must be satisfied whenever the execution path is traversed. The result type (RT) indicates what type would be returned from the execution of the code represented by the strand. A type-level error, for example, is signalled when the composition of two execution paths is found to be feasible but the two CEs cannot be successfully composed.

ESSIE's analysis of a Lisp system is expected to provide three benefits:

1. the verification of type safety, i.e. that the system does not contain any type-level inconsistencies;

2. the detection of type-level errors;

3. the signalling of anomalies which may or may not be errors.

Use of this reverse engineering technique is an attempt to reconcile the implementation freedom that supports exploratory programming with implementation constraints, such as type-level consistency, that support the development of robust software. By tackling this issue through reverse engineering, rather than strongly-typed languages (the conventional approach), perhaps we can begin to obtain the best of both worlds. Instead of forcing the programmer to work in a tight harness of *a priori* constraints, reverse engineering permits the products of exploratory freedom to be checked (and corrected if necessary) to ensure that agreed discipline and structure is, in fact, exhibited by them. As long as it is clear what the desired constraints are and how they can be satisfied, why force a programmer to work continually under them when final products can be positively vetted for adherence? And, of course, this philosophy of subsequent, rather than simultaneous, vetting makes more sense in the context of programming as an exploratory activity than when programming is seen as a formal transformation exercise. When software development is seen as a creative pursuit, we can argue that creativity demands freedom of expression, but then the need for efficiency suggests the guidance of constraints. We need both, but in what mix, and how the mix should vary with circumstances are open problems - conventional programming languages, such as Ada, offer us one extreme and Johnson's type-flow analysis tries to offer us the other.

Curiously, reverse engineering provides us with a point of contrast between software science and classical experimental sciences. The fundamental mechanism in the classical sciences is reverse engineering: they are presented with the products of say, biological science, and the role of the scientist is to figure out a plausible 'specification and design sequence'. It is not usually phrased that way, but clearly the scientist has the products as the givens and the principles and theories embodied in them as the unknowns. The classical scientist is primarily engaged in reverse engineering. Why this difference? Put another way, why is software science 'constructivist' or a process of synthesis, and classical science 'de-constructivist' (is that 'destructivist'?) or analytic? One answer is, of course, that software persons are not scientists, they are engineers. But I've already explored the ramifications of this labelling choice.

Apart from the obvious difference that technologists are primarily trying to build things rather than (or as well as) understand them, I think that this question also harks back to the fundamental belief of computer scientists that their primary concerns are with with formal abstractions and not with real artefacts. Whether there is a real artefact (i.e. a working software system) at the end of any sequence of specification, design and verification is somewhat secondary for the computer scientist who has solved (or aims to solve) all the essential problems within the formal abstractions that should (in any proper scheme) precede actual coding and running of an actual piece of software.

We shall see several of the subsequent sections in this chapter addressing problems that are part of the general problem of effective and efficient reverse engineering. But first, another major ingredient of the needed paradigm.

6.2 Reusable software

Reusability is another general concern, and one that risen quite dramatically in level of awareness within software engineering during the recent past. The term **reusable software** is, I think, self-explanatory, but perhaps I won't risk it. Here's Biggerstaff and Perlis' (1989) definition from their two-volume work on software re-usability:

> Software reuse is the reapplication of a variety of kinds of knowledge about one system to another similar system in order to reduce the effort of development and maintenance of that other system. This reused knowledge includes artefacts such as domain knowledge, development experience, design decisions, architectural structures, requirements, designs, code, documentation, and so forth.
>
> Biggerstaff and Perlis (1989) p. xv

This is, as the authors concede, a broad definition and thus covers the full scope of possibilities.

Software reusability refers to the desire to minimize reinventions of the wheel (as it were), or to avoid continual re-writing of much the same code, to be more precise. If certain functions could be specified, algorithms designed and tested thoroughly (if not verified), then subsequent software systems that involved the same functionality could use the module developed earlier. This has two big advantages: firstly, it cuts down the lengthy process of software development, and, secondly, it can provide software reliability in its strongest sense - i.e. much-reused modules will be thoroughly tried and tested in use.

So secondhand software salesmen have a much better public image than their analogs in the automotive world, or at least they would do if they existed. Software reusability has been very much more of a desire than a reality in the software world. It is true that there are, and have been for a long time, substantial libraries of statistical and mathematical functions which are reused continually with a high success rate. But mathematical software is the exception, not the rule, in this regard. And this is because mathematical functions are well-defined, context-free abstractions (recall the distinguished category of model CS problems characterized in Chapter 3). In other domains we find much similar functionality required in one program and the next, but all too often the difference between the functionality offered by an existing piece of software and the functionality you desire are sufficiently different that (when you also add interface mismatches, documentation vagaries, etc.) it is preferable to reconstruct exactly what you need rather than work on someone else's handiwork that doesn't quite fit your needs. A less defensible, but no less real, further reason for lack of reuse in the software world, is that programmers tend to prefer to write their own code than to re-work someone else's - the urge to create anew faces no real competition when the alternative is the drudgery of delving into an unknown code in order to modify it (or even to be sure that it is not in need of modification).

In sum, the lack of practical exploitation of the notion of software reuse is due to both technical problems with making it possible and the nature of programmers who would rather re-create code than re-model it. The lesson to be taken from this is that successful promotion of software reusability will require 'social' constraints on the programmer as well as purely technical advances in this field.

Halpern (1990) makes an eloquent plea for reusability of code as a key to software reliability. He credits McIlroy (1969) with being the first to write at length on reusable software. He notes that if achieving software reliability is viewed as a matter of defeating bugs (and not one of better requirements analysis and specification, nor one of proving abstract correctness) then the obvious tactic is not to introduce bugs in the first place. "This in turn suggests that we write no code, code being the swamp in which bugs breed" p.136. But not only do we need to avoid writing code we must also guard against other peoples "fresh code (that is, untested code, whether newly written or not)" p. 136. But sadly code, unlike wine, fails to register its maturity - fresh code and thoroughly well-tested code are indistinguishable. Certain portions of a much and widely used software system may be completely fresh. And only when presented with input that in some dimension exceeds anything it has been given before does the computation crash through the fresh code to our utter amazement and dismay. Halpern calls this the "crevasse problem".

So finding code rather than writing it is the general strategy advocated. But ensuring that the code is not fresh, and deciding how best to chunk-up software into reusable modules, are both open problems. To deal with the fresh-code problem, he suggests the notion of a "usage history" associated with each reusable component, and a "Software Factory" to ensure that standards are adhered to, and to maintain stocks of mature (i.e. well-tried and tested) code modules.

As Halpern notes, construction of modular software is almost universally reckoned to be a good thing: "everyone is for it, some know what it is, and few practice it." He provides three senses in which the term is used, but the one that is, he claims, relevant in the current context of reusability is:

> The gathering into one routine of all the connecting links between a program and some function it will need at many points, so as to form a single standard interface between the two. A typical subject of modularization in this sense is an I/O package, which accepts all input/output requests from a program in a machine-independent or operating system independent form, and generates from them calls on the hardware or operating system functions that actually provide the needed service. The primary motive behind this kind of modularization is that of limiting the impact of change; the adoption of a new type of printer, for example, could be dealt with in a program so modularized by changing the single I/O module rather than all the many places in the program where I/O requests originate. These objects might better be called 'damage limiters' or 'change insulators' or 'responsibility compartments.'
>
> Halpern (1990) p. 139

Nevertheless, he is not entirely happy with this definition of a module, and proposes another (but calls it a "box" to avoid the module muddle).

> A box is a unit of code whose effects within a program are exactly and only what its specification promises; it can be used in any context, and without prior knowledge of its contents, wherever these effects are wanted, provided only that its communications protocol is followed.

As you can see, Halpern's definition of boxes bears a striking similarity to my earlier description of why mathematical software is reusable. This is no coincidence (neither is it because I wrote my description after reading his definition with the intention of mimicking it!). The similarity arises because Halpern intends to achieve the same level of certainty as can be exhibited by mathematical software. He goes to outline the resultant problems and the means of dealing with them.

Halpern focuses exclusively on the code level. 'After all that's where the programs really are', he might say. He is in fact quite disdainful of approaches that are limited to abstract representations (e.g. proofs of correctness). But general interest in reusability runs through all representational levels of a typical SDLC. In fact, some people insist that the real benefits of reusability are to be found in the more abstract representations - e.g. we may have more success with composing designs from a library of design modules than composing executable code from code modules.

One of the threads of the reusability issue that connects us back to the notion of transformational implementation of software, discussed in the previous chapter, is reuse of the sequence of transformations that take a specification to an implementation. Recall, for example, the "new paradigm" of Balzer, Cheatham and Green (1983, but it is quicker to flip back a few pages and see Figure 5.6). Working on the widely accepted assumption that system evolution should work through the specification and not the implementation, they ran into the problem that this entails repeated reimplementation of the modified specification, and implementation is typically a long, tedious, and error-prone activity. The long-term solution is thus to automate it, but in the shorter-term (i.e. the next few hundred years) the answer is to semi-automate it and save the design-and-implementation sequence for reuse with the modified specification. Clearly, it can't all be used, but hopefully much of it can, thereby considerably reducing the re-implementation burden that the software engineer has to bear. This general strategy is known as **replaying a derivation sequence** or **reusing derivations**.

In the "Knowledge-Based Software Engineering" chapter of the *Handbook of AI*, volume 4 (Barr and Cohen, 1990) it is suggested that there are three contexts in which reusing derivations is feasible and profitable: adaptive maintenance, i.e. updating a system to meet changing needs; within SLDCs that view experimentation and evolution as fundamental components; and when implementing a new specification, but one that is similar to some previous derivation.

The *Handbook* goes on to address the problems posed by this general idea of reusing derivations, in particular, the problem that we never want to reuse ALL of some previous derivation sequence. So clearly, such sequences cannot be recorded as a monolithic block and replayed whenever required. Derivation sequences will have to be structured objects, and structured in such a way as to mesh with a control strategy that selects, deletes, substitutes, etc. appropriate elements to generate the new (and perhaps quite similar) derivation sequence. There is, of course, a vast fund of difficult, unsolved problems here - a limitless supply of PhDs for computer scientists perhaps. This offers the comfort that comes with job security for those researching in computer science, but for the practising software engineer it means that no comprehensive software-reuse systems are likely to be available to him or her for quite some time. Nevertheless, because this is not an all or nothing notion, we can confidently expect to see elements of reuse technology appearing in commercial software development environments in the near future.

The *Handbook* tells us that when a derivation is recorded its hierarchical structure must be made explicit. For although it appears to be merely a sequence of transformation steps, "the internal structure of a derivation is a goal/subgoal tree whose leaves are transformation steps ... A derivation is reused during adaptive maintenance by traversing down the hierarchical goal structure and replaying the derivation steps until one doesn't apply because the relevant part of the specification was changed" (draft p. 60). At this point the system might try some automatic derivation, or if all else fails it calls for human assistance. But reusing a derivation on a new specification looks like being an even more difficult problem.The key notion is one of analogy between the new specification and some previous one, and we have very little idea how to deal with this problem in general. Analogy has long been thought to be a key to much of the power of human intelligence. There is thus a long history of tinkering with it in Artificial Intelligence, but it has proved surprisingly resistant to effective understanding in terms of anything as precise as a programmable mechanism. Nevertheless, a number of research groups are pursuing this approach to reusability, but it looks like being one of the least tractable.

But some forms of software reusability are finding immediate practical application. Joyce (1988) mentions a number of current commercial exploitations of this general philosophy. The Toshiba Corporation, he claims, "realized annual productivity rates in excess of 20,000 lines of source code per person-year as a result of utilizing reusable designs" (p. 97). Another company, the Hartford Insurance Group, is quoted as realizing significant savings as a result of the establishment and use of a reusable products library. They state that "by reusing code in the library, we realize a savings [*sic*] of 250 person-days per month at a cost of 25 person-days in support and maintenance time" (p.98). A study of Hartford's 14 applications development divisions indicates that 30-40 per cent of the code in new systems comes from the reusable library. Important factors in the success of this particular reusability venture are thought to be:

1. making the library of reusable modules easy to use;

2. establishing the view that all programmers are either contributors to or consumers of library code - i.e. the company programmer can't just ignore the reusability library.

Cavalier (1989) reports on the experiences of the Hartford Insurance Group with their Reusable Code Project. Reusable code was defined "as any technique that increases productivity by eliminating redundant practices in program generation" (p. 132). As reported above, considerable resultant savings were identified by the company. They are now looking into reuse of design and specification information (both textual and graphic). And for companies contemplating their own reuse projects Cavalier give us the following recommendations generated from the Hartford experience with successful code reuse.

- Develop and maintain an automated index of the program functions existing at the installation. This serves two purposes:identification of potentially reusable modules, and identification of redundancy in the application functions which may flag a need for code reuse.

- Make full-time staff resources available to both sort out potentially reusable code modules, and make the chosen modules more generic.

- Implement productivity measurements associated with the reusability.

- Set up a 'Reusability User Group' to share experiences and ideas.

Prieto-Diaz and Freeman (1987) note that "For code reuse to be attractive, the overall effort to reuse code must be less than the effort to create new code. Code reuse involves three steps:

1. accessing the code,
2. understanding it, and
3. adapting it" (p. 6).

They proposed a classification scheme based on reusability-related attributes. The following table lists the five attributes that they selected as the most relevant indicators of reuse effort together with their associated metric.

Attribute	**Metric**
Program size	Lines of code
Program structure	Number of modules, number of links, and cyclomatic complexity
Program documentation	Subjective overall rating (1 to 10)
Programming language	Relative language closeness
Reuser experience	Proficiency levels in two areas: programming language and domain of application

Table 6.1 Metrics chosen for the five reuse attributes from Prieto-Diaz and Freeman (1987), *IEEE Software* (January) Table 3 , p. 15.

In addition, to devising this classification scheme and building an environment that helps both locate suitable components for reuse and estimate the effort that will be involved in the reuse, the authors consider that there are two levels of potential reuse:

1. the reuse of ideas and knowledge, and
2. the reuse of particular artefacts and components (p. 7).

They are clearly focusing on the second and more well-defined (although not necessarily easier in the long run) level.

Freeman's research group at the University of California, Irvine, now the Advanced Software Engineering Project (but formerly the Reuse Project) has explored many ideas centred around the notion of software reuse. The DRACO system (see, for example, Freeman, 1987) is an approach to the construction of similar software systems from reusable software components. The stated rationale behind DRACO is to improve both software productivity and quality of the systems produced. The DRACO approach includes the reuse of designs as well as of code, and thus "amortizing the cost of a piece of software over the largest possible number of systems" p.830. Clearly, this is a laudable but currently unachievable goal.

Fully recognizing the difficulty of this task, the DRACO approach is to exploit the notion of an application domain within which numerous similar systems will be created over time. And for a given application domain an analysis of this domain must be made and defined to DRACO before it can be used to generate programs in the domain. As with many of the difficult problems being addressed in this general area, DRACO does not have to be a complete solution before it will become a useful system. The initial implementation of DRACO was not (and did not have to be) a fully automatic program generator; it was designed to aid the system creator in an interactive manner - the more help it could give the better, but any automatic assistance is preferable to none. We shall see this situation recurring constantly throughout the rest of this book, and this provides a measure of comfort in an area where all the problems are daunting but partial solutions can constitute significant practical (and theoretical) advances.

What does DRACO actually do? Two things it seems:

1. it manages definitions and implementations of languages of various types (properly viewed as specification languages);

2. it provides assistance and partial automation of the task of refining a specification of a desired system (given in one of the languages known to DRACO) into another language, presumably more concrete or executable (and also known to DRACO).

Reusability in DRACO comes to the fore as it assists in the process of refining a specification to an implementation. This process of software development involves many decisions including those of design(at the specification end of the process) and those of use of specific code modules (at the implementation end). Thus there is clearly scope for the full spectrum of reusability options in this project. In addition, there is also an intent to exploit reusability in problem analysis, more than this, such reuse is seen by Neighbours (1989), DRACO's implementor, as "the most powerful brand of reuse" p.9. The analysis of new system requirements, by an organization's systems analysts, can be considered in the light of DRACO domains that already exist. Given some appreciable overlap between the new problem and the known domains (including information on the previous analyses), there is potential scope for assisting in the new analysis by reusing elements of the earlier ones.

DRACO was implemented in LISP (some few thousand lines of), but is not a production tool. The DRACO team see the key to eventual success as

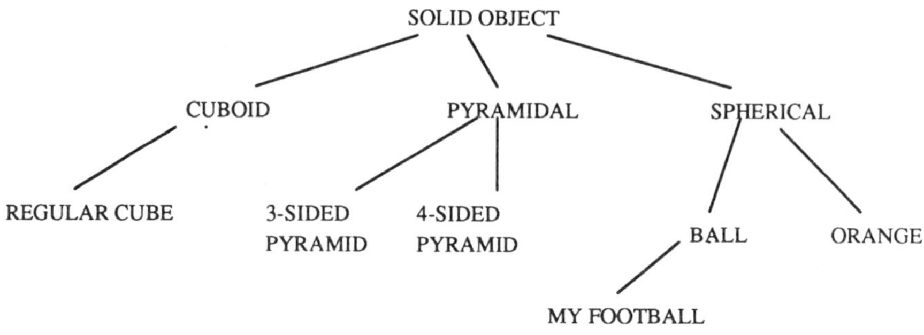

Fig 6.1 A single inheritance hierarchy

the existence of an effective library of domains - i.e. domains that can be built upon. Examples of domains already built are for augmented transition networks (i.e. sentence parsing mechanisms), for dictionary construction, and for generation of sentences in natural language.

Before moving on from the general notion of reusability we should briefly look at it within the context of OOP (object-oriented programming, introduced in Chapter 1). As mentioned in passing earlier, objects (the code-data capsules that dominate this style of programming) exist within an inheritance hierarchy. This means that any object can be viewed as a specialization of one (if only single inheritance) or more (multiple inheritance) general objects or classes - a class in OOP is roughly equivalent to a data type which is a precise characterization of the properties that a collection of entities all share. Booch (1991, p. 54) defines a **hierarchy** as follows:

Hierarchy is a ranking or ordering of abstractions.

And the notion of inheritance comes in because elements in the hierarchy can inherit properties from the more abstract levels. It is time for an example.

In Figure 6.1 the most general class, "solid objects", is specialized into three subclasses: "cuboid", "pyramid" and "sphere". Each of these subclasses is then specialized further. Inheritance comes in because the specification of, say, "ball" is partially inherited from "spherical object" and from "solid object". Thus part of the definition of "ball" might be the relationship of its volume to its radius, but this part applies to all "spherical objects" and so would be defined there and inherited by "ball" and by "my football" and by "orange". So this inheritance notion allows us to specify certain general characteristics of our computational objects just once, at the appropriate level of abstraction in the hierarchy, and then all subsequent specializations of this particular abstraction can automatically reap the benefits of our generalized characterization.

The important point about inheritance from the software reusability perspective is that once the software developer has an appropriate generalized hierarchical structure built (i.e. a hierarchy tailored to the application domain), the creation of software within this domain is primarily a process of customizing the general framework to suit specific needs - i.e. of creating objects low down in the hierarchy which will automatically inherit properties from the more abstract structure above them. In general, the lower down in the hierarchy the software developer operates the more that previously defined structure and functions are being reused. It is not too much of a distortion to claim that a significant point of difference between the conventional programming paradigm (say, programming in Pascal) and OOP is that in the former software is built up from agglomerations of elemental bricks (the statements in the language) while in the latter software is built by specializing a general framework to fit particular computational needs - one could almost say that in OOP we are 'building down'. Or as Yourdon (1990) puts it:

> People using structured methods as their development paradigm tend to treat each new project as an intellectual exercise never before contemplated; analysis and design literally begin with a blank sheet of paper. People using object-oriented methods, on the other hand, tend to practice 'design by extension.' That is, they assume that the new system they have been asked to develop is merely an extension, or refinement, of something that has already been built; so they approach the problem by asking, 'What new subclasses do I need to create, and what attributes do I need to inherit?'
>
> Yourdon (1990) p. 258

So among its many attractions OOP also seems to naturally promote the concept of reusability in software development, but only when the build-up-from-scratch mentality of programmers has been supplanted by the build-by-extension notion - and this 'not invented here' mindset has proved difficult to displace. As is often pointed out, with libraries of reusable code it is a no-lose situation from a purely technical viewpoint - there is the short-term benefit of programming at a high level of abstraction and the long-term one knowing that every contribution will be not only to the current project but to all the ones that follow it as well.

In sum, there are some immediately practical applications of the software reusability notion, and, although there are clearly some technical problems with full exploitation of this general idea, it does appear to be an underutilized notion that can provide considerable leverage once the programming milieu within a company is oriented towards capitalizing on it. Within their survey and assessment of automatic programming, Rich and Waters (1988) claim that "that the benefits of automatic programming can be traced almost exclusively to reuse" (p. 47). They also point out that "progress in any kind of automation is always obstructed by management problems as much as by technical hurdles ... [and] given that the heart of automatic programming is reuse, economic incentives in software development and acquisition need to be revised to foster reuse ... Policies whereby contractors would increase their profit by reusing software developed by others - or were paid extra if they produced something that someone else reused - would be steps in the right direction" p. 50.

6.3   Design knowledge

If we're contemplating reverse engineering or the reusability of modules that occur prior to code modules in a conventional SDLC, then we shall need to store, in a machine-manipulable form, representations of the design process - both design modules and the reasoning behind the choices made. It is this sort of information that is referred to in the term **design knowledge**.

As I've already said, it is one thing to decide that we must store design knowledge, but it is quite another to know exactly what to store and how to best store it. We've seen one suggestion that the derivation sequence should be represented as a goal/subgoal tree. Another scheme is described by Potts (1989a).

Potts describes a general scheme for representing process information,and in particular the design process in software engineering. It is a generic model which, with the aid of specialization mechanisms, can be customized for any design method. Potts lists the objects that it is necessary to represent as "design artefacts, steps and heuristics" (p. 66). The motivation for his work is presented as:

> To provide intelligent tool support for the early phases of system design, including software requirements analysis and domain modelling, it is necessary to develop a theory of the early design process that allows one to reason about design steps, sequences of steps, goals, open issues, and so forth. This ambitious goal is made even more difficult by the fact that there is no commonly accepted procedure for performing early system design (p. 66).

He lists three ways in which such a theory of design, a design method, will provide assistance to designers:

1. It provides a standard repertoire of notations, which are amenable to various analyses.

2. It helps control the technical progression of the project.

3. It contains local heuristics, in the form of standard procedures and guidance in well-defined design situations.

He draws our attention to the fact that it is the latter two points that address design as a process, and yet the first point is the only facet of design methods to be supported by traditional CASE tools (i.e. computer-

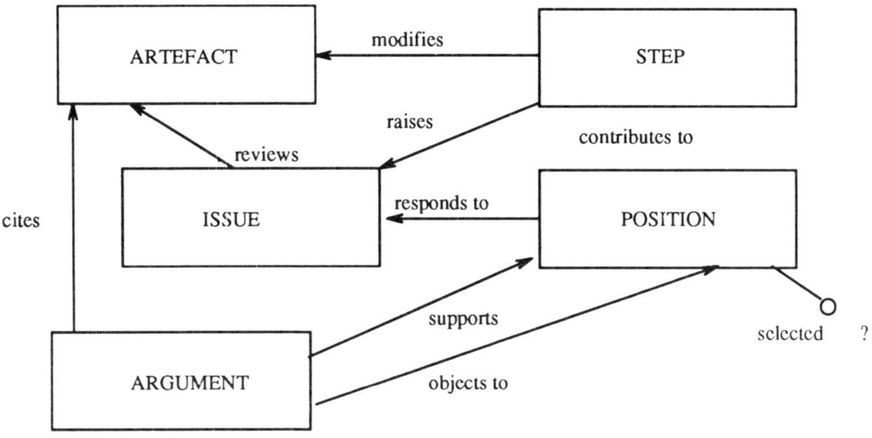

Fig 6.2 "The generic model of Potts" from Potts(1989a), Figure 1, p. 67

aided design tools). These CASE tools operate on a design state and assist in, for example, obtaining consistency. But, of course, such tools provide little assistance for the process of design - i.e. what design actions need to be performed, what issues are open and require decisions, and how to perform design actions, such as refinement of detail. Tools to assist the process of design will have to be based on explicit realizations of the design method's steps and heuristics.

Potts makes the further point that design methods are fluid. Each designer (and even the same designer at different times) will use a given design method differently. So a design method should not be a fixed procedure; we need a language or schema than can represent families of methods, at least. This leads him to address two issues:

1. What should the primitives be for generic method-independent representation?

2. How can this generic model be customized for specific methods?

For his generic schema he adopts an entity-relationship-attribute data model. The entity classes are: **artefacts**, which hold design state information, design **steps** which are the means by which refinements and revisions are performed, **issues**, **positions** and **arguments** are used to represent the reasoning behind design decisions. "Issues pose questions about some focus of concern (e.g. 'how should functionality be assigned among the processors?'). A position is a candidate response to an issue (e.g. 'Function F should be allocated to its own processor'). An argument may support or object to a position ('Function F is time-critical')" (p. 67).

There are eight legal binary relationships between the five entity types (as illustrated in Figure 6.2).

- **Modifies** - steps modify artefacts: in a revision a new version of the artefact is created, in derivation a new artefact may be created.

- **Raises** - steps raise issues: performing a step may automatically raise an issue which may, or may not, have to be addressed immediately.

- **Reviews** - issues review artefacts: e.g. an issue may be to review some property of an artefact.

- **Responds to** - a position is a response to an issue.

- **Supports** - arguments support positions.

- **Objects to** - arguments can also object to positions.

- **Cites** - arguments can cite artefacts: the artefact can provide evidence for the argument.

- **Contributes to** - positions contribute to steps: a step is performed because a set of commitments (selected positions) has been made.

Potts (1989a) then goes on to demonstrate how his generic model can be customized for the pre-implementation phases of the Jackson System Design (JSD) method (Jackson, 1983), as an example. The full details of this customization of the generic model to the "Hi-Ride Elevator" problem in Jackson (1983), can be found in Potts (1989b).

In general terms, the customization is accomplished by specialization of entity classes. "A design method's entity classes form a collection of class hierarchies, one for artefact classes, another for issue classes, and so on ... the different issue classes may be resolvable in different ways. These relational constraints dictate which steps modify which artefacts, which artefact conditions can raise which issues, which positions can respond to which issues" (p.68) etc.

Potts concludes with the observation that, although some research seeks to automate the process of requirements analysis and design,"there are many recurrent design situations where the constraints cannot be formalized strictly enough to support automatic constraint propagation. In these cases, some degree of intelligent automated task management and book-keeping of open issues and their possible solutions would nevertheless be very helpful" (p. 70) and his "issue-based information system" (IBIS) would be a possible route to kind of support for software engineering.

Just like a number of the other schemes that we have looked at, this is an ambitious project, but one whose place in a book that claims to eschew blue-sky research is justified by the fact that almost any step along the road to this long-term goal should provide immediate practical assistance to the software engineer (and the Eiffel system,described later, is one such small step within a commercial product).

6.4   Stepwise abstraction

To the software engineer who has delved into the world of software design methods and principles, the title of this subsection should elicit a feeling of *deja vu* but nevertheless seem somewhat odd. **Stepwise refinement** or **stepwise decomposition** are the terms with which I would expect you to posses some familiarity already. These terms are used to label the general process of developing an intricate algorithm from a specification - we manage the complexity by decomposing the overall problem into a collection of more-or-less independent subproblems, and we develop the necessary detail using a series of refinement steps rather than all at once. This is, of course, the dominant process in classical software engineering, i.e.engineering a specific, detailed artefact (a program) from a specification. Once we begin to countenance the possibility of reverse engineering, it should come as no great surprise that some reversal of these processes turns out to be necessary. I have called this process **stepwise abstraction** (Partridge, 1986), and it was described using, as a basis, the five points presented by Wirth (1971) in the classic description of stepwise refinement. The five points are as follows:

1. The effective communication of an AI program is based upon a sequence of abstraction steps. Typically in each step a number of substructures are condensed into a single, simple structure (often a structureless label). But on occasion, translation from an obscure to a less obscure notation may be involved.

2. The degree of conciseness and modularity of the abstract representation obtained in this way will determine the ease or difficulty with which the program can be understood and facilitate changes in the abstraction process so that the representation obtained can be understood in different ways for different purposes.

3. During the process of stepwise abstraction, a notation which is natural to the program at hand should be used as long as possible. The direction in which the notation develops during the process of abstraction is determined by the language most suitable within a particular target audience and for the type of understanding desired. This language should therefore allow us to express as naturally and as clearly as possible the structures which emerge during the design of the effectively communicable representations. At the same time, it must give guidance in the abstraction process by exhibiting each abstract representation in terms of basic features and structuring principles which are natural to the target audience.

4. Each abstraction implies a number of design decisions based upon a set of design criteria. Among these criteria are succinctness, clarity and the preservation of significant features of the program.

5. The design of an effectively communicable sequence of representations from an AI program is not a trivial process. It is a major problem area in our efforts to transform the products of a RUDE-based paradigm into practical software. It will remain a

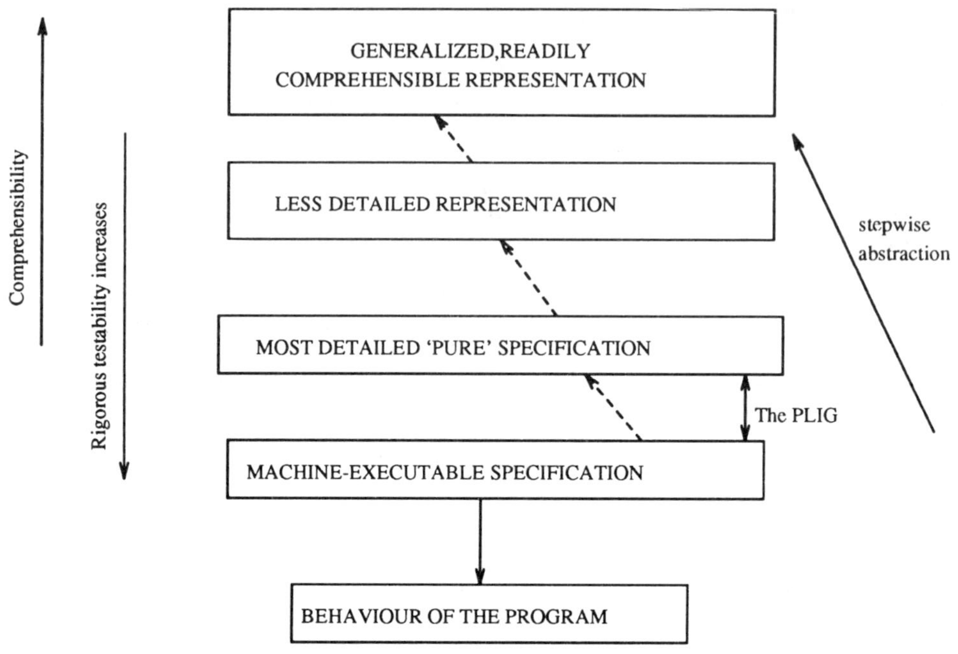

Fig 6.3 "The process of stepwise abstraction" from Partridge,1986, p.151

> problem area until guidelines for the varieties of stepwise abstraction are refined and honed to the extent that they are for stepwise refinement,or until AI problem solutions can be specified in more readily comprehensible machine-executable notations, free from the customary non-significant clutter (from Partridge, 1986, pp. 152-153).

It's an absolute certainty that the foregoing description of stepwise abstraction is not totally comprehensible on its own. Let me now try to lessen the mystification, if not eliminate it altogether. First,I can give you a picture of stepwise abstraction in action, as it were(Figure 6.3).

If the behaviour of the artefact is to be an effective force in driving system modification, we need all the support we can get for the difficult task of reasoning back from program behaviour to specification changes that will produce the desired behavioural change, and will also introduce a minimum increment to overall system complexity. The answer is to work and reason through the intervening representations that bridge the gap between specification and implementation. You may find this an acceptable approach, but still fail to see why we would need to abstract these intervening design structures. Clearly, they should be readily available if the software was developed properly in the first place. There seems to be a valid reason for traversing them in reverse order, but no real need to generate them backwards.

I suspect that full-scale stepwise abstraction is a seldom-required task, although something approaching it is necessary when faced with a pile of totally undocumented code and a pressing need to debug or enhance the system. But in the context of developing AI software, given that some incremental and exploratory methodology is necessary, minor examples (at least) of stepwise refinement are constantly in demand. There are several different reasons for this:

- There is no one 'best' sequence of representations - different types of representation will best support different types of understanding (by different target audiences) of the specification-implementation relationship. So it should not be surprising that the design sequence favoured by the original designer is not always the best (or even a good) sequence of representations to promote the understanding of an end-user, or of a software engineer charged with introducing a specific enhancement.

- Within the context of an incremental and evolutionary development methodology (and within totally conventional methodologies, if the truth were admitted), surprising system behaviour is surprising just because the design representations in use fail to support some aspect of understanding of the program - changes in the nature of abstract representations employed can be used to reduce the subsequent surprise element of the program's behaviour. This application of stepwise abstraction hinges on the obvious point that we always know a lot more about what we have, in fact, designed after we've done it, than we do about what we are designing whilst engaged in the process. The popular myth that exercise of a disciplined process of design and development allows us to maintain a full understanding of the eventual outcome - i.e. a program - does not bear close scrutiny. For any non-trivial system, further understanding can and does come through observation of behaviour, and by a process of stepwise abstraction this extra understanding can be ploughed back into the documentation.

However useful you might concede that stepwise abstraction could be, you might also point out that innumerable other seeming impossibilities have stronger claims on our interest and energy. Thus a time-machine would have enormously more potential, and it appears to be no more difficult - they are both impossible. The abstraction process is essentially the problem of decompiling, extracting form from function, and we know that's intractable, so why waste time wishing for the moon? Let's take a closer look at the fundamental process.

6.5   The problem of decompiling

Compilers are common, and decompilers are somewhere between scarce and nonexistent - it depends on the constraints employed. In the earlier discussion of the function-to-form problem (Chapter 4) we looked at how we could lessen the severity of this task by judicious choice and careful use of the 'right' representation - i.e. it is a great help if form reflects function in our programmed systems. We also mentioned how the difficulty (if not impossibility) of decompiling machine code turns out to be such an obstacle that the software industry exploits it to prevent unauthorized tampering with their products.

This is not encouraging information, but fortunately there are a number of reasons why the decompiling operations demanded by our SDLCs can be made to fall into the realm of tractable problems.

- We are not required to decompile from machine code. We can choose our implementation language wisely.

- We are not required to decompile from bare code. We should have full documentation available, including details of the system design procedure as outlined earlier.

- We are not required to decompile a complete software system. We typically have some of the necessary abstractions to hand (either as a result of earlier decompilations, or as part of the original documentation), and the demand is for a relatively small-scale decompilation exercise.

- We are not required to decompile a monolithic black box. We can look into the software and see how it is doing what we observe it to be doing in terms of the implementation language. In fact, we can do more than this. We can get the software system to show us how it is doing what it is doing. We can generate traces of the execution sequences responsible for specific behaviours (see, for example, work in 'Program Visualization' introduced by Myers, 1988, and more specifically 'self-explanation' in expert systems described in the next chapter). So we have some explicit structural information to work from, and even though it will not be precisely (or perhaps anything like) the representational form that we might wish to abstract, the explicit presence of a structure underlying the observed functionality can only lessen the severity of the decompiling task.

So, without wishing to pretend that decompiling is a simple and straightforward task, I do claim that the nature of the decompiling demanded need not be as daunting a prospect as it first appears. Nevertheless, I do maintain that it is a crucial component of the necessary discipline of ESD (as well as of quite conventional SDLCs), and one that has been largely ignored and neglected because of the belief that its use is indicative of bad practice - i.e. messing with the implementation when attention should be focused on the specification. To my mind, some degree of decompilation is unavoidable when designing and developing complex software systems. It is needed as soon as we are surprised by the behaviour of our system. And to claim that the occurrence of such surprises is itself indicative of dubious practices is like claiming that mathematical proofs have no merit - after all, they're just logical inferences from the axioms, if we missed seeing that particular inference sequence then we were clearly not paying close enough attention because it was there all the time.

I agree with the widely accepted sentiment that system development should focus on the specification and not the implementation, but I think that the degree to which we can actually do this has been grossly oversold. Such homilies ignore the real problem of complex systems, which is that the window on system adequacy is system performance. Whether we like it or not, the initial spur to system modification is often a behavioural problem, a problem with the implementation, and this must be transformed into implications for the specification before we can shift the focus to where we all agree it should be.

Hence decompilation is (or should be) an essential component of SDLCs; it is not a misconceived notion to be shunned by every right-minded software developer. A need to decompile is not indicative of a slovenly approach and thus only to be satisfied in secret behind closed doors. But decompilation is a difficult process, although not quite as difficult as it's widely believed to be. The conclusion is that considerably more time, effort and expertise than it customarily attracts should be focused on this particular subproblem.

6.6   Controlled modification

Having exposed (but by no means solved) the problem of working back from implementation to specification, we can now see how this fits into a scheme for evolutionary system development that pushes against the tide of the second law of program evolution (see Chapter 4 for the details of this law). Chapter 4 was also the place where I introduced the notion of controlled modification.

Controlled modification is the process of generating system modifications by tackling each specific problem at its source (i.e. in the specification, or in the detailed design, etc.) and then redesigning and reimplementing the changes into the system code. In addition, the 'style' of the modifications introduced should be constrained by the principles of structured growth (see next subsection).

Figure 6.4 illustrates the process of controlled modification. There are several points to note. First, you will notice that there are a couple of arrows shooting information in to support the abstraction process. On the one hand, we have the system developer's knowledge of what the software system is meant to achieve, in general, and what specific problem is behind the current need to effect a modification of the system. And, in addition, we would hope for the system to be able to assist the developer by making both original design knowledge and the results of previous abstraction sequences conveniently available.

Secondly, the move from one version of the program to the next is accomplished, on most occasions, by a (possibly substantial) detour through various abstractions from the programmed system. What level of abstraction, and what type of abstraction are needed to support controlled modification are questions that can be answered only with respect to specific problems with the programmed system. It is probably quite clear that the level of abstraction needed is the level at which the problem at hand first appears, but the notion of what type of   abstraction

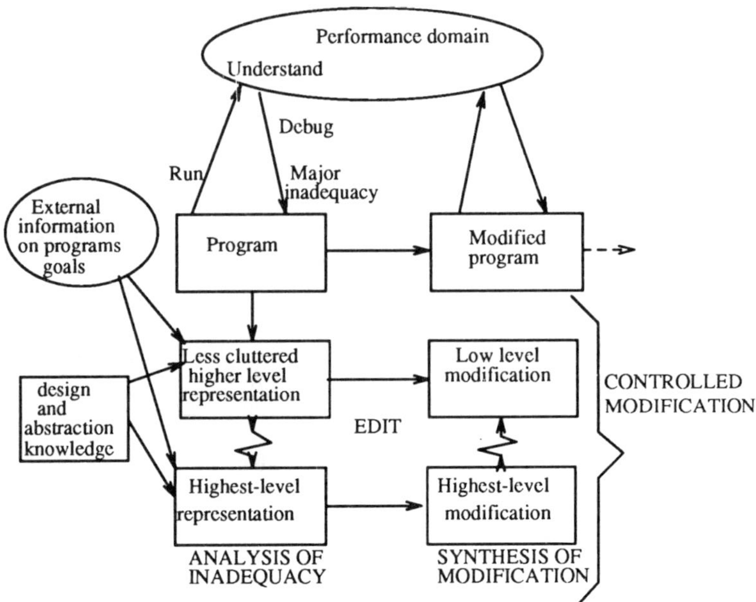

Fig 6.4 "Controlled modification as part of the RUDE cycle"

probably causes some wonderment in the software engineer who has been raised on a specific SDLC and thus sees the range of possible abstractions as very limited - i.e. there may be a requirements document, a specification, a general design and a detailed design perhaps. But, in reality, the options are much broader than this (and hence a major reason why we must practise stepwise abstraction even if we dutifully follow a structured design methodology). A sequence of abstractions may be available, but it may not be the best (or even a good) sequence to support a clear understanding of the system *from the point of view demanded by a specific inadequacy in the system's behaviour.*

For example, work on an AI system to model human learning behaviours led us to use two very different abstract representations of the programmed system. (Full results of this project can be found in Johnson, Partridge & Lopez, 1983.) In Figure 6.5 we have a conventional structure-chart representation of the overall system. It displays the basic modularity of the system design. The system modelled the behaviour of an animal in a environment, and in particular the responses that the animal generated to each new environmental input stimulus. The actual response was a function of the current input stimulus, the animal's current location, and its previous history of interaction. A last pertinent point is that the animal's cognitive processing (i.e. how it related input stimulus to response) was implemented as a neural network - i.e. a large network of primitive processing elements.

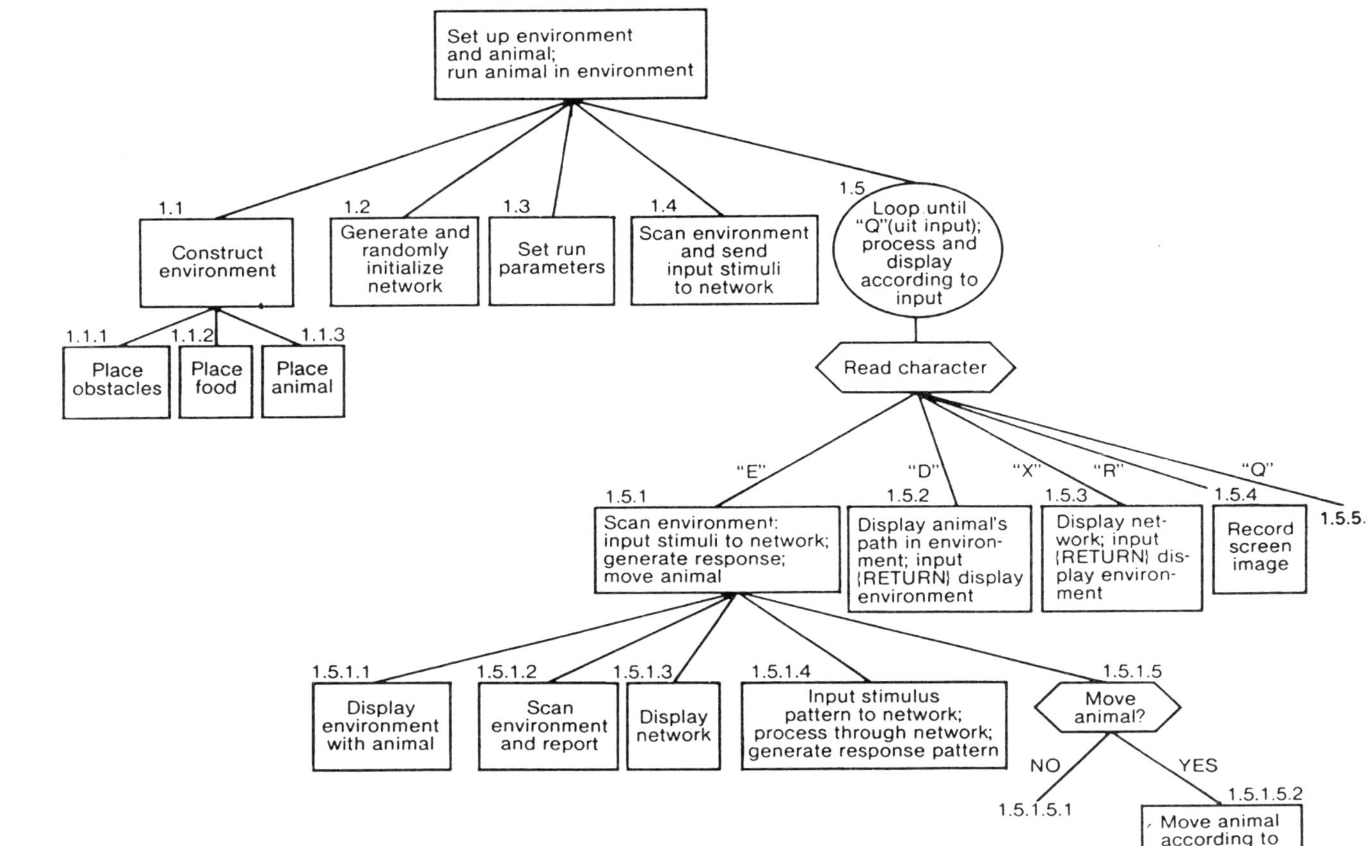

Fig 6.5 "A structure-chart representation"

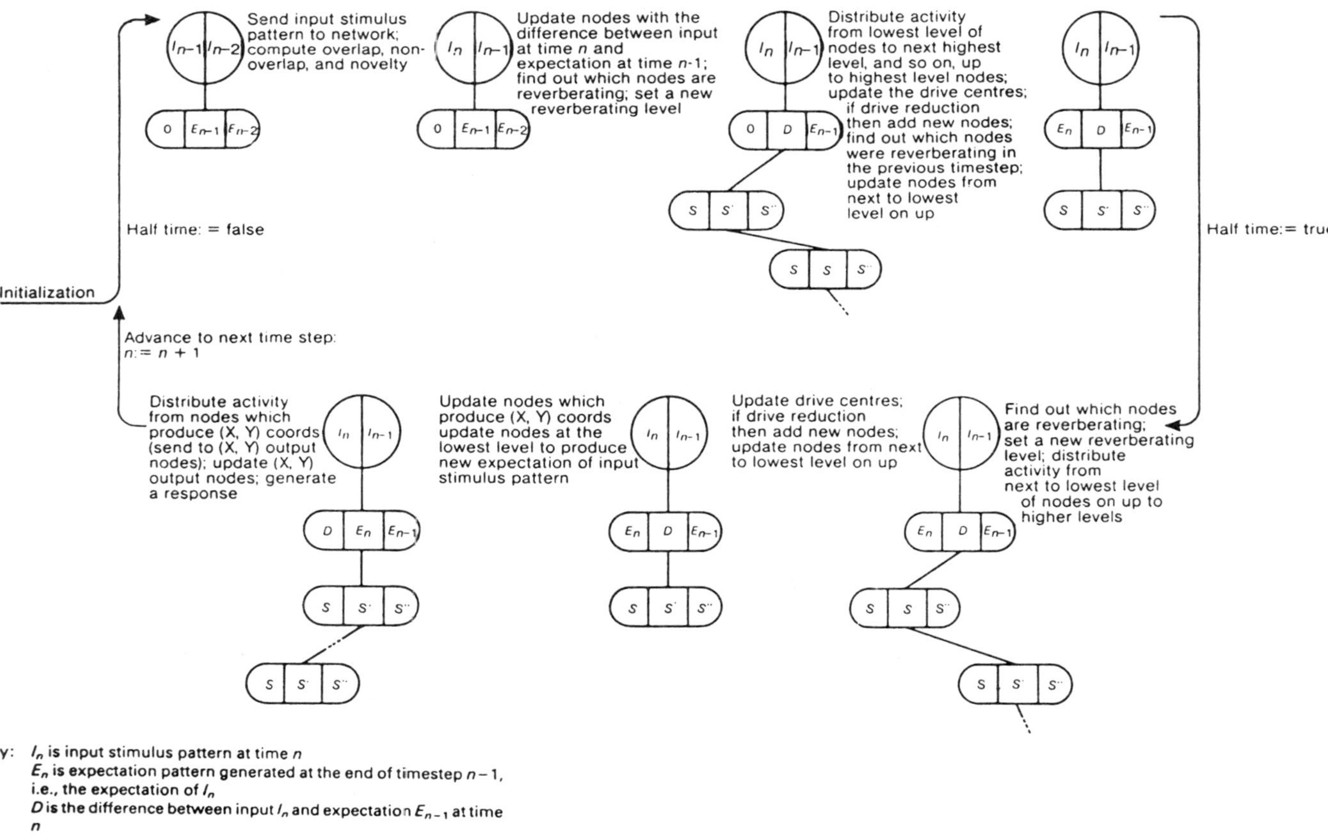

Key: I_n is input stimulus pattern at time n
E_n is expectation pattern generated at the end of timestep $n-1$, i.e., the expectation of I_n
D is the difference between input I_n and expectation E_{n-1} at time n
S is $\Sigma\,|I_n - E_{n-1}|$ divided by the number of links to other nodes
S' is $\Sigma\,|I_{n-1} - E_{n-2}|$ divided by the number of links to other nodes
S'' is $\Sigma\,|I_{n-2} - E_{n-3}|$ divided by the number of links to other nodes

Fig 6.6 "A dynamic-loop representation"

In Figure 6.6 we have an abstract representation of the stimulus-response processing mechanism that we found, through trial and error, to be the best abstract representation to support controlled modification. The AI in the system was concentrated in the network's processing of the input stimuli and the generation of a subsequent response. It was thus in the organization and detailed processing mechanisms of the network nodes (e.g. activity accumulation and transfer functions) that most exploratory system development was concentrated. Such networks are notoriously lacking in conceptual transparency because of the distributed nature of the operations that they perform. This is, of course, not good news when this is precisely the part of the system wherein we needed to develop a deep understanding of what was going on, and why.

The loop structure that comprises Figure 6.6, together with an interface for program visualization which used a dynamic graphical display, was found to be the most effective aid for understanding the system behaviour in terms of the network structures.

What is the relationship between these two abstractions? They are not different level representations of much the same information, neither are they representations of different information. They are best considered, I believe, as different perspectives on a single system.They each emphasize different aspects and neglect others, and this is entirely appropriate as they were developed to support different sorts of understanding of the system. The structure chart is fine for communicating an overall picture of the system organization and for working out the general design in a quite conventional manner. And it would of course support the understanding of problems that arose concerning say, the local and global scopes of specific implementation structures.

The 'loop diagram' in Figure 6.6 is focused on the cyclic stimulus-response behaviour of the network nodes; it covers nodes 1.5.1.4 and 1.5 of the representation in Figure 6.5. It was used to support reasoning about system behaviour with respect to changes in the network structure and processing mechanisms. Figure 6.5 is the conventional software skeleton, and Figure 6.6 focuses attention onto a concentration of AI muscle. Multiple representations of the system should assist the developer in his or her efforts both to gain a fuller understanding of the system and to modify the current version of the system in harmony with the principles of structure upon which it is constructed (see 'structured growth' later).

The construction and maintenance of the design history of a software system would be an onerous task (conventional one-time system documentation is far less demanding but often not done precisely because it is time-consuming and unappealing to the technologist). So, as we saw in the context of design records (discussed above), the prevailing view is that much of this burdensome task must be automatic, or else it will just never get done at all.

What I shall suggest here is that certain abstractions can be automatically generated provided the programmer observes certain rules in his or her programming activity.

Modern programming languages, in supporting both data structure abstraction and control abstraction bring this automatic-abstraction goal nearer. Ada (Barnes, 1983), for example, offers extensive syntactic and semantic support for the rigorous separation of the abstractions, which constitute the algorithm and abstract data structures, from the necessary (but cluttersome) implementation details. Careful system development in accordance with a set of principles and guidelines for the distribution of coded structures would allow the application of 'abstraction algorithms' which can, on a purely syntactic basis, generate the algorithmic and data structure abstractions embodied in the working system code.

To repeat an earlier example (Partridge, 1986, pp. 190-192): A 'package' in Ada contains an explicit syntactic demarcation of specification and implementation. In addition, this syntactic differentiation is supported by a semantic one - i.e. other system modules are prevented from accessing what the programmer has decided are implementation details. Such a semantically-supported syntactic distinction provides the basis for an abstraction algorithm which can generate 'specifications' from the executable code.

The Ada package is an information-hiding mechanism; it has two parts: a public or specification part, and a private or implementation part. The specification part constitutes the abstract specification of the package: it specifies all that a user can know about, and hence use in, the package. The implementation part contains (as you might guess) an implementation of the abstract specification; it is not accessible to the package user.

The programmer can thus, in effect, delineate all code as either specification or implementation. But as you should recall from our earlier discussions, these terms are not absolutes. They are relative terms (quite apart from the fact that there are many different ways to represent a given level, say, of specification). So, in practice, the situation is likely to be more complicated. A series of levels of abstract representation demands a more sophisticated decision procedure (and abstraction algorithm) than the binary choice required for two absolute categories.

Notice that the detailed distribution procedure employed will be determined by both the abstraction algorithm available and the type of abstract representation required by the system developer. A more satisfactory situation would be to have a general code distribution strategy and a selection of different abstraction algorithms for subsequent use - but this introduces severe complications which I do not want to address. The major point is that the variety of potentially useful abstractions demands some flexibility somewhere within this overall approach to automatic abstraction. It is, for example, not obvious that the best structure to abstract for supporting controlled modification of the AI muscles in the system is also the best abstract representation for supporting conventional software maintenance.

The following rather crude knowledge base is coded as an Ada package. As constructed it comprises a collection of rules, and mechanisms for adding, accessing, and removing rules. The semantics of the Ada language ensure that use of this knowledge base is limited to the three mechanisms listed as procedure and function specifications at the beginning of the package. All code from the reserved word **PRIVATE** to the end of the package is inaccessible to users of the package.

```
PACKAGE knowledge-base IS
   TYPE rule IS PRIVATE;
   PROCEDURE put rule ( condition, action: string );
   FUNCTION  next rule RETURN;
   PROCEDURE remove-rule ( item: rule );
   PRIVATE
         TYPE rule IS
         RECORD
               condition: string;
               action: string;
         END RECORD;
   END  knowledge-base;
   PACKAGE BODY knowledge-base IS
         TYPE ruleset IS array (1 .. max) OF rule;
               knowledge: ruleset;
               nextspace: integer:= 1;

               .

               .

               .

         PROCEDURE put rule (condition, action: string) IS
         BEGIN
               knowledge(nextspace):=(condition,  action);
               nextspace:=nextspace + 1;
         END;

               .

               .

               .

   END knowledge-base;
```

Clearly, construction of an algorithm that abstracts the package specification is a viable proposition. With this code, and some minor linguistic transformations (in deference to that subset of humanity that has been wise enough to avoid becoming fluent in such inhuman languages) we might automatically obtain the following abstract representation:

The knowledge base is composed of rules. A rule is composed of a condition part and an action part. The following operations on the knowledge base are possible:

1. rules can be added to the knowledge base;

2. the next rule can be obtained;

3. rules can be deleted.

In closing this Ada example, let us note that such a strategy of structure building in concert with a specific abstraction algorithm is, of course, not limited only to the coded representation of the system. It could be applied at any level in system design; it is just that with comprehensive, well-defined constraints on what is acceptable as, say, Ada code, this would appear to be the easiest level of application of automatic abstraction technology.

This sort of automatic abstraction facility is implemented within the support environment of the commercially available object-oriented language, Eiffel (see Meyer,1989, and described briefly in Chapter 9). A documentation tool, called **short**, can produce a summary version of a class showing the external interface, i.e. the exported features only and, in the case of routines, only the header and the entry and exit conditions, if stated. Meyer (1989, p. 13) tells us that "the manual for the Basic Eiffel Library is an example of Eiffel documentation produced almost entirely from output generated by **short**." He also points out that such documentation is obtained almost for free, and it is guaranteed to be consistent with the actual software as it is extracted from it.

The case for alternative (loosely equivalent) representations in software production has actually be made much earlier in this book. In Chapter 1 we viewed several alternative software design strategies (e.g. structured and object-oriented) which were presented as genuine alternatives whose relative power depended critically on the nature of the problem being tackled. In the current context we might say that the conceptual transparency (a major component of the 'power' of a representation) of a representational scheme is dependent on the nature of the problem at hand, both the intrinsic nature of the problem itself and the nature of the task that we are addressing with respect to the particular problem.

In Figures 6.5 and 6.6 we have seen examples of different alternative representations for a given computational problem. Each representation best supports a different task with respect to the particular problem - Figure 6.5 provides a traditional view of system organization and modular structure which is a useful initial perspective for general reorganization or as a precursor to focusing on specific modules, Figure 6.6 was found to be a much more powerful representation for reasoning about the input-process-output cycle, the central functionality of the system with respect to the neural network that the system contained.

We can now return to the object-oriented paradigm in order to see the power of this representational scheme (it is, of course, much more than this but for the moment we'll take this limited view of OOP). In his positive exposition of both OOA and OOD, Yourdon (1990) considers the question of what systems and applications will most effectively use the object-oriented paradigm. He notes: "A software manager at IBM recently commented to me that attempts to use standard structured techniques to build applications in an OS/2 Extended Edition Presentation Manager (PM) environment had been dismal failures; the only successes they could point to were applications developed with object-oriented techniques" p. 260. This sort of application is a typical graphical user interface and is characterized by pull-down menus, multiple windows, icons, and mouse-driven commands. In such an application (as Yourdon says) OOD excels and the traditional structured approaches typically fail.

As a direct comparison with the representations in Figures 6.5 and 6.6, Figure 6.7 is an object diagram of the same system, i.e. an animal controlled by a neural network structure which reacts to, and acts upon an environment.

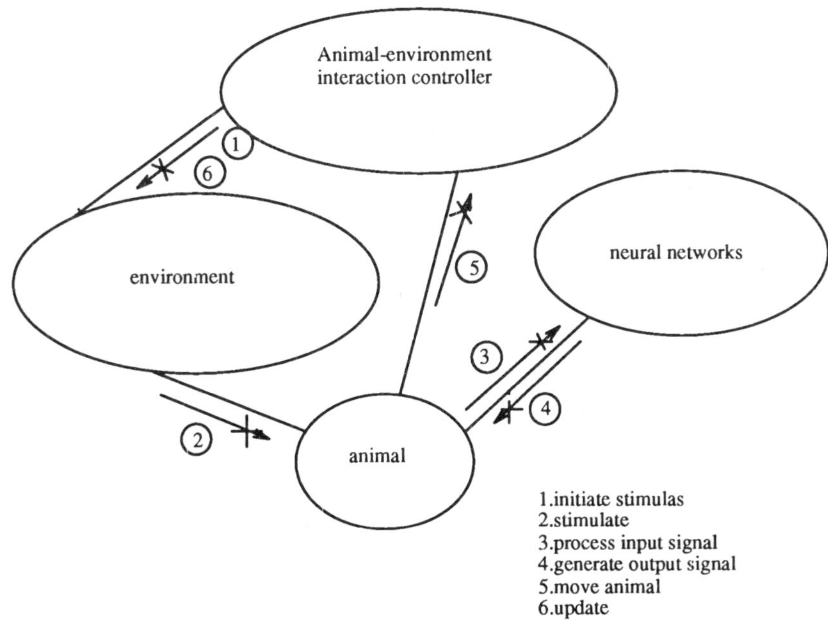

Fig 6.7 Animal-environment system object diagram

Objects are represented by an irregularly shaped, closed contour; relationships between objects, which means that they can send messages to one another, are illustrated with connecting lines; the specific messages that can be passed are named and associated with an arrow that points to the object being acted upon (the particular arrow icon used is taken from Booch, 1991, and denotes that all the messages in this system are synchronized); and the numeric labels associated with each message name specify the simple sequential synchronization required in this system.

Clearly, a whole new notation is needed in order to represent more ambitious systems, as indeed it is always needed for any new representational strategy whether it is introducing a radically new paradigm or just a new diagramming scheme within an old one. Within the object-oriented paradigm, and given its focus on message passing between objects, extensive notational impedimenta is developed for specifying and illustrating the time-ordering of events - i.e.simple sequential synchronization (as in Figure 6.7), asynchronous message passing, or more elaborate schemes such as conditional flow of control. A complete representation will be composed of several diagrams each displaying different aspects of the system. A timing diagram, for example, may be employed to show the dynamic interactions among various objects in an object diagram which is used to show the existence of objects and their relationships in the logical design of the system.

As this is not meant to be a primer on the object-oriented approach to software design, I'll go no further into notational detail. The points to conclude with here are simple: representation is important, very important, when we are trying to gain a conceptual grasp of non-trivial software, and there is no one best representation. Different representations best support different software-related activities. There may be just one specification and one design sequence for a given piece of software, but there is a variety of alternative representations that are likely to prove invaluable with respect to the software product. The software maintainer, developer or whatever should not be blinkered too much by the actual precursor representations for they will not necessarily best serve his or her current purposes.

6.7 Structured growth

Having, I hope, convinced you that there is much more to be abstracted from a program than the original design structures and specification, one further problem area needs to be highlighted. Assuming that we can effectively decompile observed behavioural inadequacies into an understanding of what is wrong with the structure of the system, how do we set about modifying the structure in such a way that overall system clarity is maintained (or even enhanced) and system complexity is kept at a minimum - which may be two ways of saying much the same thing?

Conventional software engineering, spurred on by the software crisis, has, you might think, already solved this problem. Structured programming is the common name for the motley collection of rules and looser guidelines that the responsible system developer uses in order to maximize the clarity of his or her programmed artefacts. So why not adopt, wholesale, this farrago of strictures and our problem is solved? But it is not.

Structured programming, as you ought to expect from a notion that was developed in the context of linear specify-design-implement SDLCs, was developed to be used for a one-shot, complete implementation of a detailed design and specification. This is rather different from the need to implement selected elements of a design in the context of a fairly comprehensive, existing implementation.

So, although it would be foolish to thus toss the wisdom of several decades out of the window, it would be equally foolish to expect it to solve the current problem. What we now face, as Sandewall (1978, but probably more accessible in Barstow, Shrobe & Sandewall, 1984) first termed it, is **structured growth** - although I am using it in not exactly the same way as he first introduced it, I admit.

Sandewall characterizes structured growth as follows: "an initial program with a pure and simple structure is written, tested, and then allowed to grow by increasing the ambition of its modules ... the growth can occur both "horizontally", through the addition of more facilities, and "vertically" through a deepening of existing facilities and making them more powerful in some sense" (p. 63, in Barstow, Shrobe and Sandewall, 1984).

The major difference between the two usages of this term is what drives the modification: I write of behavioural inadequacies, and he writes of the program developers desire to enhance the system. It maybe that these two driving forces are often not very different. Anyway, the point of structured growth is not why you want to modify the system,but how are you going to do it as a minimal structure-destroying act- to take the most negative viewpoint.

One of the key ideas behind the effective use of techniques of structured growth is that you are only introducing modifications to a stable, well-structured and well-tested basic system (the conventional software skeleton described in Chapter 4). If indeed it turns out that a major reorganization of the system framework is called for then we are out of the realm of structured growth and into more conventional structured programming - i.e. redesigning the system from first principles.

But given that structured growth is not taken to include major upheavals of the system, then Sandewall has several support-system features to suggest:

1. Keep track of "open statements" or "expansion points". When users type in a piece of code which they know has to be refined or rewritten later (e.g. a crude first heuristic, or a marker for where a heuristic will eventually be needed), it should be possible to tell this to the system and ask later where the (perhaps local) expansion points are. As a specific example, see the "deferred" structures in the Eiffel language (Meyer, 1989); a detailed example is given in Chapter 9.

2. "Distinguish different types of edit operations. Given an initial approximation to a program, some changes will be made to correct bugs, and some to extend the program. It would be desirable to treat these two kinds of changes separately, so that several layers of refinement or growth could be maintained in parallel. It is a common observation that early versions of a program are useful introductions to later full-grown versions. Similarly, the value of (idealized)early-refinement steps as documentation has been emphasized in Berry(1975)." (Sandewall in Barstow, Shrobe and Sandewall, 1984, p.64)

The first of Sandewall's suggestions is a structured-growth specific enhancement of the widely accepted bookkeeping (or supersecretary) role that sophisticated software development support systems should exhibit. The second feature should strike a chord with the earlier discussion on sequences of abstractions and of storing design knowledge. Clearly, the ready availability of abstract representations of earlier (and by implication more readily comprehensible as they are uncluttered with subsequent refinements) versions of the system can be merged with the general goal of maintaining on-line useful representations of the design history of the project. And, although recognizing the need for such functionality in software support environments is one thing, whereas delivering this functionality is altogether another (but see Trenouth's "version trees" in Chapter 9), such recognition is required before there is any hope of serious attention being given to the problems it involves.

In sum: in this chapter I have provided indications (little more than that I believe) of what might be the major component problems to be solved along the path to a discipline of ESD. None of them are easy problems, but none of them appear to be impossible either. And, as I've also indicated, many of them are now being addressed seriously by competent groups of software researchers. Much of what I have touched on in this chapter is still not widely accepted as necessary in mainstream software engineering - other problems such as automatic verification tools, for example, are thought to be more pressing problems - but there is sufficient activity outside of this mainstream for considerable energy and expertise to be focused on these Cinderella issues.

7
Machine Learning: Much Promise, Many Problems

It might strike you as a bit odd to see this chapter on machine learning pop-up in a book concerned with the practical application of AI. Well, your first impression would be appropriate if this chapter reviewed the theories and mechanisms that are generally taken to constitute the AI subfield of machine learning, but it will not. My goal in this chapter is to convince you that machine learning mechanisms will be a necessary part of many AI systems, and that this necessity brings with it additional aggravation for those of us that wish to engineer AI software. I do this not because I think that engineering artificially-intelligent software is a well understood and boring procedure which is in need of some injection of excitement - far from it. I do this because the potential power of machine learning mechanisms is something that we should be well aware of even though it introduces further problems on top of those that we already face. It may be wise, if not essential, to have the full picture in mind even though work on just one part of it gives us quite enough problems to be going on with.

7.1 Self-adaptive software

Mention of the possibility of self-adaptive software should, for all the old-timers in the software world, conjure up the spectre of self-modifying code. A favoured strategy, in the days when programming was largely the pastime of grappling with a mass (or better, morass) of machine code instructions in order to save a few bytes of memory or to shave a few milliseconds off the running time of a program, was to devise ingenious ways of reusing memory locations and blocks of instructions by overwriting certain critical instructions with new ones as the program executed. Thus the code that actually constitutes the program will vary as the program runs through an execution sequence. And, moreover, the details of how it actually varies are dependent upon the details of a given execution sequence.

Debugging is not one of the favoured pursuits of most software engineers. They are fundamentally creative people, system designers and builders. Looking for errors in such creations (either one's own or worse someone else's) is an exercise that few can gather great enthusiasm to pursue. Add to this inherent lack of appeal the further negative incentive of machine code, especially the early ones with (mis)mnemonic labels and glorious perceptual opacity, and it is not surprising that the queues of qualified applicants to maintain software systems have never been long. And on top of all this, in the presence of self-modifying code, the maintenance person could not even while away the hours staring at the listing hoping for inspiration in the sure knowledge that all the relevant information is in front of him, or her. For the listing, in effect, changes as the program executes. In this thoroughly dismal scenario the only serious options are to abandon the task or to collect strategically chosen snapshots of the program code and data. Octal core dumps were one favoured representation of this information (favoured by the machines that is, and in those days it was the machines that were the scarce and expensive resource). The advent of high-level languages (among other things) has done much to improve this bleak picture, but another significant improvement was introduced early on; it was a programming principle to abide by if you wanted to stand a good chance of debugging your creative efforts. The principle was:

Never write self-modifying code.

So to persons well aware of this principle and the very good reasons for its existence, a call for self-adaptive software systems is likely to be greeted with no enthusiasm. I hope to convince you that such a response would be uncalled for. But first, why do we need to contemplate the undoubted extra problems that self-adaptive software systems will bring with them?

7.2   The promise of increased software power

Way back in Chapter 1 I presented four aspects of how we might approach the problem of increasing software power - and each aspect involved AI. As it happens, not only does each of these four aspects involve AI, but they also each imply a need for machine learning in their more impressive manifestations - i.e. a need for self-adaptive software.

The central notion here is that many significant enhancements of software power require a move from static, context-free systems to dynamic context-sensitive systems. Intelligence is not a context-free phenomenon, and AI can not be either. "Machine learning," as Roger Schank has succinctly put it, "is the quintessential AI issue." This does not mean that all AI software must involve mechanisms for machine learning. But it does mean that our options in the absence of robust and reliable mechanisms for machine learning will be severely limited.

The need for self-adaptive software derives from several sources: there is a need for software that is reactive to changing circumstances, and at the more mundane level there is a need for mechanisms to lessen the difficulty of the task of incrementally upgrading knowledge bases (as argued by Michalski, Carbonell and Mitchell, 1983, in their volume entitled *Machine Learning*).

7.3   The threat of increased software problems

Given that there are some not unreasonable reasons why we might want self-adaptive software systems, what does this new need entail?   In a word: problems.   To begin with, there is the old problem of the state of a system changing over time - i.e. the program that you are asked to debug or enhance is defined by the specification plus its usage history. Now, if the old-timers were smart enough to realize that this type of software system is primarily a short cut to disaster, do we need to re-embark on this learning experience?

I think not; we must clearly not rush in, but times have changed, and, I shall argue, they have changed sufficiently for the possibility of self-adaptive software to be a viable proposition, provided we operate with caution. It is the differences more than the similarities between old-style machine-code programming and modern software system design that are most obvious - the two processes bear little resemblance except at some very basic level. So what are the modern innovations that suggest to me that self-adaptive software need not carry with it the curse of self-modifying code?

- Systems are designed and developed more systematically using appropriate abstract representations which reduce the effective complexity by several orders of magnitude.

- With the development of elaborate machine-manipulable data structures program complexity can be traded out of the algorithm and into the data structures; as a result substantial software adaptivity can be gained by merely changing data values and keeping the actual algorithm unchanged.

- Software can now be developed within a sophisticated support environment, which can remove a myriad of trivial considerations from the concern of the programmer, and this again significantly reduces the effective complexity of the overall task.

- Principles of structured system design capture the hard-won wisdom of the intervening years, and when adhered to make a well-structured system much more conceptually manageable than the equivalent monolithic list of machine code instructions.

- Within the comprehensive, multi-levelled and highly-structured framework implied by the first four points, we can constrain and limit the scope of any self-adaptive mechanisms employed.

This last point is particularly important. I am not saying that ill-considered and over-ambitious machine learning mechanisms are now fair game for the zealous software engineer. I am saying that within the constraints of a well-engineered software system there is scope for the careful deployment of self-adaptive mechanisms that will enhance the power of the software without necessarily wrecking its maintainability, and I shall provide a couple of examples in the final section of this chapter.

In particular, some types of machine learning are more inherently controllable than others, and judicious encapsulation of these mechanisms within a software system will keep the overall system intellectually manageable - especially if appropriate software management tools are developed and added to the support environment at the same time as the particular mechanisms of machine learning.

Machine learning does not have to be self-modifying code, and it should not be - at least, not in the undisciplined way that was customary in the bad old days. So what are the options for mechanisms to implement self-adaptive software?

7.4   The state of the art in machine learning

Machine learning (ML), the umbrella term for most mechanisms of self-adaptation in computer programs, is very broad with surprising depths here and there. I do not propose to subject you to a comprehensive survey, for apart from being inordinately long, it would for the most part address strategies that show little promise of being viable practical mechanisms in the near future. So I shall be highly selective, and for those readers who doubt the appropriateness of my selection (or would just like to see the big picture) I can indicate a number of comprehensive sources of information. Most general AI books are not very good on this topic, perhaps because it has blossomed so much in recent years and they have yet to catch up.   But putting modesty aside, you'll find no more comprehensive coverage than the 100-page chapter on ML in Partridge (1991) *A New Guide to AI*. Up-to-date details on individual projects can be found in the periodic edited collections entitled *Machine Learning*, published by Morgan Kaufmann (vols I, II and III published), and in the journal *Machine Learning*, published by Kluwer.

The ML mechanisms with some promise of near-term practical utility can be divided into the classical ones - such as inductive generalization- and the network learning models (the connectionistic ones - to use the common but universally disliked general label) - such as back propagation of an error signal.

In both categories, mechanisms are designed to exploit the accumulated experience of the system within a given operating environment; the major differences are the degree to which experience can be automatically exploited, and the nature of the system modifications employed in this exploitation process. Let's take the connectionistic (or parallel distributed processes - hence PDP) first.

A PDP system is typically a network of primitive processing elements that receive 'activity' values from other elements that are directly connected into them, accumulate the received activity values according to some specified function, and then pass on through further links to other elements some function of the activity which they have accumulated. A further, and crucial feature, of these models is that the activity transfer operations occur in parallel. The obvious analogy for those readers who are grappling with this description is with the brain as a network of neurons each receiving and passing on electrical pulses. Finally, each of the links between network elements has an associated 'weight' which is usually involved in the activity-transfer function through the link. So by changing these link weights activity flow paths can be effectively opened up, and closed down. Hence link-weight adjustment is the typical learning mechanism, which is, of course, totally different from learning in classical models (as you will soon see if this is not immediately obvious to you).   But this sort of information can be classed as merely implementation detail (a widely misused phrase but I think that I'm on relatively safe ground this time) and thus not of prime importance to the software designer; it is the general learning strategies that are of major concern.

Unfortunately, the general strategy for ML in PDP systems is one of error-signal feedback (and individual mechanisms dictate how to adjust link weights to reduce the observed error). This means that the capacity for self-adaptation is restricted to the training of given networks to exhibit some well-defined functionality, and not the process of learning to respond appropriately to specific, but changing, environmental idiosyncrasies. PDP models can be trained (and with formal guarantees of convergence, although the training itself may be a very lengthy process) to exhibit some 'correct' behaviour, but this is not really the type of self-adaptation that we are looking for, although it undoubtedly has some useful practical applications (e.g. in pattern recognition applications, see WISARD, Aleksander, 1983). We'll return briefly to this topic at the end of the chapter in order to view the tantalizing possibility of 'black-box' software.

So PDP models, although currently generating much excitement and hope, fall a long way short of offering us the mechanisms of self-adaption that we might use to build powerful AI systems of the type discussed earlier. This leaves us with only the classical models, but there are some bright prospects here.

ML in the classical mould (i.e. sequential reasoning in a 'space' of alternative and successive possibilities) has had some three decades to proliferate and promulgate the resultant diversity of alternative strategies. There is thus a wide selection of mechanisms to consider: learning from analogy, rote learning, advice taking, learning from examples, explanation-based learning, apprentice learning, etc. But while there is a wealth of research projects emanating from this AI subfield, very few of the current mechanisms can boast the robustness and reliability that practical software systems demand. Hence the set of actual mechanisms to consider is quite small; it is basically inductive learning schemes (i.e. the automatic generation of new information by abstracting generalities from a set of instances of some phenomenon).   In addition, I shall mention an up and coming contender from the area of deductive learning schemes - explanation-based learning (EBL) - which shows some promise of practical utility and has a great advantage in its deductive nature. For induction suffers from the inherent weakness than it cannot be guaranteed correct.   Except in totally artificial domains, induction, working as it does from the particular to the general, is always liable to generate errors.   No matter how many white swans you see, you will never be sure an inductive generalization that all swans are white is correct. Induction is a powerful mechanism (and we humans exploit it to the full) but it is one that comes with no guarantees. Nevertheless, it is the basic mechanism that has proved useful in practical software systems.

The general strategy for self-adaptation based on inductive generalization is for a system to amass a collection of instances of, say, a specific user's interaction with the system, and then to generate from this set of instances a general model of the preferred style of interaction of this user for use when he or she next appears. To the user of such a system, it should appear that the system has tailored its style of interaction to his or her personal idiosyncrasies. And furthermore, if the system continued to collect instances of the interactions with this user, subsequent inductive generalizations could be used to either fine tune this specific example of human-computer interaction or to track the changing habits of this user. Such a software system would clearly be well on the road to the greater software power that we discussed in the opening chapter of this book.

An even better mechanism would take each new instance of interaction with this user and examine it to see if it implied any change in the general strategy of interaction being used for this user. The former, what we might call 'batch-type' inductive generalization (called non-incremental generalization in ML), is mechanistically easier but behaviourally less satisfactory, and the latter is incremental inductive generalization, which can adjust the generalized information after each new instance of interaction - i.e. it can offer just the functionality that we require.

What represents an instance, and what are we aiming for with a generalization? Well, an instance is determined by the specific problem being addressed. Thus, in my example of a system customizing its user interface to accommodate a specific user's idiosyncrasies, an instance (or a training example in EBL terminology) is a particular example of an interaction with this user. But, although this may clarify things a little, it does lead us on to a number of salient subsidiary problems: What specific aspects of an actual interaction sequence constitute an instance to learn from? What does the system need to learn from the specific instances? What are the goals of this self-adaptivity? Much of the ML literature seems to assume that the world is neatly divided into 'instances', and moreover that these instances are not only clearly demarcated but are also conveniently labelled to tell us what general behaviour they are instances of, reality, even the limited reality of software systems, is just not structured in this handy way. Answers to the above questions can then be viewed as imposing the necessary structure on an unstructured reality.

The first question raises considerations of what to abstract from the individual interactive sessions, i.e. what sort of abstract representation will the inductive generalization algorithm be operating on? Surely, we will not want to record minor typing errors that the user makes? Or will we? In trying to answer this question we are led on to a consideration of the others. If one of the goals of the overall self-adaptivity of the interface is to adapt to user deficiencies, then we might well want to record all of the users slips and mistakes in the hope that the system is able to produce a general response strategy to this particular user that is tolerant of such minor flaws in communication. There are many (very many) different structures that can be abstracted from any given session of actual behaviour, and so one of the major initial decisions is which aspects of an interactive exchange will be recorded and taken to comprise an instance of behaviour for the inductive generalization process.

Even earlier issues to be addressed are the goals of the self-adaptivity within the software system. It's all very well to decide that a user-responsive interface to a piece of software is desirable, but then there are many consequent issues of the exact form that responsiveness is to take. And the final decisions here will rest on notions of exactly how and to what purpose the software system is to be used: the self-adaptivity might be seen as a means to train humans to use the underlying system as efficiently and as effectively as possible, or it might be viewed as a tolerant interface that will accept (whenever possible) the efforts of casual and sloppy (by the pedantic standards of most software systems) users and deal with them as best it can. So there are clearly many tricky decisions to be made even when it has been decided that self-adaptivity would be beneficial and that inductive generalization is the route to take.

The other major question broached earlier, but as yet unaddressed, is what form of general information can we hope that our inductive generalization mechanism will produce? Currently, there are just two answers in systems that have found practical application: decision trees and IF-THEN-type rules. And this focusing down takes us on to the current limitations of inductive generalization algorithms as mechanisms for practical self-adaptive software.

My example of automatically customizing a user interface to specific users is beyond the current state of the art in machine learning: it is unclear how best to 'model' individual users (i.e. we probably need a representation structure that is more complex than either decision trees or IF-THEN rules), and there is a similar mystery about what 'dimensions' of the human-computer interaction to model and how they might themselves interact. But this sort of self-adaptive mechanism can be, and has been, successfully applied on less ambitious tasks. I can characterize the tractable tasks as declarative, data-representation tasks rather than procedural, process-representation tasks (as a user's interaction would be most naturally represented).

So, mechanisms of inductive generalization are viable for practical software systems when the problem is one than can be realized (at a useful level) as a fixed processing algorithm operating on a dynamic data structure such as a decision tree or set of, say, production rules. It is conceivable that effective dynamic user models can be implemented in this fashion but so far we have failed to find the right combination of processing algorithm and data structure - only time will tell, perhaps.

The practical applications of this technology have so far concentrated on expert decision-making processes; this is clearly a procedural task but one that can sometimes be implemented effectively in terms of a fixed processing algorithm (say, a mechanism of logical inference) and a dynamic data structure (say, a set of IF-THEN rules). The self-adaptivity can then be realized by inducing new IF-THEN rules as a result of processing specific instances of the decision-making behaviour.

One pioneer of this sort of mechanism is Michie (see Michie, 1982, for example) who was motivated by the difficulty of extracting general rules from human experts when building expert systems. Michie observed that human experts are often quite poor at articulating, in general terms, how they do whatever it is that they are expert at doing. But, almost by definition, they are good at providing specific instances of their decision-making expertise. So why not collect a set of such instances and then inductively generate a representation of the general decision-making expertise that is expected to be implicit in the set of instances? And indeed Michie constructed a system to do this, and even produced a commercial software version called "Expertease" for use on PCs.

The core of Michie's system was an algorithm for inductive generalization developed some years earlier by Quinlan (1979) and called ID3. According to Cendrowska (1989) the limitations on the use of this algorithm derive from three requirements that the training set must meet:

- The instances of a given decision are described in terms of values for a fixed number of attributes. "The set of attributes must be adequate. The set of attributes is inadequate if there are two or more correct instances which have the same values for the attributes but are of different classes" or are from different decisions.

- The general classes or decisions must be specifiable in terms of the attribute descriptions. This seems obvious, but consider the problems of classifying system users and how to characterize, in terms of a set of attributes, examples of system usage in a way that is sufficient for the desired results.

- The classes used must be mutually exclusive - i.e. each example that the system encounters must be classifiable in only one class.

Additionally, there is the problem of the completeness. A complete training set contains all possible instances of the general class. Clearly even the possibility of completeness only comes after we have made a lot of decisions about the attribute set and the set of discrete values that are allowable for each attribute. Thus our user model may use, say, average response time as a characteristic attribute but we must further constrain the model by only allowing a discrete set of values for this attribute, e.g. <0.5 seconds, 0.5 to 0.75 seconds, and >0.75 seconds.

Once we have set up such a framework then we can entertain the notion of completeness. But if we have a complete training set then our induction algorithm would be no more than a data compression device - i.e. it would reduce a large set of instances to examples of just a few general categories. And although this information compression may be very handy on occasion, it is not the sort of functionality that we are looking towards induction to support. We want the system to generate the general classes with an incomplete set of examples. So how good are induction algorithms at this exercise?

Cendrowska (1990), who has developed PRISM (a system for inductively generating expert system rules) as an alternative to ID3, presents empirical data on the predictive power of these two induction schemes. She used data from two different problems:

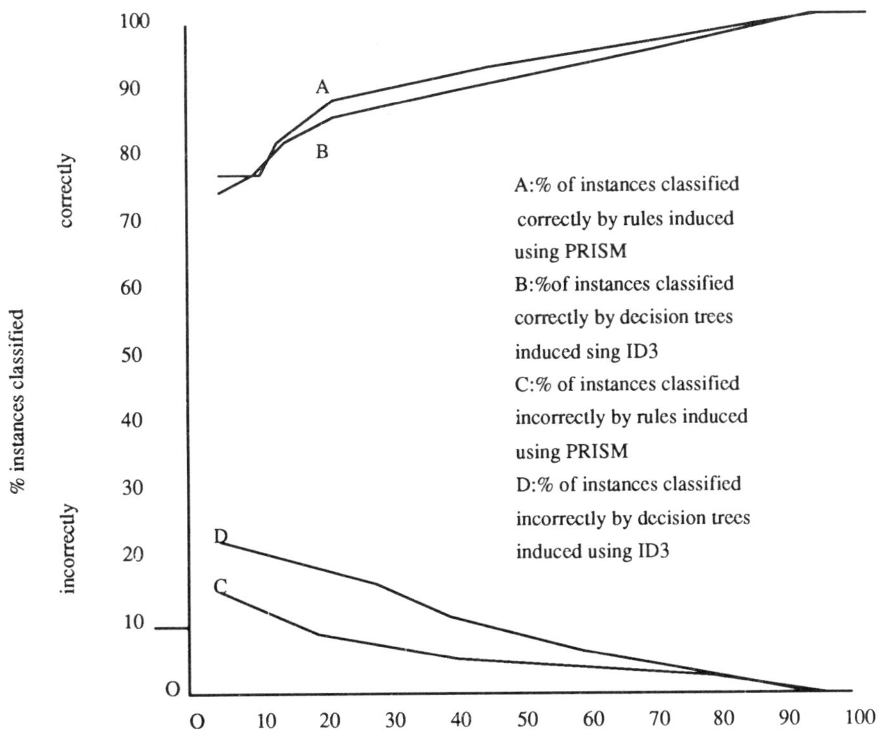

Fig 7.1 "The predictive power of induction algorithms" from Cendrowska, 1990, Figure 9.2, p. 138

1. The classification of board configurations in the King-Knight-King-Rook chess end-game (a problem that ID3 was extensively exercised on): the problem is to find a rule set which will determine for each configuration of the four pieces, whether Knight's side is lost in two-ply in a black-to-move situation.

2. The contact-lens decision procedure: the problem is to find a ruleset that will decide, on the basis of a number of characteristics of a person, whether that person is suitable for contact lens wear, and if so, which type of lens they should be fitted with.

In order to determine the relationship between size of a training set and the predictive power of a rule set induced from it, a fixed number of instances were selected at random from the complete data set ... a set of rules was induced from these instances using PRISM [or ID3], and then the induced rules were tested on the full set of instances ... This was repeated one hundred times each for training sets containing

5%, 10%, 20%, 30%, 40%, 50%, 60%, 70%, 80% and 90% of the complete data, and the results averaged for each size of training set. (p. 135)

Figure 7.1 illustrates the predictive power of both PRISM and ID3 when applied to the contact lens decision problem. With respect to correct classifications, there is little to choose between the two systems: both start at about 75% correct classification with only 5% of the training set to generalize from, and both quickly improve to about 90% correct when the induction is based on 40% of the training set. But with respect to incorrect classifications PRISM looks to be superior to ID3.

The results with the chess end-game problem are very similar, except that both systems start at nearly 90% correct (with only 5% of the training set) and attain almost 99% correct classifications when the induction is based on 40% of the training set.

But for our current purposes, we need only note that these schemes do seem to exhibit the required predictive functionality, if only we can constrain our problems to fit into the training set requirements without destroying the essence of the problem. And, in this regard, we must be aware of yet another constraint that I have so far failed to mention: the training examples must be free of 'noise' - i.e. there should be no errors in the examples presented to the system. This requirement is, of course, impossible to meet with real-world data.

Quinlan has tackled several of these important problems that separate ideal training sets from the real-world phenomena of interest; in particular, he has explored the problems of 'noise' (e.g. Quinlan,1986), and of the need to manage the uncertainties that the real-world always brings with it (e.g. Quinlan, 1987, but described later and illustrated in Figure 7.4).

A final mechanism to bring to your attention with regard to the state of the art in classical machine learning and the possibilities for practical application, is that of **explanation-based learning (EBL)**. This is a deductive scheme that uses a single training example in conjunction with domain knowledge to generate an operational version of an already known goal concept. In short, EBL attempts to transform a non-useful generalization into a useful (i.e. operational, in the jargon of EBL) one when presented with one specific example of this general behaviour and sufficient knowledge to be able to link the example and the general concept - actually, in classical EBL, it has to be able to *prove* that the specific example is indeed a specific example of the goal concept. It is this proof that is viewed as an explanation for why the supposed example is indeed an example of the goal concept, hence the name 'explanation-based'.

EBL is an exciting new idea, but it is, of course, not without its problems as well as its promise. The topic is both too involved and too contentious for us to go into the issues and do justice to them in this book. The interested reader should ferret out and consult either the two 'original' papers, Mitchell, Keller and Kedar-Cabelli (1986), and De Jong and Mooney (1986), or read Chapter 9 in Partridge (1991).

Even my sparse introduction to EBL should give rise to some knowledgeable puzzlement to the reader who is totally *au fait* with the differences between inductive and deductive inferences. The former we have been discussing at length; inductive inference mechanisms suffer from a lack of guarantees but they do permit a system to 'go beyond' the known information which is, of course, one of the major features that we require of our intelligent software. Deductive inferences, on the other hand, are as solid as logic itself - they come with a lifetime warranty, as it were - but the cost is that they add no new information to the system. So where's the gain? The benefits to be derived from a mechanism of deductive inference are several-fold. An explicit and practically useful statement is a very different thing to an implicit and non-useful (i.e. non-operational in EBL jargon) representation of exactly the same information (if it were not then the science of mathematics would be eviscerated). In addition, appropriate rearrangements of the available information can lead to better and faster solutions to problems. So there can be a lot of potential in a purely deductive mechanism but it will never have the unbounded promise of an inductive leap, but neither will it have capacity for blunder.

One particularly relevant possibility for EBL, and one that will connect us to the subsequent chapter, is its potential application in expert systems technology. Expert systems (as we shall explore in the next chapter) is a subfield of computer technology, and one that is a beacon of light for those struggling with the possibilities for AI in practical software; it is also provides a point of focus that makes a few of the nebulous problems sharply visible. One specific problem is that of the brittleness of AI systems: they perform excellently on some occasions and fail dismally on others, with no obvious indication why - i.e. seemingly very similar situations can elicit both modes of behaviour. Part of the essence of good practical software is that is does not exhibit this sort of brittleness. It should be robust and reliable.

In the context of expert systems this unsatisfactory bimodal behaviour - i.e. expert quality performance or total failure - can be viewed as a result of the fact that current expert systems are founded on purely superficial, syntactic rules. For example, a car-engine fault diagnosis system might have the rule:

> **IF** lights are dim **AND** engine will not start
> **THEN** the battery is flat

Using such a rule (in conjunction with others, of course) the expert system will be able to correctly diagnose the 'flat battery' fault on many appropriate occasions. This rule codifies a useful heuristic, and heuristics by definition will not always work. This rule can also be viewed as the codification of superficial, or syntactic knowledge. It is superficial because it contains no information as to why this heuristic actually works on many occasions. The rule allows the system to conclude the truth of 'the battery is flat' whenever it can determine the truth of 'lights are dim' and 'engine will not start'. This is a blind pattern-matching operation, and it works much of the time simply because it encodes quite a good heuristic. But when the battery has been stolen, this system will still conclude that it is flat - it doesn't know when the rule is appropriate and when it's invalidated by special circumstances (like the absence of a battery). In the jargon of expert systems: they are brittle because they have no deep knowledge - i.e. no knowledge of why certain heuristics work most of the time and hence in what circumstances they are inappropriate. There is thus currently much interest in building deep knowledge into expert systems, and perhaps automatically deriving the shallow heuristic rules from it (which would also address the problem that these shallow heuristic rules are surprisingly difficult to extract from the human experts).

Now, you can appreciate (I hope) the potential for representational change that EBL offers us. All the information necessary to make expert decisions is (presumably) present in a comprehensive deep-knowledge representation of the problem domain - e.g. for car engine diagnosis the deep knowledge would codify information that the battery supplies charge that illuminates the lights and turns the engine (via other components) when the ignition key is turned. But human expertise is typically both quick and slick: human experts give high-quality responses most of the time by focusing on just a few of the most likely possibilities virtually immediately. It seems unlikely that this sort of behaviour can come from an exhaustive evaluation of all possibilities - i.e. it seems that human experts use good heuristics most of the time. The point being that they can, and do, go beyond (or beneath) these superficial rules when necessary. To finally get to this point: the superficial rules can be considered as an operational version of the deep knowledge. So we may be able to apply EBL techniques to derive the superficial, heuristic rules from are presentation of deep knowledge. Worden (1989) provides an instructive pictorial representation of this alluring possibility (see Figure 7.2). But there are still many outstanding problems: What is deep knowledge? How do we represent it? How do we deal with the fact that we can't always *prove* that a training example is indeed an example? and so on.

And to close this section we can take a quick look at a specific example from a rather different branch of machine learning that holds promise for the engineering of practical AI software. I refer once more to the blossoming AI subfield of **connectionism**, or **parallel distributed processing(PDP)**, or **neural networks**. Work in this AI subarea is characterized by the use of networks of primitive processing elements that receive, accumulate and pass on 'activity' values and the activity-transfers occur in parallel. There are many radically different species of connectionistic models (again Partridge, 1991, reviews them, and Hinton, 1989, provides a comprehensive technical overview of the range of learning mechanisms being explored).

From our current perspective there are a couple of important points to make:

1. Some species of network are trainable with formal guarantees that the trained system will converge to some desired functionality.

2. The internal structure of these models, and their mode of operation, makes them conceptually opaque and hence not readily amenable to explicit modification by a human software engineer.

One example will serve to give you a flavour of this new brand of AI. A system called NETtalk (Sejnowski and Rosenberg, 1986) was built and

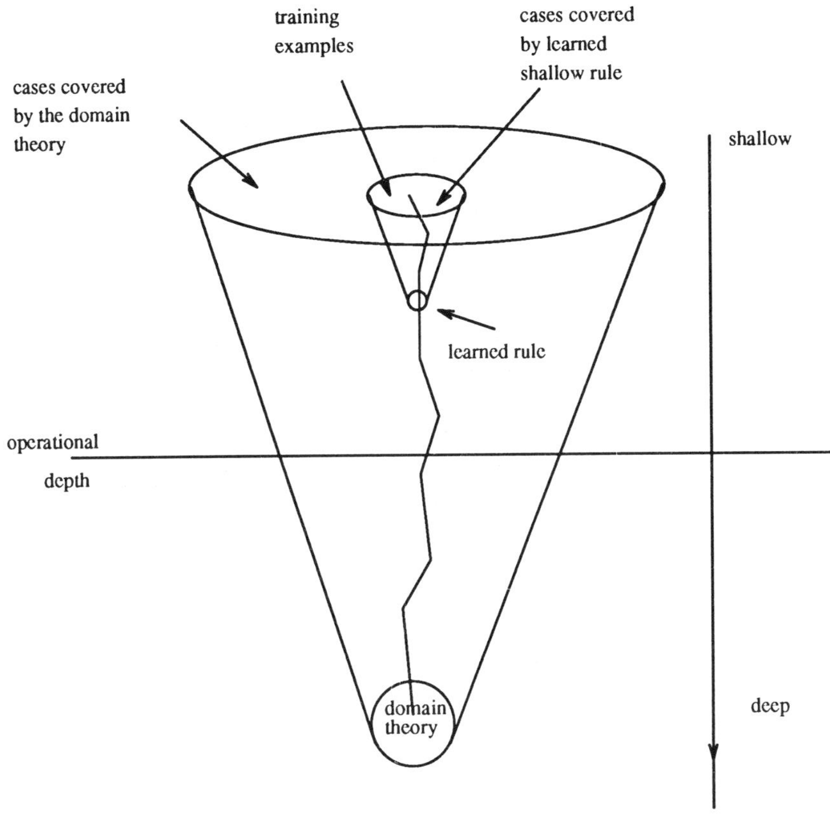

Fig 7.2 "A possible use of EBL in expert systems technology", from Worden, 1989, Figure 1, p. 146

trained to pronounce English. They used a three-layer network as illustrated in Figure 7.3.

Each of the seven input units was able to code a single letter, or a space, or one of a few punctuation marks. Thus a text sequence of seven elements (usually letters and spaces) can be presented to this network as an input. The coding of the input results in activity values being sent to each of the 80 units in the "hidden layer"; the amount of activity sent is controlled by the "weights" associated with each link. These hidden units accumulate the incoming activity values and then pass a weight-dependent amount on to the output units. Each output unit represents a pronunciation feature, and thus by thresholding the activity they all get the network generates a representation of the pronunciation of the middle letter of the 7 elements input (the three letters either side provide some context for the pronunciation of the middle letter). The

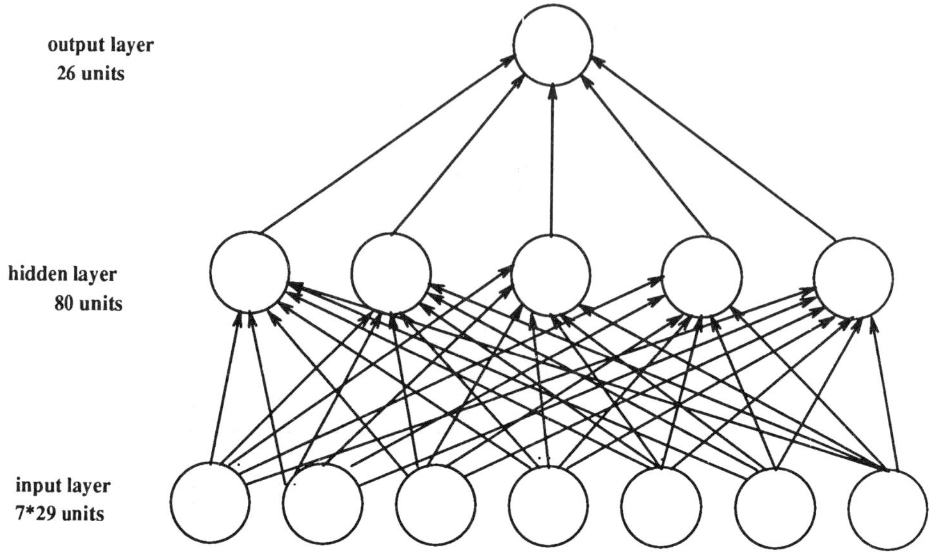

Fig 7.3 The network for NETtalk

pronunciation generated can be compared with the correct pronunciation (in terms of the features represented by the output units) and the link weights throughout the network are adjusted so that next time the letter occurs in the same context the output pronunciation will be improved.

The system output was classed as "perfect" when correct, and as "best guess" when the correct pronunciation was the closest one to the actual output pattern. The percentage of perfect pronunciation was at 55% and still rising (but very slowly) after 50,000 words of learning. But the percentage of best guesses was higher at 95%.

The great strength of this system is that it employs a well-defined link-adjustment process called **back propagation** which is also guaranteed to continually decrease overall error. The outcome is a system that after many thousands of trials (i.e. input a sequence, check output, and adjust link weights) can be heard to switch from random babbling, through very alien pronunciation, to achieve finally quite good pronunciation - i.e. it learns to pronounce English correctly. This is particularly remarkable because no pronunciation knowledge is explicitly built into the network - each network unit is initially connected to all units in the next layer and link weights are initialized by a random procedure. Yet the network learns to pronounce English from feedback of the errors it makes. This sounds a bit like magic, and perhaps just what the AI software engineer needs, but all is not sweetness and light (as you no doubt guessed).

There are considerable drawbacks. First, you have to know all the right answers and then the system can be trained to exhibit this known functionality - this is not open-ended learning. Secondly, the conceptual transparency problem: taking NETtalk as an example, when the network has learned to pronounce English, it must in some sense have learned, and thus contain, the knowledge of how to pronounce English. But within the resultant collection of link weights (which is all that is altered by the training algorithm) it is extremely difficult to identify any conceptually meaningful substructures that relate letter contexts to pronunciation patterns. This being the case, there is no way for a software engineer (or knowledge engineer, or even network engineer) to study the competent network and modify it so that the system pronounces English with say an American accent. The only known way to achieve this quite closely related goal is to retrain the network from scratch using correct American pronunciation to generate the error signals.

But it is early days yet for the subfield of connectionism, and impossible to predict what may come out of it to support the engineering of practical AI software. It does perhaps provide us with a glimpse of a radically new approach to the engineering of software systems, even if they are 'black-box' systems, and hence my reason for bringing it to your attention.

7.5   Practical machine learning examples

Having given you a quick tour of the frontiers of machine learning insofar as it relates to possibilities for practical software, it is time to look at a few of the success stories here.

Inductive generalization techniques have been used to generate expert systems from a set of examples of the expertise. Michalski and Chilausky (1980) describe the use of this general technique to generate an expert system for soybean disease diagnosis. Quite surprisingly (as the authors admit), the diagnosis system based on the inductively generated rules was repeatedly and consistently better than a similar system that was built using the traditional approach of codifying the experts' rules. "The major conclusion from this experiment is that the current computer induction techniques can already offer a viable knowledge acquisition method if the problem domain is sufficiently simple and well-defined" Michalski and Chilausky, 1980, p. 79.

In another project Quinlan (1987) presents a probabilistic classifier that begins to address the problems of real-world data (e.g. noise and uncertainty). His scheme generates a probabilistic decision tree which "can provide valuable information on the probability that a case belongs to one or more of the classes, and is less brittle with respect to unknown or imprecise attribute values and inexact thresholds" p. 37.

Figure 7.4 illustrates one such probabilistic decision tree which was generated from a set of 2800 cases of specific symptoms and the subsequent diagnosis of thyroid disease. This data was both imperfect

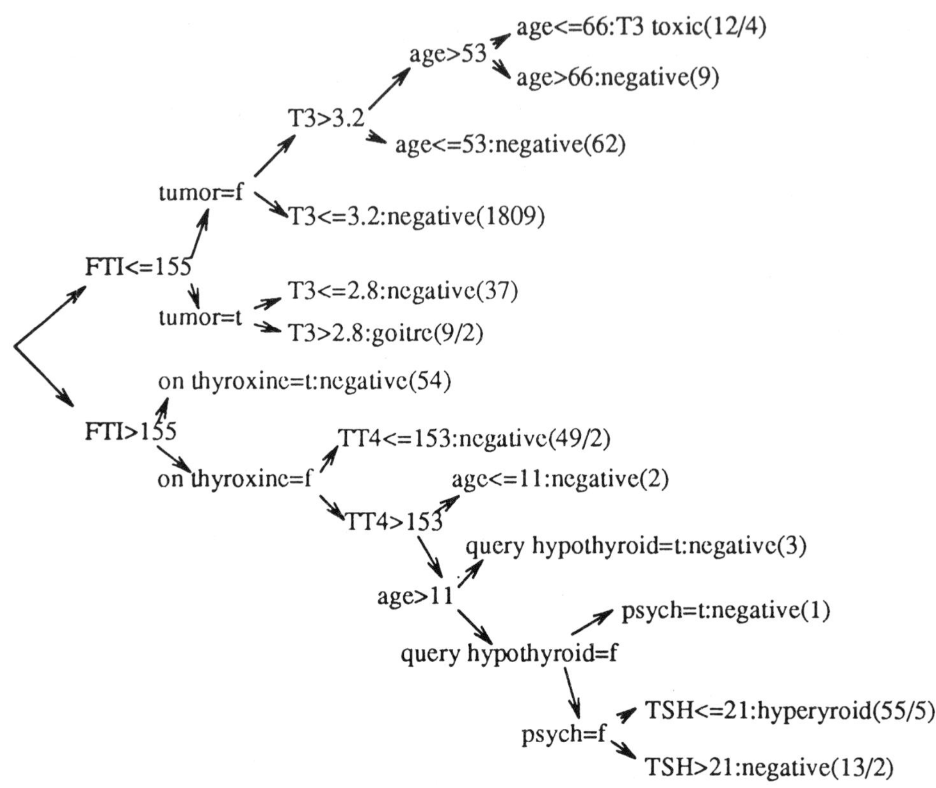

Fig 7.4 "A decision tree for hyperthyroidism" from Quinlan, 1987, Figure 1, p. 33

and noisy, as is the nature of real-world data. The tree was developed in two stages: a classical induction algorithm which generated a large tree with much complexity caused by the noise in the training set; followed by a process of 'pessimistic pruning' "which simplified the tree by replacing some subtrees with leaves ... This sort of simplification has been found to improve the accuracy when the tree is used to classify unseen cases ... A leaf produced by such pruning will generally misclassify some cases in the the training set. If each leaf is identified with the subset of training cases that it covers, some of these subsets will contain representatives from more than one class. This is indicated ... by the annotation *(n)* or*(n/e)* following each leaf; *n* is the number of training cases in the subset for that leaf, and *e*, if it appears, is the number of these cases that do not belong to the class nominated by the leaf overlap" p. 33.

These leaf annotations then provide a measure of the accuracy of the leaves, which each represent a diagnosis, or in other domains a decision, a prediction, etc. Quinlan also describes how this representation can improve decision making by "softening" absolute thresholds - i.e. it provides the information necessary to avoid making absolute decisions when the specific information at hand doesn't warrant it.

In summary, this brief excursion into the AI subworld of machine learning has, I hope, left you with some food for thought, if not with concrete ideas of how to engineer self-adaptive software. Your thoughts should now extend to the notion of self-adaptive software systems as a route to practical AI software, but with considerable reservation (given the current state of the art in ML). Nevertheless,a need for self-adaptive software systems is not to be equated with the full horror of unconstrained self-modifying code. We must proceed with caution, but proceed in this direction we must. The current technology in ML is not such as to occasion great expectations, but neither is it such as to engender great pessimism. Some ML mechanisms are now just on the edge of practical viability, and there is every reason to expect considerable progress in the next few years.

In addition to the possibility of increasing software power through the use of ML, there is the potential use of ML techniques in a new approach to software development methodology: build a basic system and then train it to the required level. PDP systems demonstrate one means of achieving this goal, and inductive generalization techniques provide us with another.

8
Expert Systems: The Success Story

Far too much has been written about expert systems already, and in this brief chapter I have no intention of rehashing the time-worn examples of MYCIN, TEIRESIAS, R1, etc. going through their repertoire of tricks. The purpose of this chapter is to satisfy the obligation to provide some survey of this AI subfield in a book that is about the engineering of AI-software systems, for expert systems do have a strong claim to be *the* major area of practical application of AI tools and techniques. But this claim is not accepted by all who are in a position to evaluate it critically. This subfield, like most AI-related phenomena, is not devoid of contention and disputation, far from it.

My goal is not to go into the arguments for and against the various claims for expert systems technology; it is simply to look at, and see what is to be learned from, the short but intense history of trying to build expert systems - practical AI-software (in some cases at least). Provided that we steer clear of the more grandiose systems (and the more mundane ones) there is, I believe, a growing body of practical AI-system building know-how being amassed within the general area of expert systems.

8.1 Expert systems as AI software

Part of the argument that surrounds this AI subfield hinges on the claims for the AI nature of the software systems constructed. At this distance into this book, the less than totally inattentive reader will appreciate the fruitlessness of attempts to definitionally circumscribe the subclass of expert systems that are AI software. We shall do better to begin to characterize the extremes (of AI-ishness in expert systems), and then accept that the large intervening grey area is full of specific examples that could be argued for and against endlessly when we have nothing better to do.

It is clear that some expert systems are examples of practical AI software, and equally clearly some are not. At the non-AI end of this spectrum, we find knowledge bases that are known to contain all of the relevant information (with respect to the specific problem that the proposed expert system tackles), that are operated on with a straightforward mechanism of logical inference, and that generate results (i.e. decisions, predictions, etc.) which are decidably correct or incorrect on the basis of an abstract decision procedure. As any of these three constraints are relaxed, so we begin to move in the direction of AI-ish expert systems. These non-AI expert systems are conventional software engineering problems implemented by means of AI techniques, which may, or may not, be the most effective implementation strategy.

At the clearly-AI end of the spectrum, we find that it is necessary to use knowledge bases which are (and will always be) incomplete, that mechanisms for reasoning with uncertainty or probabilistic inference are needed to operate effectively on these knowledge bases, and that system results are not always classifiable as simply correct or incorrect: we have to come to grips with some notion of adequacy. Another, almost complementary, way to view this point is that AI systems must use heuristics: some rules will be heuristic and mechanisms of reasoning with uncertainty will involve heuristics. And heuristics, by their very nature, are not guaranteed always to give good results. They sometimes lead to poor results and even to errors - such, sadly, is the nature of heuristics.

One further point to bear in mind is the 'level' at which the original problem is tackled - or the scope of the problem to be addressed as it is termed below. For example, at the non-AI end of our spectrum we can aim to implement a system that simply plays legal chess; at the other extreme we can aim to construct the next world chess champion. They are both chess-playing programs, but there the similarity ends.

Between these two extremes of expert systems there are all combinations of possibilities - a continuum of AI-ishness in expert systems, if you will. Luckily we do not have to untangle the mess, but I hope that the foregoing will enable you to understand how such widely differing opinions, all from informed persons, can arise in this general area.

8.2 Engineering expert systems

So some expert systems are definitely AI software, and some lesser portion of these are robust and reliable AI software (we must beware of what is perhaps a small proportion of a small proportion, but we are still clearly in the realms of the finite, as opposed to the infinitesimal, I believe). How were they built?

Although not exactly hot off the press, Hayes-Roth, Waterman and Lenat (1983) still make a good attempt to answer this question. They take it for granted that the development of an expert system is an evolutionary, incremental process, and because of the nature of classical expert systems' technology the process boils down to one of the extraction and representation of a human expert's knowledge. Figure 8.1 illustrates their five stages in the evolution of an expert system.

A critical part of the first stage, **Identification**, is determining the scope of the problem to be addressed. This is probably a general characteristic of all attempts to implement AI-software and was referred to above in our discussion of the AI-ishness of expert systems. My unsubtle example of two sorts of chess-playing program might lead you to

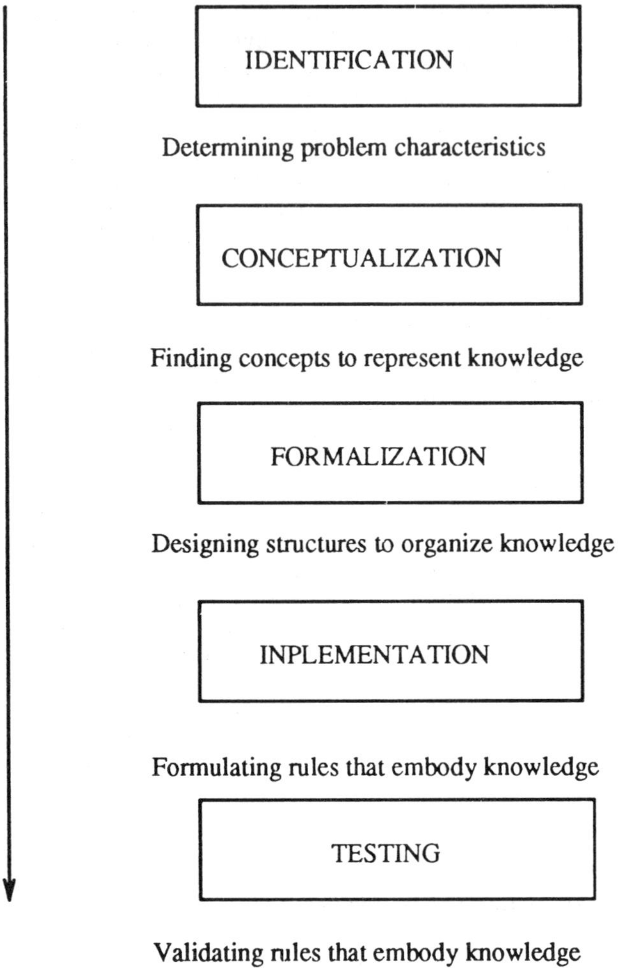

IDENTIFICATION

Determining problem characteristics

CONCEPTUALIZATION

Finding concepts to represent knowledge

FORMALIZATION

Designing structures to organize knowledge

INPLEMENTATION

Formulating rules that embody knowledge

TESTING

Validating rules that embody knowledge

Fig 8.1 "Stages in the evolution of an expert system" from Hayes-Roth, Waterman and Lenat, 1983, Table 1.3 p. 24

think that this is a fairly trivial point; it is not. In fact, deciding on the exact scope of the problem to be tackled can be a crucial determinant of whether the project will blossom and flourish, or wither and die. Most AI-type problems at the level that many humans can deal with effectively are way beyond the current state of the art for practical software engineering. So most problems need to be trimmed down drastically. But if you trim them too much, you may have a tractable problem that is, however, lacking all semblance of AI-ishness. And what's more disastrous, it may be resistant to subsequent attempts to broaden its scope to include some AI features. You may recall our earlier discussions of building AI muscles on a conventional software engineering skeleton, for this sort of strategy to succeed the skeleton must have appropriate places upon which the muscles can be developed. We must design for change, but for change in ways that are quite alien to conventional software engineering. We must address the basic problem of evolutionary software development: we must ensure that "the user's operational system will be flexible enough to accommodate unplanned evolution paths" (Boehm, 1988, p.63).

In the **Conceptualization** stage, the task is to identify and explicate the key concepts, relations and information flow patterns in the particular perspective on the problem identified in the previous stage. This is the stage where the problem is carved up, in an informal way, into the major modules, subtasks, and control strategies for inter-task interactions. In this stage the intertangled web of the real-world problem is broken into independent parts, and then decisions have to be made as to how to satisfactorily approximate the original problem by adding well-defined control strategies to allow the selected modules to communicate with each other.

This is a critical stage for the subsequent evolutionary development of the implemented system: certain modularization schemes will inhibit subsequent development of the heuristics that will be needed to add AI to the system, while others, in which the heuristic in question operates totally within a module, will not.

The **Formalization** stage is self-explanatory, but we should note that formalization usually has a side-effect of introducing further constraints in our conceptualization of the problem. The cautions given with respect to the **Conceptualization** stage also apply here.

In terms of current expert systems' technology, the **Implementation** stage amounts to formulating the rules that constitute the knowledge base, and the control strategy to be used for reasoning over this knowledge base. After this we are in a position to produce an executable prototype system.

The last stage, which Hayes-Roth, Waterman and Lenat call **Testing**, concerns evaluating the performance of the prototype and introducing modifications as indicated by the domain expert's critique of the system.

All of the foregoing might lead you to believe that the development of an expert system is a linear process rather like the development of conventional software with just the names of the stages changed in order to pretend that something new is happening. This is quite wrong, but also quite understandable, for Figure 8.1 gives us only part of the picture, as it were. Figure 8.2 indicates that the stages do not form a simple linear progression.

As you can now see (in Figure 8.2) there are a number of control paths back from each stage to an earlier stage - i.e. there are loops in the methodology which suddenly makes it reminiscent of the RUDE cycle and iterative development schemes in general. But, if you want to be awkward, you might insist that this sort of diagram is not really different from the old waterfall model of conventional software development (see Figure 4.6).

The main point of difference (apart from the stages involved) is the weight and 'meaning' associated with the arrows that take us back to an earlier stage in the development process. In the waterfall model there is

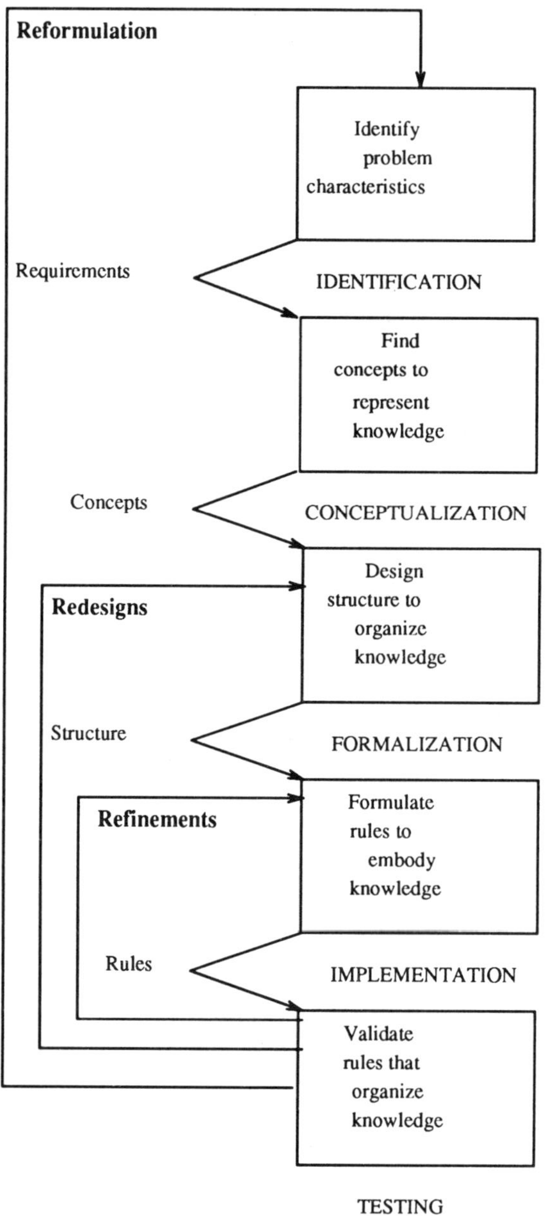

Fig 8.2 "Control flow in expert systems' development" from Hayes-Roth, Waterman and Lenat, 1983, Figure 5.5, p. 139

meant to be steady linear progress from left to right, and only an occasional need to nip back to an earlier stage to correct an oversight or minor error. In fact, the use made of the 'back' arrows can be equated with the lack of time, attention and expertise of the system developer. Whereas in Figure 8.2, the back arrows are expected to carry more traffic and are not simply a result of a poor attempt at system development (although that will, of course, add to the degree to which the back arrows are used). In expert systems' development it is accepted at the outset that a smooth linear progression from initial idea to adequate system is not possible. The nature of the problems and of the target systems is such that iteration (i.e. use of the back arrows) is a crucial feature of the development methodology itself.

One further and important point to make about the development of expert systems, which the above illustrations do not bring out, is that they are *never* 'finished'. The cynical software engineer might want to say much the same thing about conventional software systems - they too are often never finished. But this putative similarity is itself very similar in nature to the previous one about back arrows in the development process - i.e. there is an 'echo' of the AI-system phenomenon in conventional software system development, but in practice there is a qualitative difference between these two manifestations of superficially similar phenomena. In conventional software engineering there is (or ought to be if things are done properly) a comprehensive, well-defined specification of the desired system, and in principle at least the software is finished when it meets this specification. In expert systems there is no such detailed and comprehensive specification of the desired software, and not because of any inadequacy on the part of the expert-system developers but because of the nature of the problem - it is typically a performance-based specification (recall this general feature of AI problems from Chapter 2). In this particular AI domain, the behaviour of human experts is the main source of information as to what we might expect to accomplish with an expert system, and this, of course, provides a problem 'specification' that is a far cry from the sort of specification that we can and do generate for say, a conventional inventory management system.

The more specific reason why an expert system is never finished is two-fold:

1. The knowledge base is never complete. There is thus always the possibility of adding more knowledge to improve performance or broaden the scope of the system.

2. There is often no absolutely correct answer for the system to produce. There is thus always the possibility of adding (or improving existing) heuristics in order to achieve better results - better diagnoses, better predictions, etc.

Clearly, these points of difference mesh with the characteristics of AI-ish expert systems that I gave earlier. As we move away from the AI-end of the spectrum these characteristics diminish in importance or disappear altogether, and similarly so will these points of difference.

8.3   The lessons of expert systems for engineering AI software

The first lesson to be learned from our whistle-stop tour of expert systems technology is that it constitutes an existence proof of the possibility of engineering AI software. Some would dispute this claim, but I think that there are definitely some (perhaps quite a small number) of AI-ish expert systems out and about in the real world and doing a useful job. The number of such systems and the level of AI that we find in them is not such as to warrant great jubilation but it is a beginning: a small step for expert systems but a big step for AI-systems engineering - to coin a phrase.

An important cache of examples of practical AI software is to be found at the Digital Equipment Corporation (DEC). For well over ten years, DEC has been collaborating with researchers at Carnegie Mellon University with the express aim of developing expert systems to tackle various problems associated with the selling of sophisticated computer systems. The fruits of this collaborative effort have the somewhat cryptic names of R1, XSEL, XCON, etc. The R1 system, for example, checks customer orders of computer systems. It is designed to minimize the shipping out of wrong or incompatible components. This example is of particular interest for a number of reasons: firstly, expert system technology was explicitly employed to address an outstanding problem that a conventional software engineering approach failed to solve; secondly, the benefits of the R1 system were easily quantifiable (at least in terms of dollars saved as a result of less incorrect orders shipped out); and thirdly, the systems has now been successfully used for many years and a lot of empirical data has been collected and published (e.g. frequency of occurrence of errors, ease of maintainability). This last point is particularly important because so very few expert systems have been subjected to close study during prolonged usage, and we know that maintenance (i.e. post-delivery activities) is an extremely important element of practical software technology. It is one thing to build a piece of software that passes all acceptance tests for immediate use; it is quite another for that software to be amenable to subsequent modification (either to remove the residual errors as and when they surface, or to enhance its functionality in response to changing needs). DEC's expert systems seem to satisfy both sorts of requirement. Figure 8.3 gives us some data from the R1 expert system collected over a period of three years. It illustrates the contention that basic software problems (such as the number of different kinds of situations that R1 did not deal effectively with - graphed as "total distinct problems") are no worse for expert systems than they are for conventional software. This discovery is not one that is greeted with great jubilation but it is, nevertheless, quite a comfort within a technology as new and untried, and potentially unstable, as that of expert systems.

A general introduction to this family of expert systems and the full results of empirical study of the R1 system can be found in McDermott (1981) and in McDermott and Bachant (1984). And a long-term study of XSEL is provided by Mumford and MacDonald (1989).

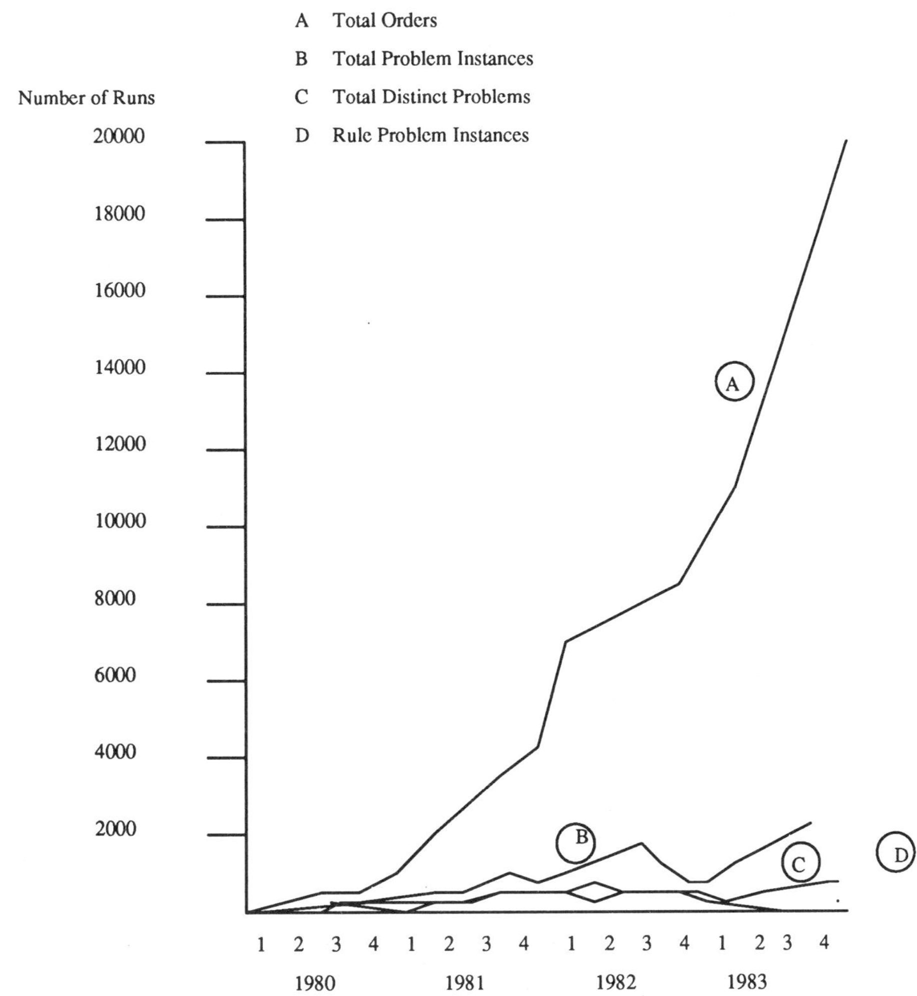

Fig 8.3 A sketch of R1's performance (from McDermott and Bachant, 1984, p. 31)

A second lesson, with more immediate impact but still quite general, is that the development of AI software cannot be squeezed into the conventional mould. We must come to grips with the notions of partial specifications whose adequacy is explored by means of working prototype systems. And we must similarly learn to do without the comfort of thinking that system behaviour is provably correct even in principle. The relatively recent flurry of expert system building activity and its failure to result in a similar flurry of practical expert systems should teach us that the problems posed by AI software are not to be taken lightly. They are deep and difficult problems, and we must recognize this fact.

A further twist to the conventional wisdom that experience with expert systems has exemplified is the importance of the **HOW** in building AI software. It is important that the system's reasoning is (or can be presented as if it is) analogous to human reasoning in similar situations. Expert systems' technology, based as it is on a knowledge base of rules and a mechanism of logical inference, shows us the importance of this point. Self-explanation capabilities are made much of in expert systems' technology (too much of, but that's beside the current point). Many expert systems have the ability to 'explain' their line of reasoning that led to a particular outcome. This 'explanation' of how a specific conclusion was generated, which is a simple chaining of IF...THEN...IF...THEN... from the rules that the inference mechanism employed, is designed to be easy for the human expert to understand.

As an example, a car engine diagnosis system when given a set of symptoms (such as 'engine won't start' and 'turns over slowly') might, en route to a diagnosis, ask the question 'are the lights dim?' The user is then at liberty to ask the expert system 'why are you asking this question?', and the system's explanation will come from the particular chain of inferences that it is building. It might respond:

It has been established that
1. the car won't start, and
2. the engine turns over slowly
Therefore, if
2. the engine turns over slowly, and
3. the lights are dim
then
there is evidence that the problem is
4. the battery is flat [Rule 123].

Of course, the reasoning is likely to be much more complex that this, but the point is that a fairly good explanation can be automatically generated from a rule-based and logical-inference-driven system. In the above example, the clauses numbered 2,3 and 4 constitute one of the car-engine diagnostic rules in the rule base. If we can suspend disbelief for one moment and assume that the explanation is not transparently obvious, the user might want to further clarify this explanation. Further probing can typically be done using 'how' queries. For example, 'how did you know that the engine turns over slowly?' In this case the system should respond that 'the engine turns over slowly was a given fact', but it might have been an inference from another rule in which case the system would have retrieved and displayed the relevant rule. This could in turn suggest more 'how' queries and so the system-user explanatory dialogue can continue.

The real point is not whether he or she *actually uses* such rule-chaining reasoning but that he or she can readily appreciate the validity (or not) of such an 'explanation' of specific system behaviour. Now, why is this so important? You may recall Michie and Johnston's (1984) argument, (presented in Chapter 4) which elevates this benefit of rule-based systems to become the supreme goal of AI - i.e. the goal of making complex technology more readily understandable. And while I'm setting up links back to earlier topics, recall also the decompiling problem and how it must be tackled (a Chapter 6 topic).

The importance of this **HOW** constraint on AI-software function stems from the nature of the basic problems. Iterative system development requires that someone can understand the specific system behaviour in terms of general system structure - the closer the human developer can relate to the way the computer system is operating, the easier it is to achieve the necessary understanding. So the **HOW** constraint is necessary for system development. It is also necessary for both validation and use of an adequate system. Validation of AI software is problematic, as we discussed in Chapter 4. A long-term process of building confidence in the behaviour of the system seems to be an essential component of AI software validation, and a major feature of this confidence-building process is for the human experts to 'see' how the behaviour is generated. In addition, an AI system is expected to produce surprising results, but this class of results is composed of two different categories which must be clearly separated: there are surprising results because of intelligent reasoning that the human overlooked, and there are surprising results from problems within the system - not just outright errors but possibly a generally good heuristic having a bad moment (as they necessarily will from time to time). Again an understanding of the the system's reasoning behind the surprising result will provide the basis for the necessary discrimination.

A third lesson from experience with expert systems is that part (perhaps a large part) of the secret of success is choosing the right sort of problem, and the fact that most expert systems projects do not get beyond the prototype stage tells us that it is all too easy to make the wrong choice. So, do we know what the characteristics of an appropriate problem are? We know that configuration of complex computer systems was an appropriate choice, and we know that medical diagnosis wasn't. But do we know why, in general, this is so? A number of people have tried to provide the general characterization that we now seek. Luger and Stubblefield (1989) present the following criteria for selecting a problem for expert system development:

1. The need for the solution justifies the cost and effort of building an expert system.

2. Human expertise is not available in all situations where it is needed.

3. The problem does not require either perceptual or motor skills - i.e. it is a purely cognitive problem.

4. The problem is relatively self-contained, in particular, that high quality solutions do not require common-sense reasoning.

5. The problem cannot be solved as a conventional software engineering problem.

6. Co-operative and articulate experts exist in the problem domain.

7. The problem can be limited in scope and still be usefully solvable - it can be fitted within the current scope of the technology, say, a few hundred rules per module (knowledge-base partition).

A fourth lesson to be learnt is that the so-called knowledge acquisition problem is far from solved. The codification of the information upon which human expertise is widely believed to be founded - i.e. the knowledge acquisition problem - has proved to be surprisingly resistant to the straightforward strategy of inducing the expert to simply articulate his or her rules and heuristics. As a consequence, we might observe that within the expert systems community there are substantial breakaway groups who are employing alternative tactics to solve this problem. Automatically inducing a general decision tree from a set of tutorial examples is one such alternative approach that we've seen in the previous chapter. Another group of alternatives is based upon traditional psychological techniques of collecting large amounts of relatively simple data from the experts (e.g. judgements from the experts of relatedness of pairs of specific concepts), and applying statistics to yield an appropriate representation of the knowledge (see Cooke, 1990, for a representative example). There are also radically different approaches which deny the existence of rule-based knowledge (e.g. Dreyfus and Dreyfus, 1986) and thus champion a fundamentally different solution strategies (e.g. PDP implementations, such as the "harmony theory" model of electronic circuit expertise constructed by Smolensky, 1986).

In sum, the very existence of practical expert systems should boost our confidence that the many (very many) problems to be faced by the developer of practical AI software are not insurmountable. But at the same time, the ratio of expert systems started to expert systems as delivered products is sufficiently large (perhaps 100:1) to warn us against over-confidence. The few successes do not, I believe, encapsulate the silver bullet that AI-software developers might hope to discover. Success with expert systems technology must be predicated upon right choice of problem, a supportive exploratory programming environment (i.e. the right basic tools and continual behavioural feedback from the experts), and no small measure of sheer good fortune, I suspect. And what we can gain from experience with this technology (both successes and failures) is not a neat new methodology for AI-software development, but only a knowledge of where much of the conventional wisdom on software development is deficient and where future emphasis needs to be placed - e.g. in evolutionary prototyping, in in-use validation.

A last, but very important point, which conveniently leads us into the next chapter, is that the leap in software development complexity that the move from conventional to expert system development entails has given considerable impetus to efforts to produce software development tools. We now see a plethora of expert system building tools and shells on the market. One of the most important decisions for the novice expert system builder is which, if any, tool or shells to purchase. Having the right tool (or shell) for the job can make the difference between having a working prototype to explore at an early stage, and becoming bogged down in knowledge-base and inference-engine implementation details so that time, patience and money runs out before any working system is forthcoming.

The general point here, and the one that introduces the next chapter, is that the complexity of AI-software engineering demands significant and substantial software tools as a prerequisite - the demand is, in fact, greater than this: we must have comprehensive software support environments before there will be any chance of engineering AI Software.

9
AI into Practical Software

At this late stage in the book there are a number of things that should be crystal clear. To begin with, engineering practical AI software is a very difficult task, and we are only just beginning to sort out the individual problems that need to be solved. Part of the difficulty here stems from the apparent similarities between conventional software engineering and AI-software engineering. There are indeed some real and useful similarities, but there are also some deep differences masquerading as similarities. The presence of these differences does not mean that we should abandon the challenge, nor that we must 're-model' the AI systems to fit the conventional mould; recognition of these differences should lead to the development of new techniques and to radical changes of emphasis in order to devise an appropriate methodology for the engineering of artificially intelligent software.

The exact nature and extent of the differences is still a subject for debate, but what is indisputable (I think) is that the move to AI software entails a leap in complexity for the software developer. And with many tasks within conventional software development straining the limits of manageable complexity, how can we hope to cope with a non-trivial further escalation of the problem? The short answer is, we can't, but what we can do is to reduce the effective complexity for the human system developer. How do we do this? We get the computer to manage much of the complexity for us, and this is done by means of a programming support environment within which we provide a comprehensive set of power tools for system designers and developers (to steal a phrase from Sheil, 1983).

9.1 Support environments

The notion of providing a computational environment to assist the programmer in the programming task is not new. Significantly, it was a major feature of AI programming in the days before conventional programmers fully realized its importance. And this is quite understandable once we accept the fundamental difference between what is called "programming" in this two areas. In conventional programming we are translating a formal specification into an alternative (formal) notation that will result in an effectively computable algorithm. This translation is by no means trivial, nor is it devoid of the need for insight and imagination, but it is, at bottom, a transformation between formal notations in which some equivalence is to be preserved.

Programming, from the conventional computer science viewpoint, is the transformation of a formal specification into a computational procedure for correctly realizing the given specification.

Dijkstra (1989), for example, might well support this statement about programming, although I suspect he might object that it is too weak. For Dijkstra "the programmer's ... main task is to give a formal proof that the program he proposes meets the equally formal functional specification" p. 1404. Programming in AI has never been this process - some would say, "that's its big mistake", but I don't think so. AI programming has always been a process of exploring prototypes and evolutionary system development.

Programming in AI is the exploration of behaviourally adequate approximations to an incompletely specified (and probably computationally intractable) problem.

Thus "programming" in its most limited sense is just one stage in the overall process (and not a major one) - the implementation or coding stage. Clearly, I am using the term in the looser sense of system design and development as well as actual coding. But as you can see from the two statements given above, the meaning of the word "programming" is quite context-dependent, and not subtly so. The practising software engineer is likely to view programming as an activity that falls somewhere between my two extreme statements, but interestingly the person at the code face may well find himself somewhat closer to the AI characterization than to the computer science one. Several of the invited commentaries to Dijkstra's (1989) article took exception to what they saw as his extreme view. Karp(1989), for example, quoted with approval the following statement:

> I do not view the process of programming, especially programming in the large, as that of discovering an algorithm to a pre-specified and unalterable logic. It is more often a process of discovery and adaptation, as various relevant components of a problem are examined in turn, and a goal, initially specified incompletely, is reached. (attributed to Richard Fateman, p. 1411)

First, notice that a crucial word in this domain, "programming", can mean quite different things to different people (in Chapter 1 I have previously drawn attention to the problems posed by these multiple-meaning words). Bahrami (1988), in his book entitled *Designing AI-Based Software*, distinguishes between "AI-based programming" and "traditional" or "algorithmic programming". But he offers us no more than a separation between "program (control)" and "knowledge" as characteristic of AI-based programming. This is, in fact, no more than a crude characterization of expert systems' technology, which is (as we know from the previous chapter) just one facet of AI.

Second, notice that once again the AI viewpoint seems to be closer to that of conventional software engineering than to what I have labelled the computer science viewpoint (earlier, in Chapter 2, I distinguished model computer science problems to first make this point). And finally, if we accept the AI viewpoint, rather than the computer science one, the function of a programming language expands considerably. New demands emerge - e.g. the need to support reasoning back from observation of behaviour to structural cause. As a result, the management-of-complexity demand goes up as we move from conventional to AI programming. Hence support environments were needed by AI programmers almost at the outset. The emphasis in formal computer science has been more on the avoidance of complexity by, for example, erecting a "fire wall" between whether the specification meets the user's need and whether an algorithm correctly implements the specification (Dijkstra, 1989, p. 1414). The approach to the complexity problem is different; it remains to be seen how much (and what sort of) complexity can and cannot be avoided.

Indirect evidence of this difference of approach can be found in the nature of the favoured programming languages. Thus LISP is a terrible programming language when considered *in isolation* and as a vehicle for conventional programming. It can't hold a candle to, say, Pascal as a computable notation for easing the task of designing a correct and efficient implementation of a given specification and minimizing the number and severity of the inevitable bugs. But the LISP language embedded in a powerful support environment, such as INTERLISP-D, is a totally different beast. Programming in the formal computer science sense puts a premium on a succinct formal notation that can deliver correctness when employed from within a comprehensive framework of fixed and frozen constraints. Features such as strong typing have been developed in response to such pressures. AI programming raises flexibility, as demanded by experimentation and evolutionary development, as a major desideratum of the programming medium. The resultant, differently prioritized collections of requirements have led to rather different sorts of programming languages being preferred within each domain. And although some of difference in programming language preferences can be accounted for by historical accident and simple prejudice, it does seem to be difficult to reconcile these two sets of desiderata in one and the same programming language (but see type-flow analysis in the section on reverse engineering in Chapter 6). Effective and efficient programming in AI has always demanded the support of a programming environment, and not just the availability of a programming language, so it is not at all surprising that many important features of the environment notion have arisen in the AI domain.

9.2   Reduction of effective complexity

With the task of programming not restricted to the problems of deriving a correct algorithm from a fixed and well-defined specification, and the lack of built-in constraints in typical AI languages, AI programming becomes an unmanageably complex process. The programmer, or system developer if you prefer, has to manage machine-executable approximations designed to exhibit some ill-defined, ideal (but probably unattainable) patterns of behaviour - e.g. the way native speakers recognize and generate language, or the sorts of diagnoses that an expert diagnostician generates.

The programming environments of the first generation were designed to support just the task of actually writing and debugging code. Their role was primarily one of increasing the efficiency of the code-development task. But what we now require of a support environment is something much more than this: we need complete life-cycle support from requirements analysis through to system maintenance, and rather than just increasing efficiency we need substantial help just to make the overall task doable at all. On the bright side, we should notice that, although we demand extensive and diverse assistance from the desired support environment, it is not an all-or-nothing requirement. Any useful functionality that we can add to a system-development environment may prove to be a positive step down the long road to our final goal. Even better than this, the achievement of such small steps should make further steps easier, for it is by experience with a useful working system that we gain practical insight into what is necessary to get a more useful working system.

My insistence on complete life-cycle support refers to the need to extend the role of the computer to help both before programming begins and after the system achieves adequacy. Prior to the actual programming we have the system requirements to be organized and documented, then the specification, and most importantly the design sequence to be recorded (recall our discussion of maintaining an on-line history of design knowledge of a system, Chapter 6). When an adequate system has been delivered and is in use there will be system maintenance - traditionally considered as part of the unavoidable pain of using computer software, but not much to do with the system development process. Hence we hear much of system development environments, but precious little on system maintenance environments, and even less on life-cycle support environments that cover both ends of the process under one roof (as it were). But AI software promises to be at least as hard as conventional software to maintain, and probably much harder when we have to deal with the extra complexities of machine-learning mechanisms.

The maintenance task is, of course, just basic system development within the RUDE cycle, and thus involves all of the same problems (with probably the extra one that the original developer is not the maintainer). Just as design history and on-line documentation are expected to ease the 'understanding', 'debug' and 'edit' stages of the development cycle, they can also be expected to aid the system maintainer. Hence the benefits of a complete life-cycle environment: all useful design and development information (or knowledge if you prefer) can be made available to the system maintainer. The Eiffel system (Meyer, 1989, and described in outline later in this chapter) provides us with an example of the beginnings of automatically generated, on-line documentation in a commercial product. This documentation tool was briefly described in Chapter 6 immediately following the Ada example.

Similarly, the change of emphasis in the goals of the necessary environment - from that of merely speeding-up system development to one of making the unmanageable manageable - is due to the extra complexities of AI-software development. And while we might expect the desired environments to continue in their role of adding efficiency to the processes, the *raison d'être* for life-cycle environments is to make the construction of AI software possible.

There are a number of quite straightforward ways that support environments can be (and have been) developed to reduce the effective complexity of system development. The effectiveness of these environments is based on the computer's fast, vast and accurate information storage and retrieval abilities. A classic paper by Winograd (1975) was one of the first to outline what we might expect from a fairly sophisticated support environment. He labelled the role that he envisaged these environments playing as moderately stupid assistance.

9.3 Moderately stupid assistance

Winograd argued for the necessity of computerized assistance to offset the complexity of the software development process. Even in those early days his vision was such that it is still seen as appropriate. He outlines features that we are still striving to realize today. "The key to future programming", he wrote, "lies in systems which understand what they are doing." We are, as I'm sure you realize, still very far from achieving this goal, but we'll return to this grand goal in a later section of this chapter.

He outlined four features of the 'assistant' he envisaged:

1. Semantic, as well as syntactic, error checking could be a feature of such a system, thus eliminating many errors before the program is ever run. Static errors and even implications for the dynamic semantics could be brought to the programmer's attention.

2. Answering questions such as, "Is variable X global to any other subprogram?", will be based upon a supersecretary (i.e. fast, accurate storage of and retrieval from vast amounts of cross-referenced information) function. Moving to more ambitious functionality: questions such as "Are there any likely problems arising from the modification proposed?" Good answers to this type of question will require that our environment contains considerable intelligence about programming at least.

3. The system should be capable of filling in trivia without bothering the programmer with the actual details that it automatically generates. The programmer might decide to expand a set, S, by two elements. It should not be necessary for the programmer to clutter his or her thinking with the implementation details of set S. "Expand set S by two elements", is the sort of command that the programmer should be able to issue, and let the system take care of the minutiae required to implement this action.

4. The system should also possess some expertise in debugging programs, nothing really grand like the tracking down and analysis of errors, but the ability to apply debugging strategies (such as tracing and backtracking) as a result of high-level human directives. The programmer might ask, "Where was the value of Z last changed?", and the system should be able to rerun and trace (i.e. do whatever's necessary, or say why it can't) an execution sequence in order to answer the question.

As you can see from the date of the original reference these suggestions are not new - in fact, they're ancient by AI standards - but many are still largely future events. Why is this? It is not because of disagreement with Winograd's vision, although there is opposition in some quarters (see, for example, Scherlis, 1989, who "summarize[s] roughly" Dijkstra's, 1989, views on teaching computing science: "software engineering as a worthy cause is eyewash, and the very notion of a 'programming tool' is corrupt" p. 1406). And the lack of a concrete realization is not because no one has tried to implement these sorts of ideas: it is because an efficient and effective implementation of these modest-seeming proposals turns out to be exceedingly difficult. Any departure from a straightforward storage and retrieval capability seems to demand the introduction of AI techniques - heuristics, plausible inference, etc. And, of course, it is because support for AI programming is essential that we need such environments in the first place. We are in a Catch-22 situation: it takes AI to make AI.

But the picture is not actually this dark: more than a glimmer of light is provided by the observation that we can start small and from anywhere. We don't have to solve all of AI's problems before we can hope to solve all of AI's problems. But you can now see that Winograd's phrase "moderately stupid" entails a significant amount of intelligence in any system worthy of the epithet. It did (in 1975) and still does capture a range of environment-support characteristics which would constitute a real advance, and yet it straddles the frontiers of the state of the art: some of this functionality is now commonplace and some is still the subject of research, but with a firm promise of concrete successes to further ameliorate the programmer's lot in the near future.

A second justification for this level of assistance (if one is not enough for you) comes from the nature of assistance. Assistance can be entirely passive (help is only provided as and when it is asked for), or it can have an active element which I have taken as part of the essence of 'assistance'. It is not too inaccurate (certainly no more than the norm in this book) to say that the degree of active help and of intelligence in an assistant go hand in hand. It is not at all clear how much active 'help' the programmer will want. The answer, of course, depends on many factors including the programmer, the task at hand, the quality of the assistance, etc. Winograd opted for the conservative view, a minimum of active help, an assistant that will do just what is asked, no more no less, i.e. a moderately stupid assistant.

Ramamoorthy, Shekhar and Garg(1987) provide an update on *Software Development Support for AI Programs*. They make the point that "existing AI development environments support just the implementation phase,   resulting in less reliable and   hard-to-maintain

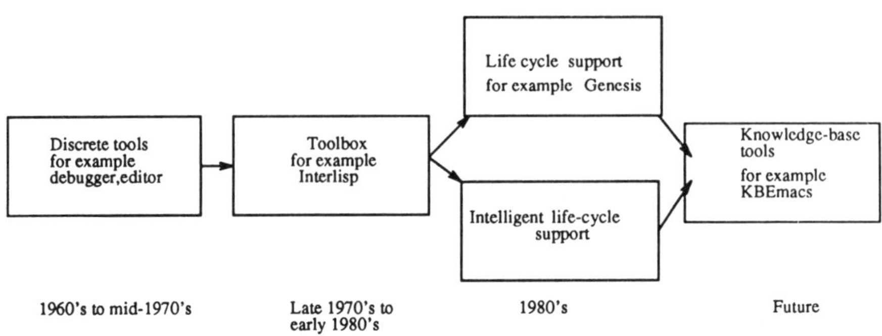

Fig 9.1 "Classification of development environments" from Ramamoorthy et al., 1987, Figure 4, p. 34

programs "(p. 30-31). "An ideal software development environment should provide a powerful language for the application, as well as appropriate methodology and tools for program development" (p. 31) - in a phrase, an intelligent life-cycle support environment. They classify development environments as illustrated in Figure 9.1.

As is apparent from Figure 9.1, the authors see life-cycle support environments as a future event, although they do list three "efforts in this direction": Genesis (their own work, see Ramamoorthy et al.,1985), Gandalf (Haberman et al., 1985), and SAGA (Kirlis et al.,1985). But for the frontiers of the current state of the art they look towards expert system building shells, such as Intellicorp's KEE system. These sorts of systems constitute their category called "knowledge-based tools". But there are others which are not wedded to expert systems only, but which also tend to be less robust and therefore less usable in practice at the present time.

A major example here is the work of Rich and Waters on the "Programmer's Apprentice" system. KBEmacs, their knowledge-based editor, provides "plans" and "cliches" to assist the system developer. They characterize "the assistant approach" as illustrated in Figure 9.2.

"The assistant interacts with the tools in the environment ... in the same way as the programmer and is capable of helping the programmer do what needs to be done" (Waters, 1986, p. 352). A "cliche" is "a standard method for dealing with a task" (p. 353). They are implemented as generic parameterized procedures, so all the system developer need do is to invoke a cliche and fill it with right parameter values in order to obtain a substantial chunk of program. A "plan" is an abstract representation of a program. The "plan formalism" is designed to represent two basic types of information: "the structure of particular programs and knowledge about cliches" (p. 354).

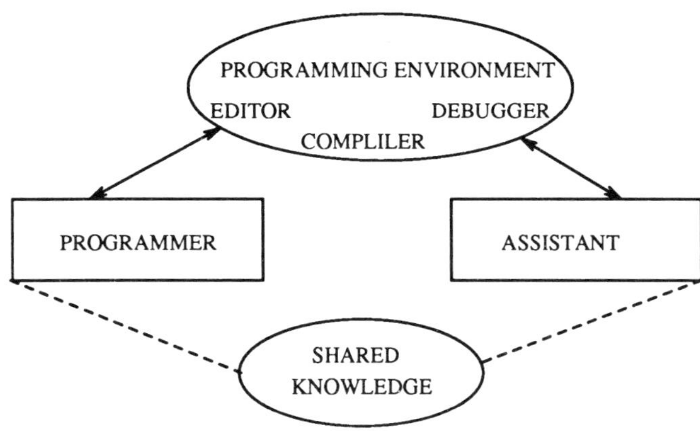

Fig 9.2 "A programming assistant" from Waters, Figure 2 p. 353 in Rich and Waters, 1986

Rich (1986) elaborates the nature of plans and presents details of the formal approach that has been used. Figure 9.3 is his plan for a search loop.

Rich describes a search loop in English thus: "A **search loop** is a loop that has two exits in which a given predicate (the same each time) is applied to a succession of objects until either the predicate is satisfied (in which case that object is made available for use outside the loop), or the objects to be searched are exhausted" (p. 492). He observes that this type of program construct can be programmed in many different forms which can be structurally very different. Within the plan calculus the essential nature of this loop can be specified (as illustrated in Figure 9.3), and this plan will accommodate most (if not all) of the variants which are only distinguished by details that are often arbitrary and conceptually unimportant. The goal is, then, for structures, such as those illustrated in Figure 9.3, to contribute to a library of standard forms. System development will then become more a task of selecting an appropriate standard form and particularizing it with the important specific details of the problem at hand, and the 'assistant' will take care of the necessary "filling in of trivia" (as Winograd suggested it should).

These plans, and thus the bones of the Programmer's Assistant, rest on formal foundations, a situational calculus in point of fact. My reason for drawing your attention to this aspect of the Programmer's Assistant is not to lead in to an elaboration of all the gruesome details of the formalism but to expose an underlying trend in the nature of support environment work - the progression from eclectic ad hoc-ery to formally founded design. The initial emergence of support environments was largely a result of evolutionary growth - handy functions were 'tied' or just lumped together as it became apparent that a particular function could serve a useful purpose in the system development process. When there is a

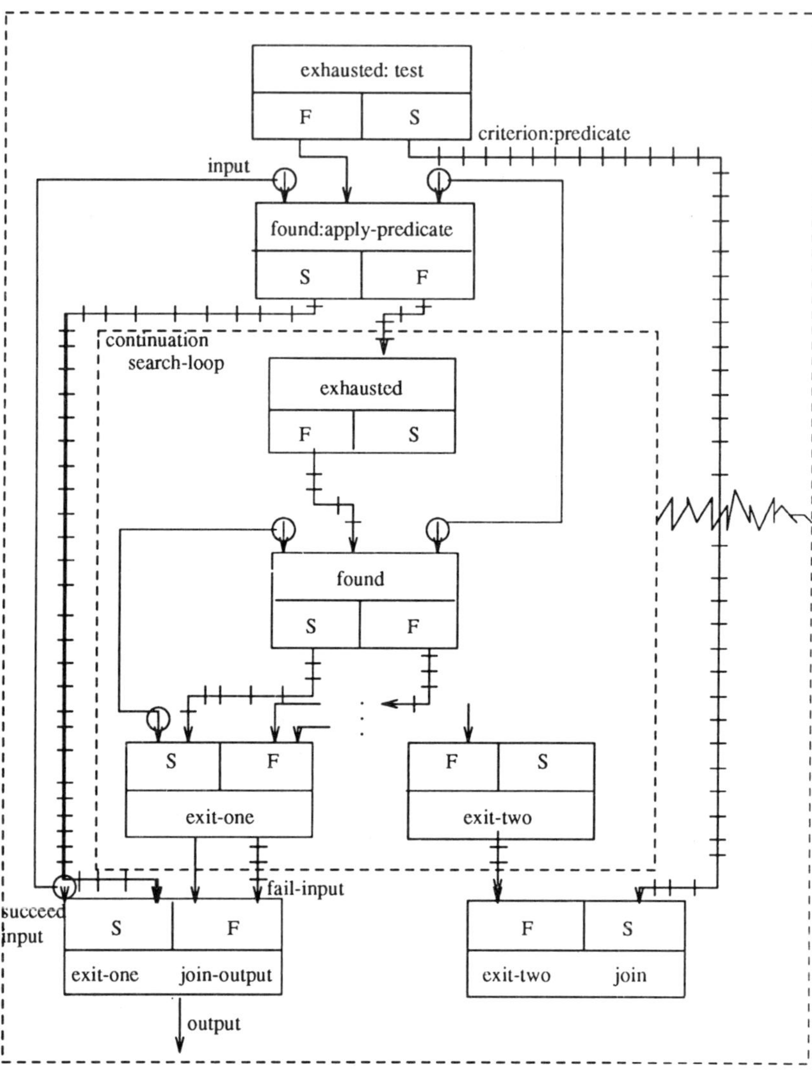

Fig 9.3 "Plan for a search loop" from Rich, 1986,Figure 2.1, p. 493

critical mass of such handy functions, we have a support environment. This may then be viewed as an object in its own right (and not just as a fortuitous collection of handy functions) which leads on to a more conscious effort to assess its strengths and weaknesses with respect to the general goal of effective support for the programming task. The next stage (which is also the current one) is to take one step back from specific environments, grasp the essentials of what an environment is to achieve, and then search for a well-defined basis upon which the details of the sought-after functionality can be realized.

An example of this type of development, and one that addresses a fundamental problem for system developers working within an evolutionary development paradigm, is described and demonstrated by Trenouth (1990a and 1990b). He provides a formally based framework for managing (and thus relieving the human of the necessity to manage) a population of different versions of the 'same' system. Why would you be silly enough to attempt to juggle (conceptually, of course) a variety of different versions of the same system? The answer is that, although the effects of some modifications will be clearly undesirable (and thus the modified version can be discarded), many modifications will exhibit both strong and weak points according to individual circumstances. It turns out to be necessary to explore different aspects of (or different alternatives to) system development for some period of time without having to commit ourselves irrevocably to any one particular choice.

Each new version of the system has a parent (the version that was modified in order to obtain the new version), and may be the parent of any number of descendants. The basic arrangement of versions to be managed is that of a tree. Each node in the tree is a version of the system under development. The version tree is defined by intervals of existence that are attached to each software object (see below). Figure 9.4 is a schematic abstraction of such a tree of versions.

Figure 9.4 is abstracted from a version tree that emerged in the development of a system to implement the solution to a classic AI search-space problem. The development sequence proceeds (in a general sense) from left to right, and, as you can see, various searching strategies were tried. Only eight versions (or states of the system) are illustrated, many more were actually generated. In this illustration we can see that from the initial version, labelled *S0*, the system developer first tried a depth-first search strategy which resulted in a working system, *S1*. But the search space of the particular problem addressed was infinite along certain paths, so this version failed to terminate on occasion. The user then experimented with alternative search strategies as the figure illustrates. By modifying version *S1*, in different ways, the versions *S2*, *S3* and *S4* were obtained. From each of these alternatives a series of modifications (not illustrated) eventually led to three working versions that solved the initial problem with different search strategies. An important point that is not brought out in the figure is that these three alternative development paths could have been generated in almost any order (the "almost" refers simply to the fact that within a given path there is a left-to-right ordering in time).

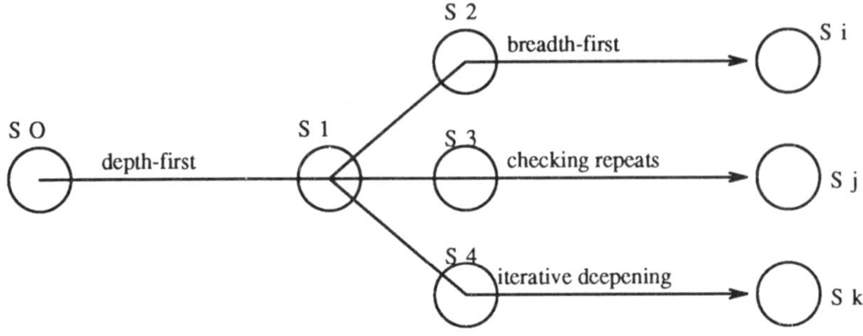

Fig 9.4 "A tree of versions" adapted from Trenouth, 1990b

The formal basis selected for the management of this 'space' of versions is an event calculus. It is a new method of supporting software version control that uses event-annotations on objects in a project knowledge base. The events are used to generate intervals of existence for the software objects (e.g. procedures or comments). The basic types of events are creations, deletions, or modifications. Given a procedure P it can be annotated as follows:

P : (Ei,Ej)

The semantics for this notation are that P exists from after event Ei to before event Ej. In fact, an object can have an ordered sequence of intervals attached to it, and most environmental changes are realized very simply in terms of these annotations. The representation allows project objects (i.e. entities, relationships and attributes - see Figure 9.5) to be shared across any number of project states. It also delivers a mapping between the project objects and events, and this is used to provide a flexible way of referring to an event or state: only the project objects which it must or must not contain need be mentioned. The user can jump to any previous version of the system and continue on from there (a generalization of part of the **undo** function of INTERLISP) by referring to the desired state in any one of a number of different ways.

The implemented prototype of this approach to **Exploratory System Development Environments (ESDEs)**, ESDE-P, has a number of other features such as hierarchical change logging, plan and problem posting, stepwise abstraction support, and intelligent housekeeping advice to the developer (e.g. "You should write code the forparent/2 - mentioned in ancestor"). These other features take account of the context in which they are invoked. Thus the output of the advice component will depend on the current position of the programmer in the version tree.

In addition to providing us with another example of a formally based approach to environment development, Trenouth's system is an example of an attempt to build a basic framework to support exploratory programming. This sort of emphasis comes with a well-defined basis and

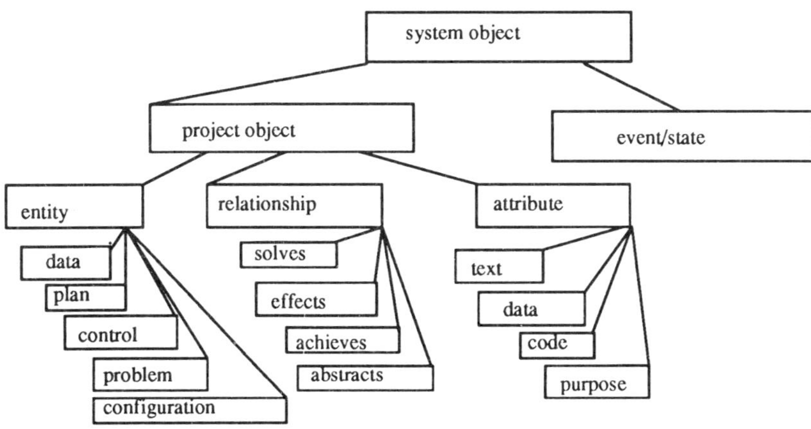

Fig 9.5 A Taxonomy of software development concepts in ESDE-P (from Trenouth, 1990b)

can be contrasted with approaches that can be characterized as collections of functional components integrated into a coherent whole. Both types of approach are required, and are required to be properly integrated in order to provide the software support environments that the AI-software engineer sorely needs.

9.4 An engineering toolbox

A second metaphor often used in conjunction with attempts to get the computer to assist the programmer is that of an environment being a repository for powerful 'tools' - "Power tools for programmers" (Sheil, 1983) is the classic paper here. The 'assistant' metaphor emphasizes the the active role that the computer may play, offering unsolicited help, advice and words of caution. The 'toolbox' metaphor promotes the more passive possibilities: a homogeneous collection of powerful tools just sitting there in the environment simply waiting for the system developer to select one and use it. And, although each individual tool may or may not involve AI, the toolbox approach is the less contentious one in that the human system designer initiates tool usage, whereas the software assistant has the scope to interrupt normal proceedings - the desirability of such functionality is a debatable issue. But, the toolbox approach also contains less potential for exploiting the environment idea. Having separated these two conceptions of how we might develop support environments, let me say that this convenient distinction is not adhered to by exponents of these notions - the terminology is mixed and muddled, so be warned.

Clearly some of the functions of our moderately stupid assistant are (or can be) entirely passive tools. The supersecretary function, for example, can be an extensive database management function that only retrieves specific information on request. This would be simply a tool under my classification scheme.

The seminal exposition of this general viewpoint (as mentioned earlier) is that of Sheil (1983). He doesn't mention AI much but talks instead of "large, complex programs whose implementations will require significant resources. Their more interesting similarity, however, is that it is extremely difficult to give complete specifications for any of them. The reasons range from sheer complexity (the circuit designer can't anticipate all the ways in which his design rules will interact), through continually changing requirements (the equipment in the oil rig changes, as do the information bases that the government department is required to consult), to the subtle human factors issues that determine the effectiveness of [say] an interactive graphics interface" p. 574 of Rich and Waters, 1986, reprint (as are all further quotations from Sheil). If you recall our earlier discussion of the software-specification problem (Chapter 3) and the myth of complete specification, then you will realize that I don't fully share Sheil's view of the basis for lack of complete specifications. But to whatever cause we attribute the problem, there is agreement that there is a need to build software systems in the absence of a complete and precise specification.

Given this need, he suggests that "some applications are best thought of as design problems, rather than implementation projects. These problems require programming systems that allow the design to emerge from experimentation with the program, so that design and program develop together" (p. 577).

He notes that the first advance towards a power-packed personal programming environment was the inclusion within a single shell (i.e.the environment) of standard features of the programming milieu - text editors, file management software, electronic mail, etc.

As Barstow and Shrobe (1984) say in their concluding paper in *Interactive Programming Environments* (Barstow, Shrobe and Sandewall,1984): "the idea of a programming environment is clearly an evolving one; what we today consider to be a programming environment will probably be considered primitive and limited by future standards" (p.559). They provide a perspective on the developmental history of programming environments. It portrays this development as a move from initially just harnessing the raw power of the computer to handle large volumes of data rapidly and accurately (i.e. the supersecretary function) to producing moulds for how system development should be structured. The "mould" metaphor is much too static; modern environments provide a flexible and dynamic set of constraints that favour certain styles of software development. Barstow and Shrobe offer us a tripartite classification:

1. **Environments concerned with the entire life cycle of a program or system**. These environments are generally focused on managing the development of large systems built by many programmers. They serve as the repository of all information on the system and thus contain databases of the relevant information from each stage of the development process. The authors add: "Finally, they assume that a

system's specifications are clearly understood before coding begins"(p. 560).

2. **Environments concerned primarily with the coding phase and whose tools are relatively independent from each other**. This is the classic 'toolbox' environment - a collection of goodies bundled together.

3. **Environments which regard coding, debugging, testing and maintenance as a single process of program development through incremental enrichment**. This type of environment is contrasted with (1) above within which these subprocesses (or subtasks) are viewed as separate modules with distinct boundaries.

It is clearly the type 3 environment that is demanded when we want to engineer AI software, but we would also want to see such type 3 environments extended to include also the type 1 capability of being able to accommodate large systems that many people have worked on. Barstow and Shrobe focus their discussion on state-of-the-art LISP environments which are by no means the whole story but they do constitute the most advanced robust and reliable environments (as opposed to fragile demonstration systems) currently available.

A survey of the state of the art in the UK is provided by Bereton (1988) edited collection *Software Engineering Environments* which, as its name tells us, concentrates on the use of IPSEs (Integrated Project Support Environments) for conventional software development - roughly, type 1 environments.

One last point about software support environments is that it appears to be the case that support for effective exploratory programming is also support for speculative code hacking. For example, the Interlisp-D environment allows broken computations to be back-stepped and restarted after making, say, some minor code alteration. There is no need to restart the computation from the beginning and no need to recompile after a modification to the code. This sort of support makes a code-and-fix approach incredibly quick and easy, and thus tempting (in the short term). So one of the (many) challenges for the software support environment developer is to decouple these two modes of software development such that the environment both encourages good practice and discourages, or ideally prohibits, bad practice. The environment needs to function as an intelligent filter, letting good software-development activities pass smoothly through but straining off and thereby blocking the undesirable ones. But can this be done? It may not be easy, however it's probably not impossible; it might even be quite easy to eliminate certain elements of bad practice, and any step in this direction has to be beneficial in the long run.

As support environments become more comprehensive the filter role should be easier to realize. If, for example, program abstractions such as design documents are represented within the system, then an appropriate filtering strategy might be to allow substantial code changes only after design representation changes. This sort of thing is quite easy to say but difficult to implement in a satisfactory manner, but bear in mind that a good partial implementation could be valuable - it's not an all-

or-nothing strategy. What we see here is a second (and perhaps secondary) role for software support environments: they should reduce the effective complexity of software development, and they might also be used to curb bad practice.

9.5   Self-reflective software

Apart from a drive to realize sophisticated support environments, are there other targets to aim for in our efforts to engineer practical AI software? There seem to be at least two major features of the AI software itself that will repay close attention - one highly speculative, and the other quite down to earth. The title of this section introduces the more nebulous possibility.

One of the reasons for suggesting that complete life-cycle environments have the potential to do much to alleviate the problems of AI-software development is that if the environment mediates in the system design, say, then there is the possibility of siphoning off 'design knowledge' for later reuse in subsequent activities, such as system maintenance. What we hope to capitalize on here is an environment that can assist in system maintenance because it 'knows about' how and why the system was designed the way it was. If this is viewed as a viable (although quite long-term) possibility, then the next step is to move this knowledge about the whys and wherefores of a given software system's structure from the environment and into the software system itself. Such a system would then possess the basic information to become self-reflective (the term metaknowledge is used in the expert systems' world). Such a system would contain the potential to consider and reflect upon its own functioning and structure. If this begins to suggest that rather awkward and doomed situation which involves ever-decreasing circles, then remember that there is no requirement of completeness here. Such a system would not have to know everything about itself (whatever that might mean). It would be very handy for it to know just some useful things about itself, although probably the more the better.

Why might we want such self-reflective software? The obvious reason is exactly the same as the reason for wanting design and development knowledge within a complete life-cycle environment, viz. it should provide a basis for automating support of all subsequent operations on the software system. The extra step that we've now taken is to place this metaknowledge within the software system itself rather than leave it in the development environment. The advantage of this is that the software system is self-contained, with its own 'power pack' as it were, but the disadvantage is that every piece of software would be much bigger and much more complex as a result.

In order to bring the discussion in this section down to earth, let me suggest that such self-reflectivity (in a crude form, I admit) is manifest in many expert systems. A number of expert systems boast a self-explanation capability, as we saw in Chapter 8. When the system asks a question, the user can ask 'why' in response, and the expert system will then explain the reasoning behind the particular question that was originally asked. In addition, it is typically possible for the user to query an expert system's decision by asking 'how'. In which case the expert system will explain the line of reasoning that led to the specific decision that was queried. In truth, this is only a rather straightforward trace capability which just happens to work quite impressively in conjunction with a logical, rule-based inferencing mechanism. Rather more generously, we might say that it is one of the triumphs of current expert systems' technology that a useful self-reflective capability can be so easily implemented.

9.6 Overengineering software

The more down-to-earth approach that I want to explore a little is that of overengineering AI software. If we can't prove that a piece of software is correct, and we can't (you must know my biases by now), then we should do what is done with every other engineered product: we should build in some redundancy. We've already touched on this possibility when we discussed differences between software as an engineered artifact, and the more traditional products of the engineer (Chapter 1).

The main problem is that, unlike most products of traditional engineering, we don't know how to overengineer software systems. The terms 'overengineering' or 'adding redundancy' might be the same in these two domains, but it seems that the processes needed to implement them are totally different. Addition of redundancy seems to score a bullseye on several of the major differences between software systems and bridges, buildings, or motor cars. The functional complexity of software systems, together with the narrow bounds of acceptable variation associated with some of these functions, seems to mean that significant general redundancy cannot be added to software systems by any one (or few) simple expedient - like doubling the size of main structural beams say.

A number of approaches to this problem have been tried, and they all help to some extent, but what they have all failed to do is to provide a straightforward general strategy for increasing software reliability through redundancy.

The addition of extra checks and traps is one route to software reliability that has been, and always should be, employed. In its simplest form it amounts to the system developer overengineering the system by threading the basic system with a mesh of detailed check statements and error-trapping functions. For example, if a variable AV is supposed to contain the average of a set of values, say, A1 through to A10 then there are a number of checks that could be implemented. We might check that the value of AV is larger than or equal to the smallest value averaged, and that it is smaller than or equal to the largest. This check does not, of course, guarantee that the value of AV is indeed the correct average, but it will catch certain errors that may occur in the averaging procedure, and so does provide some measure of redundancy.

This thoroughly pragmatic approach to programming, which assumes that errors will inevitably occur, has long been sanctioned and encouraged in software engineering. Yourdon (1975), for example, calls it "antibugging" or "defensive programming", and devotes a whole chapter to the programming principles and guidelines that will contribute to this practice. As a strategy to promote software reliability, it may be viewed as good practice, which the programmer must institute making the best of whatever facilities a particular programming language contains. But, more positively, programming languages can be designed to provide sophisticated support explicitly for defensive programming. This defensive programming can be, and has been, given official status in certain (usually unofficial versions of) programming languages. Thus an **ASSERT** statement has been added to the language Pascal. This is a statement that allows the programmer to assert that a certain relationship is true. So the earlier example might be programmed as:

ASSERT(Aleast <= AV <= Amost)

The semantics of this sort of statement are that when during program execution the control flow encounters an **ASSERT** statement the boolean expression it contains is evaluated. The value should be TRUE or FALSE. If the value is TRUE then no action is taken and control flow passes on to the next statement. But if the expression evaluates as FALSE then an error (or at least warning) interrupt is initiated.

The use of such a strategy for overengineering programs can be 'enforced' by the development of appropriate principles of programming, such as: one fifth of computation statements in a program should be **ASSERT** statements.

This example also provides us with an example of why such *ad hoc* overengineering is not completely satisfactory. Firstly, the check is at the level of fine implementation detail. In order to add this check you have to get right down to the fine details of the implemented system. Secondly, it is an *ad hoc* test. There are many other similar ones that could have been used instead or as well - which do you choose and where do you stop? Thirdly, such checks will make the system larger and slower, and are quite likely to miss the real problems in the software. This is because the very fact that the system designer (or implementor) dreamed up and added this check means that he or she consciously thought about the possibility of the averaging function malfunctioning in this particular way. But all too often, the source of the insidious system errors is the unusual combination of circumstances that no one consciously foresaw. So, by its very nature, it is unlikely that a check for this error condition will have been built in.

A relevant, blossoming field of logic programming is that of **constraint logic programming (CLP)** - see Cohen (1990) for a survey of CLP. There are many rather different routes that development of this notion can, and probably will, take, but of interest here is the view that CLP encompasses the notion of automatically asserted constraints in a Prolog-style language. Put simplistically, instead of proving the truth of, say, A (from A:-B and the truth of B as in standard Prolog), some constraints to the truth of this statement may be automatically generated. So A might be true when, say, "X < 23" if we assume that B (and perhaps A) contains the variable "X". In general, we thus generate, not simply truth values, but truth subject to certain constraints. To return to our **sort** example, the query:

sort([X1,X2,X3], S)?

would fail in standard Prolog, because unbound variables (i.e. X1,X2 and

X3) cannot be sorted - i.e. compared using the <= operator. But in CLP we can expect the result:

    S=[X1,X2,X3], X1<=X2, X2<=X3

That is, the sorted list S is [X1,X2,X3] when the constraints X1<=X2 and X2<=X3 are satisfied.

One of the promises of this enhancement of standard Prolog is that it provides a neat and natural way for the system to automatically tell us the detailed conditions under which the computation is correct. Instead of the programmer having to devise these detailed constraints on the correctness of the algorithm (i.e. the ASSERT statements in effect), they are generated automatically as part of the computation. In CLP we get the result of the computation and an explicit statement of the detailed conditions under which it is correct. And although these constraints are not redundant in the sense that ASSERT statements are, they do represent additional information which the programmer can use to ensure system reliability. The drawback is, of course, that the correctness of the constraints depends upon the correctness of the algorithms from which they were generated rather than upon some (at least partially) independent source, like the programmer's second thoughts. In this sense they are a weaker strategy than assertional programming.

In an effort to provide a more independent checking mechanism, a result can be recomputed and the two values can be compared to see if we get exactly the same value twice. Nothing is easier. We can make a copy of the code and compute all significant values twice, but this would not solve our problem: it will just mean that the system makes all the same errors twice. We must add useful redundancy; not just any redundancy. If the programmer were to redesign and recode critical functions twice over then the results of these two different computations could indeed be usefully compared.

A frequently used technique for improving software system reliability in this manner is through replication of the critical software components together with a 'comparator' module that cross-checks for consistency and might accept, for example, agreement in two out of three replicated channels. The replication envisaged is not simple duplication, but an exploitation of **software diversity** "which is a particular form of redundancy involving the design and coding of separate software for each of the replicated channels" (Smith and Wood, 1989, p. 161). This approach to reliability through redundancy is also called **N version programming**. Figure 9.6 illustrates this sort of approach to software system redundancy.

Careful statistical analyses of the products of N version programming - i.e. different implementations of the problem developed independently by different people - shows that the versions are not independent (Eckhardt and Lee, 1985). In fact, it appears that these independently developed versions display considerable similarity with respect to their weaknesses - e.g. they are all fragile with respect to the same inputs. This finding does, of course, undermine the rationale for the N version programming approach to software redundancy: it fails to provide the necessary redundancy.

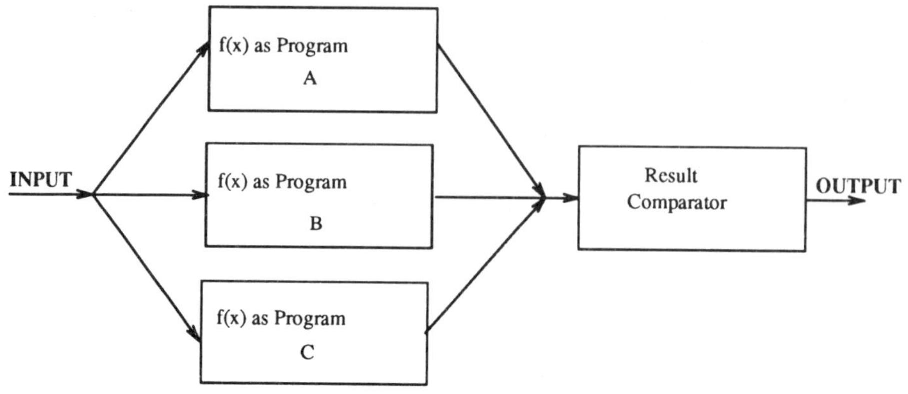

Fig 9.6 Simple software diversity providing system redundancy

It is perhaps not too surprising that two people, although working totally independently, produce similar programs, after all they are probably using similar structured design methodologies and similar procedural programming languages. Such similarities in the design process provide powerful constraints on the program that will be produced. The statistical analyses seem to bare this view out. A recent extension of this approach to software reliability has found that considerable independence among the N versions does occur if radically different programming paradigms are used. In the empirical study of Adams and Taha (1991) the two different paradigms were procedural and declarative as imposed by programming in Pascal and in Prolog, respectively. A further increase in effective redundancy within this N version approach might be gained by enforcing fundamentally different design methodologies such as object-oriented design and traditional structured design. Clearly, although the simplistic view of N version programming fails to yield the necessary redundancy, there is much potential scope for generating effective redundancy within this general framework; many possibilities remain to be explored.

This strategy of diverse programming paradigms has been explored in the context of developing a bifacial programming language (Smartt, 1983, and Adams and Smartt, 1985). The prototype language was a loose amalgam of Pascal and Prolog such that a given problem could be implemented in each language, and at strategic points within the calculations intermediate values could be checked for equivalence. This is a neat-sounding idea for overengineering software. It is true that 'double-programming' each problem is not quite as simple and straightforward as, say, doubling the size of the main supports of a bridge, but, given the nature of software artifacts, it may be pointless to hope for anything that simple. Unfortunately, this nice idea of having two very different, intermeshed computations cross-checking each other does not work too well. And the reason is simple: if you have two totally different

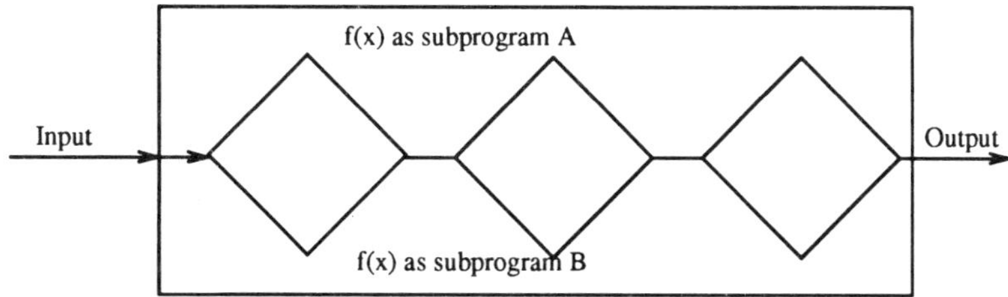

Fig 9.7 Redundancy through 'bifacial' computation

computations (one procedural and one declarative, in this particular case) computing the same overall function, there may be few intermediate stages within the two computations that are usefully comparable, and even fewer that are easily identified as comparable. The bifacial language used abstract data types to solve the problem of determining when two results were equal when their concrete representations differed. But this approach to the when-to-compare problem did put an excessive burden on the programmer, who first had to master a non-trivial algebra for abstract data types in order to properly exploit the consistency-checking feature of the language. Figure 9.7 is a schematic illustration of the redundancy promised by such a bifacial language.

A subsequent thought was that a Prolog program might be used to check a given result, a result given by a procedural, say Pascal, computation. This is a sequential use of double-programming redundancy, but it is perhaps not quite as bad as a doubling of the simple-program computation time, for, intuitively, one might expect checking a given result to be faster than actually computing the result. This project then evolved into a study of the relative efficiency of checking a given result in Prolog and computing that result. Guthrie (1985) showed that the time-complexity of verifying a result (i.e. checking a given result) is never greater than the time-complexity of finding that result (i.e. computing the result) with the same program. She also characterized a substantial class of Prolog programs for which these two time-complexities are the same, and showed that there is no algorithm for deciding whether or not a Prolog program will verify a result in less time that it would take to compute that same result. Figure 9.8 provides a schematic illustration of this possibility for achieving software reliability through useful redundancy.

In an effort to avoid the problems of this type of overengineering at the level of programming detail, there have been attempts to introduce the necessary redundancy at an earlier stage in the overall process. The general idea is to design useful redundancy into the system long before the questions of implementation details are addressed. This sort of approach to software reliability, quite outside of concerns for AI software, has long been advocated by some software specialists (see, for example, Randell, 1975). Randell suggests a scheme of "stand-by sparing" in which

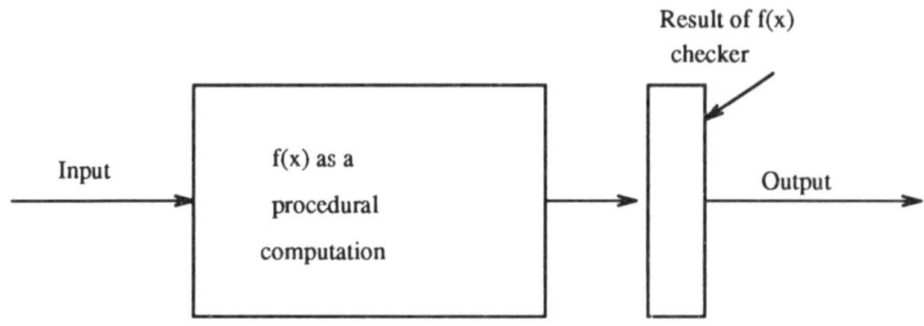

Fig 9.8 A declarative check on a procedural computation

there are built-in checks for critical system components, and when a check fails a 'spare' software component is switched in to deal with the particular set of circumstances that caused the failure. Such failures, which are assumed to be exceptional, are taken to be due to "residual design inadequacies" (Randell, 1975, p. 438).

He goes on to describe two important characteristics of a "recovery block scheme for achieving software fault tolerance by means of stand-by sparing":

1. It incorporates a general solution to the problem of switching to the use of the spare component, i.e. of repairing any damage done by the erroneous main component, and of transferring control to the appropriate spare component.

2. It provides a method of explicitly structuring the software system which has the effect of ensuring that the extra software involved in the error detection and in the spare components does not add to the complexity of the system, and so reduce rather than increase overall system reliability. (Randell, 1975, p. 438)

So, what we now see as crucial to the production of reliable AI software (i.e. designing in useful redundancy) has in some sectors of the conventional software community long been viewed as a route to software reliability. It is interesting to see in these old papers the hedge that this approach is needed until such time as proofs of program correctness can be applied to practical software systems. It is worth pointing out, at this juncture, that a belief in the possibility of formal verification of algorithms undermines the incentives to explore methods for designing in useful redundancy. The provision of any form of redundancy has a cost (in system size, complexity, or execution time), and if the system can be guaranteed to be correct then its plain silly to pay the price of redundancy. (The reader might also recall the conspicuous lack of testing strategies in treatises on the 'science' of programming - see Chapter 3 for a memory jog if necessary.) Clearly, if the ship is unsinkable, then lifeboats are an unnecessary expense. No one would accept this argument about ships. Why is it any less unpalatable when applied to software systems? I'm not sure, but I suspect it is something to do with the confusion between mathematical abstractions and software systems as engineered artifacts.

Once more the object-oriented paradigm provides us with an up-to-date perspective on the assertion-based approach to software reliability. The programming language Eiffel and its environment, from Interactive Software Engineering Inc., "apply the concepts of object-oriented design and programming to the construction of high-quality software" (Meyer, 1989, in abstract). Eiffel offers us reusability (as we've already considered within OOP), extendibility (Eiffel programs are readily modifiable - another OOP goodie), and reliability through various means including assertions and the traditional approach of strict static typechecking. It is, of course, reliability through systematic use of assertions that I shall focus on here.

In Eiffel, assertions may be used in the following roles:

1. As routine **preconditions** to express conditions that must be satisfied whenever a routine is called.
2. As routine **postconditions** that express conditions which are guaranteed to be true when a routine terminates (if the precondition was satisfied on entry).
3. As **class invariants** that must be satisfied by objects of the class at all times.

In order to avoid the run-time penalty of assertion-checking, such monitoring, at two levels (preconditions only or all assertions), maybe enabled or not individually for each particular class. A violated assertion will trigger an exception which will cause an error message and termination unless customized exception-handling has been provided.

At first sight, it seems that Eiffel offers us merely an integrated and slightly more elaborate assertional capability than we had in Pascal many years ago. But there is at least one substantial advance which begins to address the problem of the low-level of traditional assertional checks. This particular innovation results from a combination of assertional checking and the OOP notion of inheritance, which (in Eiffel) encompasses the idea of deferred classes. A **deferred class** is a class that contains at least one **deferred routine**, which is a routine whose implementations will only be provided by descendants (and thus need not be provided until later). Deferred classes allow Eiffel to function as a high-level design language, i.e. certain general features of the deferred class can be specified without the necessity to provide a specific, detailed implementation. Yet pre- and post-condition assertions can be associated with a deferred routine, and invariant assertions with deferred classes. Clearly, there is some scope here for a high-level assertional capability at the design stage, and, in addition, because Eiffel is an efficiently executable language, we gain the benefits of a fast prototyping tool.

Meyer (1989, p. 10) provides the following example of the use of Eiffel; it illustrates the design-level assertional capability.

```
deferred class VEHICLE export
    dues_paid, valid_plate, register, ...
feature
    dues_paid(year:INTEGER):BOOLEAN is

        ...
        end; - dues_paid
    valid_plate(year:INTEGER):BOOLEAN is

        ...
        end; - valid_plate
    register(year:INTEGER) is
            - Register vehicle for year
        require
            dues\_paid(year)
        deferred
        ensure    valid_plate(year)
        end; -- register

    ... Other features ...
end  -- class VEHICLE
```

In this example there is no commitment to the details of the registration algorithm for a vehicle, or indeed to the assumption that a single algorithm will apply to all vehicles - cars, motorcycles, etc. But whatever the details of the actual registration procedures, the same assertions can be made (a precondition introduced by **require**, and a postcondition introduced by **ensure**).

So Eiffel can be employed as a high-level design language by exploiting the notion of deferred classes and routines. A first version may be composed of deferred classes and routines (in effect, a design). Later refinements will then supply details to replace the deferred components. Further features such as **polymorphism** and **late binding**, which permit considerable type flexibility, give the programmer significant freedom to design systems using deferred classes and routines.

Let me conclude this chapter by drawing your attention to the fact that, although overengineering (under various alternative names) has long been recognized as a route to reliable software systems, we have yet to see good generalized approaches to the problem emerge. And finally, let me point you back to the section **Reusable software** in Chapter 6, and in particular to Halpern's (1990) argument for the avoidance of "fresh" code as a key to software reliability: in terms of this approach the redundancy resides in the repeated successful usage of a piece of code and not in the structure of the code itself. And the associated costs are removed from the actual software system itself; they manifest themselves in the proper maintenance of the library of reusable software components, which seems like a much better place to put them.

10
Summary and What the Future Holds

In this final, wrap-up chapter, I shall draw together all that has been discussed in the previous chapters and, in addition, I shall bring some other, broader issues to your attention. Software development is not a purely technical issue. Software products operate in society, but general acceptance of this viewpoint has been sluggish, to say the least.

Let's take what we might call the internal societal problems of software development first. Many software systems are built by a team of people, and not by just one lone hacker, as we often seem to tacitly assume. Once a group of people are involved certain problems are reduced (e.g. each programmer has less code to write and something less than the full system to manage conceptually), but certain new problems emerge (e.g. the task of maintaining consistency between modules designed and developed by different people). The pros and cons of software teams versus single virtuoso performances is a much debated issue, and even more so is the optimum size of team for particular sorts of tasks. I shall not reopen the debate here. My point is just to bring to your attention the fact that the awkward technical problems that we have been grappling with throughout this book can become further aggravated by the presence of a software development team in place of a single-handed approach.

Outside of the team, the society of software developers, there is yet another world, and an even bigger and more problematic one. But before we plunge into it, I shall spare a few words for the essential link man, the manager who is typically the project's interface with the external world. This person, who is typically not a computer technologist, can be a major source of headaches to the project team. System reliability, which is in no small part founded on extensive careful testing and subsequent examination of the outcomes, can be threatened by the manager who sees only a deadline for delivery. The manager also knows that by the time many of the residual bugs are making their presence known to the community of users, he or she will be somewhere else and not indisputably responsible for any particular bug anyway. So the team-manager interaction can be an important determinant of the quality of the software produced.

Good software is software that satisfies intangible user needs, and it's almost axiomatic that a 'frozen' software system, however good, will soon fail to give satisfaction. Most users are only human (some software vendors might dispute this), and given a good piece of software their attention and interest quickly moves on to extensions of the current task that are possibly, or almost, solvable with the system at hand. We can hope that self-adaptive software, when it arrives, will allow the investigative user to retrain the current version of the system so as to satisfy this desire for something "just a little bit different".

The unfortunate fact that software systems have to operate in conjunction with some sectors of humanity and are supposed to satisfy their demands raises a further important point of difference between software as an engineered artefact and buildings, bridges, and tin-openers. In Chapter 1 we looked at exactly this question of similarity and difference, but we did not consider the impact of human inquisitiveness (which is perhaps just a nice way of saying "human perversity").

Give a man (or woman for that matter) a good tool for the job at hand and he or she will soon find a smart way to misuse it, or will break it in the attempt. Some would claim that this sort of activity is the hallmark of intelligence - man is not only the tool-using animal par excellence, he and she are the creative tool-misusing animals. Well, our behaviour with software tools is no different, except that our propensity for change is more easily satisfied: there are many, more readily apparent ways to misuse a software tool than say a tin-opener. A bridge is a bridge, and although it's true that you can hang banners on it and jump off it, etc., there are only so many different ways to (mis)use it. More importantly, very few of these misuses will threaten the designed function of the bridge (target practice from a battleship springs to mind as an exception, but there are few of them).

But give a user a new piece of software and it will soon be being used in ways that the system designer never dreamed of - a database system, for example, will be required to manipulate data structures that the system designer could not have imagined even in the wildest of dreams. The malleability of software systems can contribute to this problem because the user is tempted to make small (but potentially fundamental) changes in the software. The delivery of object code rather than source code is the means by which this particular embellishment to the general perversity is stamped out. But, given that the software is itself effectively unalterable, there will be many ways to misuse it, and ways that misuse its basic functionality - i.e. not just hanging banners on a bridge. Software is soft - but it's also brittle. It is easy to modify, but difficult to modify correctly.

This is the problem of the **open functionality** of software systems, and it goes some way towards accounting for the seeming unreliability of software when compared to the products of conventional engineering. The wide variety of innovative uses (or misuses) of a software system will, sooner or later (usually sooner), uncover a weakness (if not an honest-to-goodness dormant bug) in the system. And sometimes, the reason is that the system designer did not foresee, and could not reasonably have foreseen, the particular set of circumstances under which the software has crashed. As one system designer succinctly put it: "Writing code isn't the problem; understanding the problem is the problem" (quoted by Curtis, Krasner and Iscoe, 1988, p. 1271). A thorough understanding of a software system within its full range of possible user environments is an open-ended problem. So, yet again, we see that the difference in reliability is not due to a lack of proper developmental principles on the part of software developers; it is, in no small part, due to the nature of human users combined with the open functionality of software systems - a property that few conventionally engineered artefacts happen to possess.

This societally driven problem seems, at first sight, to point to a contradiction in my attempted characterization of software-engineered artefacts *vis-a-vis* conventional artefacts. In Chapter 1 I claimed that a distinguishing characteristic of software systems was their tight functionality - i.e. software only works properly when component functions are operating within certain, narrow bounds. But, in reality, the open functionality of software does not contradict the tight-functionality characteristic. The former refers to the opportunities, almost an invitation, to try to misuse software systems, and the latter refers to the problems that this may cause with respect to certain functions within the software. There's no contradiction, but there is interaction. Users will invariably use the system in ways never intended by the system designer: sometimes they get away with and sometimes they don't. The big problems occur when they think they are getting away with it, but in fact they are not.

Use of sophisticated life-cycle environments is, I have advocated, a (perhaps *the*) 'answer' to our problems in trying to engineer AI software - although it's not much of an answer, more another set of problems as I'm sure you're well aware by now. An environment that persists throughout the use and maintenance stages of a software system does, of course, provide a context for that software. Such an environment can therefore be constructed to 'filter' the impacts of the external users. This should help alleviate some of the worst problems, but that is perhaps all, for the environment itself is just another software system and will thus exhibit open-functionality vulnerability.

As an example of current concerns about these larger issues, the ones beyond the purely technical problems, we can look at the work of Curtis and "The Design Process Group" at MCC. Curtis, Krasner, Shen and Iscoe (1987) criticize software development models for focusing on the objects that exist at the end of each phase of the model (e.g. requirements specification, detailed design) and for failing to describe the actual processes that occur during software development - i.e. models, such as the waterfall model, fail to treat software development as a problem-solving process. "It is our primary thesis that this focus should be on activities that account for the most variation in software productivity and quality" (p. 98). And for Curtis et al. this means empirical research based on large system development projects which are developed within a context of individuals, teams, projects, and even companies. In Curtis, Krasner and Iscoe (1988), they illustrate these successively wider contexts as a series of layers (see Figure 10.1) and present the results of a field study of seventeen large software projects.

In sum, they maintain that the traditional, artefact-oriented, software development model must be integrated with a model that "analyzes the behavioural processes of systems development at the cognitive, team, project, and company levels. When we layer these behavioural processes

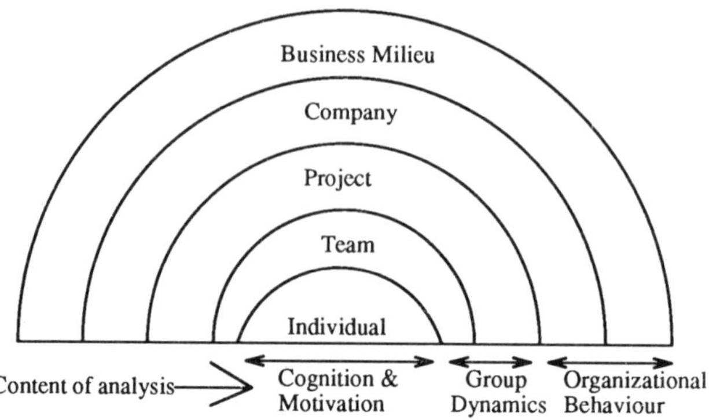

Fig 10.1 "The layered behavioural model of software development" from Curtis et al. (1988), Figure 1, p. 1269

on the growth process of artefacts, we begin to see the causes for bottlenecks and inefficiencies in the systems development process" (p. 98). "The process of developing large software systems must be treated, at least in part, as a learning and communication process ... Design is in part an educational process, trial and error learning (prototyping) is only one approach to education, albeit a powerful one ... From observations gathered on actual projects, we have concluded that processes such as learning, technical communication, negotiation, and customer interaction are among those crucial to project success which are poorly provided for in most existing models" (p.102-103). Curtis et al. (1988) present one potential set of relationships that may be present when building software systems (Figure 10.2).

To take another, but methodologically similar viewpoint, one that again suggests that no small part of the answer to the software reliability problem is to be found in the people concerned rather than in purely technical considerations, an IBM employee told me when questioned about his software team's approach to the reliability problem: "Well-trained, talented, motivated and dedicated programmers are the only solution" (an opinion that occurs repeatedly in the field studies of Curtis et al., 1988). This may be a silver bullet, but one that's difficult to lay your hands on most of the time. This particular problem is aggravated by the fact that programming is typically not viewed by companies as a long-term career job which involves an apprenticeship and substantial training, and, until it is, this particular road to reliable software will remain little used.

Educating software engineers is problematic. The root of the problems is that of 'size'. Example projects in a formal educational environment are necessarily small-scale and of short duration. A move to the real world of large-scale, long-term, widely used software causes completely new problems to emerge. The successful code hacker learns to view actual

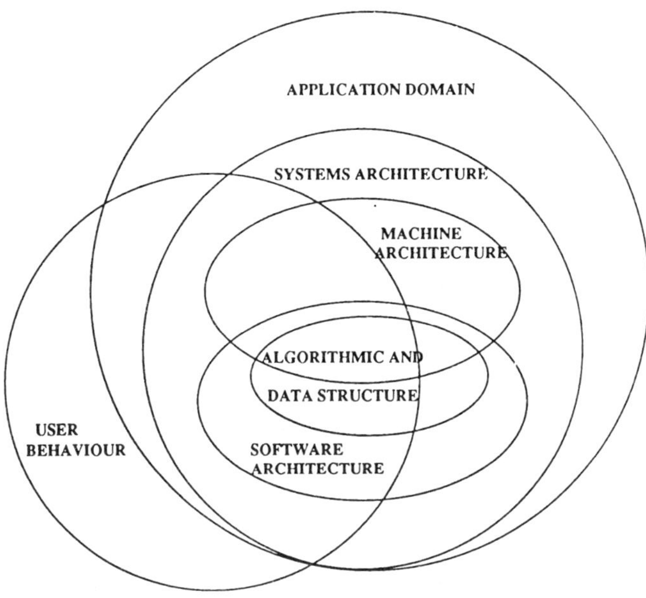

Fig 10.2   "Knowledge domains involved in system building" from Curtis et al., 1988, Figure 4, p. 1273

coding as about 90 per cent of the problem, whereas in reality it is more like 1 per cent of the large-scale commercial problem. Similarly, in the practice situation the system builder is usually also the user. When these two roles are filled by different individuals, who have no direct contact with each other, the fundamental problem of satisfying user needs changes beyond recognition. Again societal issues, which are difficult to address within the constraints of a formal educational context, distort and disfigure the purely technical ones.

Returning once more to the extra problems raised by the possibility of AI-software, I should mention the philosophy espoused by Winograd and Flores (1986). Winograd, once a prime mover in the optimistic AI camp, has now backed off to advocate extreme caution in the development of AI-ish software systems. These two authors write that "the development of any computer-based system will have to proceed in a cycle from design to experience and back again. It is impossible to anticipate all of the relevant breakdowns and their domains. They emerge gradually in practice. System development methodologies need to take this as a fundamental condition of generating the relevant domains, and to facilitate it through techniques such as building prototypes early in the design process and applying them in situations as close as possible to those in which they will eventually be used" (p. 171). Clearly, our authors are echoing a number of the issues that we have discussed, from the need for iterative development and prototyping to open functionality in the human propensity to exploit it.

Winograd and Flores point out that the source of much user dissatisfaction with AI-ish software is that the glossy but thin veneer of AI (say, an English-like interface) leads the user to expect far more than the system can actually deliver. Better AI software will involve techniques for making the system's actual capabilities transparent to the user instead of generating unfulfillable expectations. This point is very important with respect to the engineering of AI software, for such software will only ever embody certain aspects of intelligence, yet we are only used to interacting with fully intelligent systems. The concept of powerful, but severely limited intelligence is not one that humans have needed to entertain seriously. Hence our propensity to infer general intelligence when confronted with a very limited demonstration of just one aspect of intelligence. This human proclivity will (and already does) lead to error and misunderstanding between humans and computer systems; AI-software systems, unless well engineered to dispel unwarranted assumptions of grandiose capabilities, can only aggravate this problem.

To change course one last time, let me say just a few words about a recurring worry which if resolved would go some considerable way to softening the confrontation between the advocates of SAV and of RUDE methodologies. When we supply the system developer with a power-tool kit it can be used either wisely and to great beneficial effect, or misused cavalierly to great detrimental effect. And I think that much of the SAV(wo)man's distaste for the RUDE-based approach can be traced to a concern about all the bad ways in which the available tools may be used. I'm not sure if it is possible to decouple power for good from potential for misuse (as I said above, it's a "worry"). But it seems that once more a well-designed environment ought to be able to go some way towards promoting proper use of the available tools and preventing misuse - another 'filter' function for the environment to perform.

Finally, software design and development (including AI-software design and development) should be more like engineering, but more like engineering as it actually is, rather than like engineering as the scientists dream that it might one day be. But software artefacts, especially AI-ish ones, are different from conventionally engineered artefacts in a number of significant respects. These differences should not be trampled in the stampede for software development in the mould of "sound engineering principles". Hidden interactions, and tight functionality, make for extra complexity, while malleability and apparently open functionality tempt the user to misuse. The classical engineer has none of these problems to face, or at worst only faint echoes of them. In large part, software reliability will come from solutions to these special problems, and not from following slavishly in the footsteps of traditional engineers.

Additionally, a preoccupation with logic and formal methods has diverted considerable effort and attention away from the tasks of identifying and solving other problems that are at least as important, and probably more important in the long run. The possibility of AI software holds much promise but brings with it many problems. The problems involved with building practical AI software are many, diverse, and mostly unsolved. But we are focusing in on the problems, and that's a necessary prerequisite to finding solutions. Part of this problem-identification task concerns the proper role of specification and verification. Much conventional software seems to be, or seems like it ought to be, amenable to complete specification and verification, but for many AI problems this possibility seems increasingly unlikely. And so, one service to the software development community in general that attempts to engineer AI software will bring is recognition of the central role that prototyping, reverse engineering, etc. should play in the production of reliable software. Logic, complete formal specifications and formal verification, undoubtedly have a place in the game, but it's not centre field and our efforts to engineer AI software make that perfectly clear.

So, efforts to engineer AI software, while directed ostensibly at a vast and limitless problem, will, as a side-effect, continue to expose and illuminate misconceptions in entirely conventional software system design and development. The emergent methodology of a discipline of ESD will thus find application in areas completely devoid of AI content. For AI is not really a special case: it is merely an extreme, and as such it serves the very useful purpose of highlighting problems that run throughout the software spectrum, as well as presenting us with a challenge in its own right.

References

Adams, J.M. and Smartt, M. (1985) Software reliability through redundancy, *Proc. 18th Hawaii International Conference on Systems Sciences*

Adams, J.M. and Taha, A. (1991) *An experiment in software redundancy with diverse methodologies*, Technical Report, Dept Computer Science, New Mexico State University, Las Cruces NM88003, USA.

Andrews, D. (1990) The Vienna Development Method, in D. Ince & D. Andrews (Eds.) *The Software Life Cycle*, London: Butterworths, pp. 221-259.

Agresti, William W. (ed.) (1986) *New Paradigms for Software Development*, Washington, DC: IEEE Computer Society Press, p.295.

Aleksander, I. (1983) Emergent intelligence from pattern recognition nets, in *Artificial Vision for Robots*, I. Aleksander (Ed.), London: Kogan Page.

Arango, G., Baxter, I. and Freeman, P. (1991) A framework for incremental progress in the application of artificial intelligence to software engineering, in D. Partridge (Ed.), *Artificial Intelligence and Software Engineering*, Norwood, NJ: Ablex Pub.Corp., pp 425-437

Ashworth, C. and Goodland, M. (1990) *SSADM: A practical approach*, London: McGraw-Hill.

Bader, J., Edwards, J., Harris-Jones, C., and Hannaford, D. (1988). *Practical Engineering of Knowledge-Based Systems, Information and Software Technology*, **30**(5), pp. 266-277.

Bahrami, A. (1988) *Designing Artificial Intelligence Based Software*, Wilmslow, UK: Sigma Press.

Balzer, Robert., Cheatham, Thomas E. Jr., and Green, Cordell (1983) "Software Technology in the 1990's: Using a New Paradigm,"*IEEE Computer*, November, pp. 39-45.

Barnes, J.G.P., (1983) *Programming in ADA*, Reading, Mass.: Addison-Wesley.

Barstow, D.R., Shrobe, H.E. and Sandewall, E. (1984) *Interactive Programming Environments*, New York: McGraw-Hill, p. 609.

Bereton, Pearl (Ed.), (1988) *Software Engineering Environments,*

Chicester, UK: Ellis Horwood

Berry, D. (1975) Structured Documentation, SIGPLAN Newsletter (November).

Biggerstaff, T.J., and Perlis, A.J. (Eds.) (1989) *Software Reusability*, 2 vols., Reading, Mass: Addison-Wesley.

Boehm, B.W. (1976) Software Engineering, *IEEE Transactions on Computers*, vol. C-25, no. 12, December, pp.1226-1241.

Boehm, B.W. (1988) A spiral model of software development and enhancement, *IEEE Computer*, May, pp. 61-72.

Boehm, B.W., Gray, T.E., and Seewaldt, T. (1984) Prototyping versus verifying: a multiproject experiment, *IEEE Transactions on Software Engineering*, **10**(3), 290-302 (reprinted in Agresti, 1986).

Booch, G. *Object-Oriented Design with applications*, Redwood City, CA: Benjamin/Cummins.

Brooks, F.P. (1979) *The Mythical Man-Month*, Reading, MA: Addison-Wesley.

Burt, A.D., Hill, P.M. and Lloyd, J.W. (1990) Preliminary Report on the Logic Programming Language Godel, TR-90-02, Computer Science Dept., University of Bristol, Bristol BS8 1TR.

Buxton, J.N. and Randell, B. eds. (1970) Software Engineering Techniques, A report on a conference sponsored by the NATO Science Committee, Brussels 39, Belgium: NATO Science Committee.

Cendrowska, J., (1989) *Knowledge acquisition for expert systems: Inducing modular rules from examples*, PhD Thesis, Open University, Milton Keynes, UK.

Cohen, J. (1990) Constraint logic programming languages, *Communications of ACM*, **33**(7), pp. 52-68.

Cooke, N.J. (1990) Using pathfinder as a knowledge elicitation tool: Link interpretation, In R.W. Schvaneveldt (Ed.) *Pathfinder Associative Networks*, pp. 227-239, Norwood, NJ: Ablex.

Curtis, B., Krasner, H., Shen, V. and Iscoe, N. (1987) On building software process models under the lamppost, *Association for Computing Machinery*, pp. 96-103.

Curtis, B., Krasner, H. and Iscoe, N. (1988) A field study of the software design process for large systems, *Communications of the ACM*, **31**(11), 1268-1287.

De Jong, G., and Mooney, R. (1986) Explanation-based learning: An alternative view, *Machine Learning*, (1), 145-176.

DeMarco, Thomas, (1979) *Structured Analysis and System Specification*, New York: Yourdon Inc.

DeMillo, R.A., Lipton, R.J. and Perlis, A.J. (1979) Social Processes and Proofs of Theorems and Programs, *Communications of ACM* **22**(5), pp. 271-280.

Dijkstra, E.W. (1989) On the cruelty of really teaching computing science, *Communications of ACM*, **32**(12), pp. 1398-1404 and 1414.

Dreyfus, H.L. and Dreyfus, S.E. (1986) *Mind over Machine*, New York: The Free Press.

Eckhardt, D.E. and Lee, L.D. (1985) A theoretical basis for the analysis of multiversion software subject to coincident errors, *IEEE Transactions on Software Engineering*, vol. SE-11, no. 12, pp. 1511-1517.

Edwards, J.S. (1991) *Building Knowledge-based Systems*, London: Pitman.

Fetzer, J.H., (1988) Program Verification: the Very Idea, *Communications of ACM* **9**(31), pp. 1048-1063.

Floyd, Christiane, (1984) A Systematic Look at Prototyping, in Budde, R., K. Kuhlenkamp, L. Mathiassen, and H. Zullighoven (Eds.), *Approaches to Prototyping*, Berlin: Springer-Verlag, pp. 1-18.

Freeman, P. (1987) A conceptual analysis of the DRACO approach to constructing software systems, *IEEE Trans. on Software Engineering*, **13**(7) (July) pp. 830-844.

Gibbins, P. (1990) What are formal methods? in D. Ince and D. Andrews (Eds.)*The Software Life Cycle*, pp. 278-290, Butterworths: London.

Gilb, T. (1988) *Principles of Software Engineering Management*, Reading, Mass.: Addison-Wesley.

Gries, David (1981) *The Science of Programming*, New York : Springer-Verlag.

Guthrie, L. (1985) Some results on evaluating and checking functions for software redundancy, PhD Thesis, New Mexico State University, Computer Science Department, NM 88003, USA.

Haberman, A.N. et al. (1985) Special issue on the Gandalf project, *Journal of Systems and Software*, **5**(2).

Hayes-Roth, F., Waterman, D.A., and Lenat, D.B. (1983) *Building Expert Systems*, Reading, MA: Addison-Wesley.

Hill, I.D. (1972) Wouldn't it be nice to write programs in English - or would it?, *Computer Bulletin*, vol. 16.

Hinton, G.E. (1989) Connectionist learning procedures, *Artificial Intelligence*, 40, pp. 185-234.

Hogger, C.J. (1988) Programming environments, *Proc. ECAI 88*, Milan, Italy, pp. 698-706.

Horowitz, E., Kemper, A., and Narasimham, B. (1985) A Survey of Application Generators, *IEEE Software*, January, pp. 40-54.

Ince, D. (1988) *An Introduction to Discrete Mathematics and Formal System Specification*, Oxford, UK: Oxford Univ. Press.

Ince, D. C. (1989) *Software Engineering*, London: Van Nostrand Reinhold.

Ince, D. (1990) Z and system specification, in D.Ince & D. Andrews (Eds.) *The Software Life Cycle*, London: Butterworths, pp. 260-277

Jackson, M. A., (1983) *System Development*, Englewood Cliffs, NJ : Prentice-Hall.

Johnson, P. (1990) Type flow analysis for robust exploratory software, Dept. of Information and Computer Science, Univ. Hawaii, Honolulu, HI 96822.

Johnston, V.S., Partridge, D. and Lopez, P.D. (1983) A neural theory of cognitive development, *J. Theoretical Biology*, vol. 100, pp. 485-509.

Jones, C.B. (1980) *Software Development: a formal approach*, London: Prentice-Hall International.

Jones, C.B. (1986) *Systematic Software Development Using VDM*, Englewood Cliffs, NJ: Prentice-Hall.

Joyce, E.J. (1988) Reusable Software: Passage to productivity?, *Datamation*, pp. 34, 18, 97-102.

Karp, R. (1989) Commentary on Dijkstra's "On the cruelty of really teaching computer science," *Communications of the ACM*, **32**(12), pp. 1410-1412.

Kirlis, P.A. et al. (1985) The SAGA approach to large program development in an integrated modular environment, *Proc. GTE workshop on software engineering environments for programming-in the-large*, June.

Kodratoff, Y., Franova, M. and Partridge, D. (1990) Logic Programming and Program Synthesis, *Proc. 1st International Conference on Systems Integration*, Morristown, NJ, pp. 346-355.

Kowalski, Robert, (1984) AI and Software Engineering, *Datamation*, **30**(10), pp. 92-102.

Ledgard, Henry F. (1975) Programming Proverbs, Rochelle Park : New Jersey.

Lehman, M.M., and Belady, L.A. (Eds.) (1985) Program Evolution: processes of software change, London : Academic Press, 539 pp.

Luger, G.F. and Stubblefield, W. A. (1989) *Artificial Intelligence and the design of Expert Systems*, Redwood City,CA: Benjamin/Cummings.

McDermott, J. (1981) R1, the formative years, *The AI Magazine* **2**(2), pp. 21-29.

McDermott, J. and Bachant, J. (1984) R1 revisited: Four years in the trenches, *The AI Magazine*, **5**(3), pp. 21-32.

McIlroy, M.D. (1960) Macro Instruction Extensions of Compiler Languages, *Communications of ACM* **4**(3), pp. 214-220

Mc Kevitt, P. (1990) Acquiring user models for natural language dialogue systems, Proc. 2nd International Workshop on User Modelling, University of Hawaii.

Mc Kevitt, P. and Partridge, D. (1991) Problem description and hypothesis testing in AI, in McTear, M.F. and Creaney, N. (eds) *AI and Cognitive Science ' 90*, pp. 26-47, London: Springer-Verlag.

MacLennan, Bruce J. (1987, 2nd Edition) *Principles of Programming Languages*, New York: Holt, Rinehart and Winston.

Meyer, B. (1985) On formalism in specifications, *IEEE Software*, **2**(1). pp. 6-26.

Meyer, B. (1989) *Eiffel: An introduction*, Interactive Software Engineering Inc., 270 Storke Rd., suite 7, Goleta, CA 93117.

Michalski, R.S., Carbonell, J.G. and Mitchell, T.M. (1983) *Machine Learning I*, Los Altos, CA: Tioga.

Michalski, R.S. and Chilausky, R.L. (1980) Knowledge acquisition by encoding expert rules versus computer induction from examples: a case study involving soybean pathology, *Internat. Journal of Man-Machine Studies*, **12**(?), pp. 63-87.

Michie, D. and Johnston, R. (1984) *The Creative Computer*, London: Viking

Mitchell, T.M., Keller, R.M., and Kedar-Cabelli, S.T. (1986) Explanation based generalization: A unifying view, *Machine Learning*, (1) , 47-

80.

Mostow, J., (1985) Responses to Derek Partridge, *The AI Magazine,* **3**(6), pp. 52-52.

Mumford, E. and MacDonald, W.B. (1989) *XSEL's Progress, the continuing journey of an expert system,* Chichester, Sussex: Wiley.

Myers, B.A. (1988) The state of the art in visual programming and program visualization, In A.C. Kilgour & R.A. Earnshaw (Eds.), *Graphics tools for software engineering,* The British Computer Society: London.

Neighbours, J.M. (1989) Draco: A method for engineering reusable software systems, In T.J. Biggerstaff & A.J. Perlis (Eds.) *Reusable Software,* Reading, Mass.: Addison-Wesley.

Parnas, D.L. (1989) Commentary on "On the cruelty of really teaching computing science" by E.W. Dijkstra, *Communications of the ACM,* **32**(12), pp. 1405-1406.

Partridge, D. (1986) *AI: Applications in the future of software engineering,* Chichester, UK: Ellis Horwood.

Partridge, D. (1991) *A new guide to artificial intelligence,* Norwood, NJ: Ablex Publishing Co.

Potts, Colin (1989a) Representing recurrent issues and decisions in software design methods, *AAAI Spring Symposium on AI and software engineering,* Stanford University, March 28-30th, pp. 66-70.

Potts, Colin (1989b) A generic model for representing design methods, *Proc. 11th Internat. Conf. on Software Engineering,* IEEE Computer Society Press.

Prieto-Diaz, R. and Freeman, P. (1987) Classifying software for reusability, *IEEE Software,* January, pp.6-16.

Quinlan, J.R. (1979) Discovering rules by induction from large collections of examples: a case study, in D. Michie (Ed.), *Expert systems in the Micro-Electronic Age,* Edinburgh, Scotland: Edinburgh University Press.

Quinlan, J.R. (1986) The effect of noise on concept learning, in R. S. Michalski, J.G. Carbonell and T.M. Mitchell (Eds.), *Machine Learning I,* Los Altos, CA: Morgan Kaufmann, pp. 149-166.

Quinlan, J.R. (1987) Decision trees as probablistic classifiers, *Proc. 4th Internat. Workshop on Machine Learning,* Irvine, CA, pp. 31-37.

Ramamoorthy, C.V., Shekhar, S. and Garg, V. (1987) Software development support environments, *IEEE Computer,* **20**(1), pp. 30-40.

Ramamoorthy, C.V. et al. (1985) Genesis - An integrated environment for development and evolution of software, *COMPSAC.*

Randell, B. (1975) System structure for software fault tolerance, *Proc. International Conference on Reliable Software,* SIGPLAN Notices **10**(6), pp. 437-449.

Rich, C. (1986) A formal representation of plans in the Programmer's Apprentice, in C.Rich & R.C.Waters, *Readings in Artificial Intelligence and Software Engineering,* pp. 491-506.

Rich, C., and Waters, R. C. (1986) *Readings in Artificial Intelligence and Software Engineering,* Los Altos, CA : Morgan Kaufmann, p. 602.

Rich, C.R., and Waters, R.C. (1988) Automatic Programming: Myths and Prospects, *IEEE Computer*, (August) **21**(8), pp. 40-51.

Sandewall, Erik. (1978) Programming in an interactive environment: the LISP experience, *ACM Computing Surveys*, 10, 1, pp. 35-71.

Scherlis, W.L. (1989) Commentary on Dijkstra's "On the cruelty of really teaching computing science," *Communications of the ACM*, **32**(12), pp. 1406-1407.

Sejnowski, T., and Rosenberg, C. (1986) NETtalk: A parallel network that learns to read aloud, Tech. rep. JHU/EECS-86/01, Dept. of Elect. Eng. and Computer Science, Johns Hopkins Univ., Baltimore, MD.

Sheil, B. (1983) Power tools for programmers, *Datamation*, (February), pp. 131-144 (reprinted in Rich & Waters, 1986, 574-580).

Smartt, M. (1983) A language designed for redundancy, PhD Thesis, New Mexico State University, Computer Science Dept., NM 88003, USA.

Smith, D.J. and Wood, K.B. (1989) *Engineering Quality Software*, London: Elsevier.

Smolensky, P. (1986) Formal modelling of subsymbolic processes: An introduction to harmony theory, In N.E. Sharkey (Ed.) *Advances in Cognitive Science 1*, pp. 204-235, Chichester, UK: Ellis Horwood.

Sparck Jones, Karen. (1990) What sort of thing is an AI experiment?, in D. Partridge & Y. Wilks (Eds.), *The Foundations of AI: a sourcebook*, Cambridge, UK: Cambridge University Press, pp. 274-281.

Swartout, W., and Balzer, R. (1983) On the inevitable intertwining of specification and implementation, *Communications of ACM*, **25**(7), pp. 438-440 (reprinted in Agresti, 1986).

Trenouth, J. (1990a) "Version Control via Temporal Annotations for an Exploratory Software Development Environment," *Information and Software Technology*, July/August.

Trenouth, J. (1990b) "Exploratory Software Development," PhD Thesis, Computer Science Department, University of Exeter.

Turski, W.M. and Maibaum, T.S.E. (1987)*The specification of computer programs*, Reading, Mass: Addison-Wesley.

Vaudet, J., and Kerdiles, P.F. (1989) VALID: a proposition to advance capabilities for knowledge-based systems validation, ESPRIT Conference '89, Brussels.

Waters, R.C. (1986) The Programmer's Apprentice: A session with KBEmacs, in C. Rich & R.C. Waters, *Readings in Artificial Intelligence and Software Engineering*, 351-375.

Waters, R. C. (1989) Programming in the year 2009, in Preprints of the International Workshop on AI and Software Engineering, Department of Computer Science, University of Exeter, pp. 1-5.

Winograd, T. (1975) Breaking the complexity barrier again, *SIGPLAN Notices*, **10**(1), pp. 13-30.

Winograd, T. and Flores, F. (1986) *Understanding Computers and Cognition*, Norwood, NJ: Ablex Pub. Corp.

Wirth, N. (1971) Program Development by Stepwise Refinement, *Communications of ACM*, **14**(4), pp. 221-227.

Worden, R. (1989) Processes of Knowledge and Software, *Proc.*

Expert Systems 88, Brighton, UK, pp. 139-159.

Yourdon, E. (1975) *Techniques of program structure and design*, Englewood Cliffs, NJ: Prentice-Hall.

Yourdon, E. (1990) Auld Lang Syne, *BYTE*, October, **15**(10), pp. 257-262.

Index